Praise for
Walking Him Home

"Joanne is to be commended for sharing a very personal view on the impossible choices facing patients and families living with, and dying of, a serious and progressive neurologic illness. There is much here for patients, families, policymakers, and healthcare providers to take in and wrestle with in coming to terms with medical aid in dying."

—Dr. Benzi Kluger, Julius, Helen, and Robert Fine Distinguished Professor in Neurology at University of Rochester School of Medicine and president of the International Neuropalliative Care Society

"Joanne Tubbs Kelly skillfully narrates an intimate memoir about helping her husband end his life using Colorado's End-of-Life Options Act. Kelly provides a moving illustration of the ethical tensions at play and makes an important contribution to the conversation on death and dying."

—Kerry Landsman, medical ethics consultant

"An unvarnished account of a loving marriage and medical aid in dying."

—*Kirkus Reviews*

walking him home

walking him home

helping my husband die with dignity

JOANNE TUBBS KELLY

SHE WRITES PRESS

Published 2022

Printed in the United States of America

Print ISBN: 978-1-64742-089-5
E-ISBN: 978-1-64742-090-1
Library of Congress Control Number: 2022903328

For information, address:
She Writes Press
1569 Solano Ave #546
Berkeley, CA 94707

She Writes Press is a division of SparkPoint Studio, LLC.

Names and identifying characteristics have been changed to protect the privacy of certain individuals and companies.

To Alan,
my sweetie forever

"Why does death so catch us by surprise,
and why love?"

—Annie Dillard, *The Writing Life*

CHAPTER 1

January 11, 2020

Willie Nelson crooned a lament from an iPad in the next room as Alan took the deadly cocktail from Beverly's outstretched hands. When Alan let go of my hand to reach for the mug, I shook some feeling back into my cramped fingers, which Alan had been gripping as if his life depended on it. Beverly, our housemate and friend, had prepared the beverage Alan would drink to end his life, mixing the prescription powder with apple juice according to the pharmacist's instructions. I had talked her into taking on this task because I wanted to spend every minute of Alan's last conscious hours with him, at his bedside, not in the kitchen fretting over details. And now the poison was ready to drink. Beverly made sure Alan had a good grip on the mug before she let go.

Two members of Alan's hospice team—tall and lanky Josh, whose arms teemed with tattoos, and sweet, petite Cara—had stopped by our house earlier to give Alan a sponge bath. When he was clean, I had helped them dress him in his fire-engine-red pullover. He looked almost chipper, as if he might jump out of bed and make lunch for our assembled guests. Never mind that it wasn't even a remote possibility at that point, given that Alan couldn't stand up or even sit upright in his wheelchair for very long—he looked so dapper, anything *seemed* possible.

How could this kind and funny man, this beloved husband of mine, be about to end his life?

Alan's eyes, brimming with love and gratitude, locked on mine momentarily before he took a slug of the cocktail. I had been dreading this moment for weeks, but I was determined to be strong for Alan. I wanted to sink to the floor and keen, but I couldn't do it now. It would have to wait until everyone was gone, especially Alan.

His reaction to that first gulp was as swift as it was vehement: "Yuck! This tastes disgusting!" He spit the straw out of his mouth as if a wasp had stung his tongue.

I didn't know whether to laugh or cry. I can't tell you whether his daughters laughed or not. Or our minister, who hovered in the background. At that moment, I was tuned to Alan's wavelength, and everything else was static.

The pharmacist's instructions had been clear: Once the powder—composed of diazepam, digoxin, morphine, and propranolol—was mixed with liquid, it had to be consumed within two minutes or it would start to solidify. After another minute, it would be too solid to drink. They didn't send us any extra powder for a do-over.

Leaning in closer, I reminded Alan, "Sweetie, if you want to die, you need to drink it now, even if it tastes awful." A spark of hope exploded like fireworks in the back of my brain: *Maybe the repulsive taste will make him change his mind!*

For weeks I'd been waiting for Alan's determination to waver. *You know, maybe I'll hang around for another week, or maybe another month*, I imagined him saying. I knew he was fed up with being in pain, with the indignities he suffered because he couldn't take care of his own body, with not being able to talk clearly enough for people to understand him. But why was he in such a big rush? He could always ask for more morphine to help him with the physical pain. I didn't want him to suffer, but even more, I didn't want him to vanish from my life. I had asked him to postpone his dying until the holidays were over so his daughters, granddaughters, and I would not be mourning every Christmas for the rest of our lives. He had reluctantly agreed, but now, eleven days into the new year, he was impatient to move on. Part of me wished he would at least pretend he was reluctant to die, reluctant to leave me.

From the time I first met him, Alan had proclaimed to anyone who would listen that we treat our pets better than we treat our elders. We euthanize our four-legged family members when their suffering becomes too heavy, so he could not understand why we allowed our human loved ones to endure unbearable pain and unspeakable indignities.

Alan was overjoyed when the voters of Colorado passed the End-of-Life Options Act in 2016, which was before he was diagnosed with a fatal illness. He claimed his worst nightmare was dying of bedsores. It was Alan's shorthand way of saying he didn't want to lie in bed—in pain, unable to move, unable to communicate, unable to swallow—for weeks on end, until his heart finally stopped beating. He wanted to die with dignity at a time he chose, at home in his own bedroom, surrounded by family. Which was exactly what he was about to do.

And, despite the fact that he had been my best friend and lover for more than a quarter of a century, my soulmate, my partner in adventures of all sizes and shapes—including making homemade limoncello in Tuscany, hiking through a cloud forest on the Inca Trail to Machu Picchu, and remodeling a house from top to bottom while living in it—despite the fact that I loved him dearly and did not want him to die, I had helped him get to this point. Maybe I wasn't exactly the genie in the magic lamp who granted his wish, but he couldn't have pulled it off if I had refused to help him.

CHAPTER 2

1993

When people asked Alan and me how we met, Alan always replied immediately that he had hired me, without adding any further details. He'd raise an eyebrow and smile a mysterious little smile, giving the impression that maybe something salacious had occurred. Not wanting people to think I was a hooker, I would hurry to fill in the blanks: I was a freelance writer producing marketing materials for high-tech and medical companies; Alan was marketing manager for a company that made precision injection–molded plastic parts for medical equipment. He was looking for someone to write a bimonthly newsletter for his company's customers.

My memory of the interview is blurry at best, but I know that a half-dozen people, all of them men, were present in the windowless, fluorescent-lit conference room decorated with whiteboards and industrial carpeting. The acrid smell of industrial solvents wafted in whenever someone opened the door. I wore my dress-for-success suit and sensible-heeled pumps, and I carried a leather briefcase that had been expensive when I bought it, although at that point it was worn around the edges but not yet shabby. I hoped it conveyed the impression that I was a seasoned professional. Most likely, nobody even noticed my briefcase. I covered up my nervousness with my practiced "How can I help you solve your problems?" job-interview persona and hoped my underarm perspiration was not noticeable. Perhaps I impressed the team with my portfolio of materials produced for previous clients, or maybe I was the only candidate they found to interview. Either way, I got the job.

What I remember most about the interview was the sparkle in Alan's eyes, the heat waves emanating from his skin, his eagerness to work with me, as if I were the answer to his most fervent prayers. Oh yes, and the wedding band on his left-hand ring finger.

I had been divorced from my second husband for five years at that point, and it was the first time in my life I had spent a significant stretch of time living alone. My job during most of those years, as marketing communications manager for a small start-up company, gave me the opportunity to travel, both in the US and abroad. Under the tutelage of the company's chairman of the board, a fun-loving, financially savvy man named Daryl, I began investing in the stock market and enjoyed modest success.

I cashed in some of my stock market winnings and some of the stock options Daryl's company had used to lure me on board to make a down payment on a house in Boulder, a small brick ranch with a two-car garage, a large yard, a mature peach tree off the corner of the deck, and a view of the Flatirons—gigantic rock slabs tilted at precarious angles that form Boulder's iconic skyline—out the kitchen window. I told friends it was my purple-ceilings house, not that I would ever *really* paint my ceilings purple. The important point was that I *could* paint my ceilings purple if I wanted to. I didn't have to convince anyone it was a good idea or ask anyone's permission. I didn't have to get buy-in on the exact shade of purple from anyone. I could do it the way I wanted just because I wanted to. I felt free and unfettered. But at the same time, I longed for a man to share my life with, to go on adventures with, to grow old with. So I dated a lot of men, enjoying the process of looking for the perfect partner.

One of the men I dated, an architect, broke up with me abruptly after several months of dating. His timing was lousy, as I had spent the entire afternoon bonding with his nine-year-old son, oohing and aahing over every one of the baseball cards in his mind-numbing collection. But even worse than the bad timing were his reasons for dumping me: I was too smart, too successful, and too sophisticated for him. Three deadly S-words for a single woman in the 1990s.

At first, I was devastated by being rejected and his reasons for rejecting me. It took me a while to figure out that his inability to accept those S-qualities in me was more of a statement about who *he* was than about who *I* was. But it raised a big question for me: Was I ever going to find a man who was comfortable with my brains, my independence, and my career success? I wanted a man who would love me for who I was, who was not going to require me to "dumb down" to make him feel okay about himself. I started being a lot more selective about the men I dated. I even gave up men altogether for a while. That's when I met Alan.

We were careful with each other, both of us acutely aware of the electricity arcing between us, but neither of us wanting to cross the line into actions we might regret. But I do admit to teasing him a bit. I remember a working lunch at a quiet restaurant, just the two of us, where I wore a tight, black miniskirt I would never have dared wear for a meeting with any other client. It was more of a hot-date skirt than a business-meeting skirt, and I knew it.

Alan followed me as we made our way to our table, and I could feel his eyes burning into my back. As I turned to sit down, I caught him staring at my ass. When our eyes met, a bright blush bloomed on his checks. I probably blushed too. My miniskirt had elicited the response my bratty self had hoped for, but my responsible adult self was ashamed I had intentionally provoked him.

As we waited for our food to arrive, I opened my briefcase and pulled out two copies of my proposed editorial calendar for the next several issues of *The Vanguard*, the newsletter I was writing for him. My hand brushed his as I handed him his copy, and I wondered if people at nearby tables could see the sparks that flew, or if they were only visible to Alan and me.

Alan perused my proposed story lineup and looked at me appreciatively. "I like the idea of doing a three-part series on statistical process control," he said. "It will help our customers get a better idea of what goes into producing parts that meet their quality requirements. Steve can teach you what you need to know about statistics and capability ratios. He can get lost in the weeds sometimes, but I'm sure you can keep him on track and get the details you need."

I was delighted he liked my story ideas and pleased by his confidence in my abilities to understand the statistics involved. I didn't tell him how much I had struggled with statistics in grad school, although it wasn't as much about the math as it was my inability to understand the heavy accent of the teaching assistant who taught the course. What baffled me now was how Alan could make my gut do a flip-flop while discussing statistical process control.

As we ate, we talked about possible graphics and photographs we could use to accompany each article. We did not talk about our lust. It sat at the table with us like a silent elephant, an uninvited guest. Mostly uninvited, at least.

I spent about a year working with Alan and his colleagues, writing newsletter articles, press releases and brochures, managing photo shoots, and coaching the management team on communications strategy. During that time, Alan and I did well at keeping our relationship professional.

Then, out of the blue, everything changed.

June 1994

One night, as I was getting ready for bed, my phone rang. It was Alan calling me from a tradeshow he was attending in Chicago. I did have a few clients who called me occasionally in the evening—usually when they were traveling in a different time zone—but never Alan. I knew something was wrong.

"My wife left me for another man," he moaned into the receiver. He sounded lost.

My heart beat loudly in my ears. How do I respond appropriately? I had no idea his marriage was shaky. "I am so sorry," I told him, sincerely. I *was* sorry he was in pain, true, but I was elated he might soon be available. My alter ego turned cartwheels down the hall, while my adult self consoled him on the phone.

"It sounds like she didn't give you much warning," I ventured.

"None at all. Over the last few weeks, I could tell something had shifted, but I couldn't put my finger on what was different. She seemed distracted, but it was subtle."

"Hmm. Do you know the guy?"

"It's someone she works with. I met him at a party once, but it barely registered. If I'd known he was going to run off with my wife, I would've paid more attention."

I was amazed he could make jokes when he was in such obvious pain.

"You're the first person I've told," he added. I didn't need to ask him why.

Later, I told friends that finding Alan was much like finding a parking place at the library when I attended grad school. With parking spaces scarce in the library lot, the best strategy was to wait in your car, engine running, where the building's sidewalk emptied into the lot. As a library patron exited the building, you'd slowly cruise behind her, following her to her soon-to-be-empty parking spot.

As Alan's wife headed for the exit, I swooped in.

July 1994

The first time Alan cooked dinner for me, it was in his sparsely furnished bachelor pad, just weeks after his wife had bailed on their marriage. Alan had responded to a classified ad in the newspaper placed by a University of Colorado student named Chris, who was looking for a roommate. Alan and Chris hit it off, even though Chris was almost twenty years younger than Alan. The only furniture in the living room was Chris's weight bench, but at least there was a card table in the dining area and a couple of folding chairs so we could sit to eat.

Alan sang and danced his way through the preparation of a pot of spaghetti with homemade marinara sauce. The fact that he was tone deaf didn't slow him down or mute his volume. He was happy to be alive and overjoyed to be chopping onions, mincing garlic, sipping red wine, and belting out a Willie Nelson classic—albeit horribly off-key—all for me.

I stood at the far end of the kitchen counter prepping ingredients for a salad. Every few minutes, Alan danced his way down to where I stood. If I held a knife in my hands, he'd settle for a peck on my cheek, but if not, he'd wrap me in his arms for a passionate, toe-tingly kiss or he'd twirl me around the narrow room as he showed off his jitterbug moves.

"Do you always dance while you cook?" I asked.

"Only when I cook for you."

I laughed. "I bet you say that to all the girls."

"Only the ones I'm trying to seduce." His eyes twinkled as he refilled my wine glass.

Later, I told him how much I liked his marinara. I didn't tell him how much I disliked Willie Nelson. That came later.

October 1994

For the first few months of our relationship, I floated around my house with the imaginary purple ceilings, my feet barely touching the floor, and Alan lived with Chris in their apartment on the other side of Boulder. Most days, we talked on the phone or saw each other, and most weekends we spent all our time together. I had found the man I wanted to spend the rest of my life with, but Alan was so newly out of his marriage he was still in shock.

Alan was much more of a party person than I was, and unlike me, he had no qualms about going to gatherings where he hardly knew a soul. He sounded excited when I invited him to be my date for an upcoming party where he would meet the people I had worked with before I became a freelancer. Daryl had planned a huge Halloween extravaganza to be held at his horse stables, and he assigned costumes to each of his guests. I was instructed to come as Madonna, and my date, as a cowboy. Despite the regrettable miniskirt I had worn to lunch with Alan so many months earlier, I had misgivings about wearing anything too risqué in front of people with whom I had professional relationships, but I suspected Daryl's motive in asking me to come as Madonna was to get me out of my comfort zone. With a cowboy on my arm, I'd feel safe enough, I figured.

I found a purple bustier at The Ritz, Boulder's iconic costume emporium, with stiff and sparkly cones jutting from the front like gaudy party hats. I experimented with stuffing the spiky cups with various socks and shoulder pads and whatnot until I found a look that worked. I practiced prancing around the house in it to make sure the padding would stay in place. I kept my fingers crossed no neighbors would drop by unexpectedly during my trial runs. Once my stuffed bustier passed the at-home dancing test, I borrowed a fringed black leather jacket and picked up a leopard-print miniskirt at a thrift store. My costume was close to ready.

A week before the party, Alan and I were sitting at my dining room table amidst a clutter of dirty dishes and the remains of a lasagna we had created together and stuffed ourselves with, when I realized Alan hadn't said much about *his* costume.

"Do you want help with your cowboy outfit?" I asked.

Alan looked down at his lap and refolded his soiled napkin. "Umm. I think we need to talk."

"Uh-oh. What's up? You don't want to go as a cowboy?"

"I don't want to go to Daryl's party," he said softly, still focused on his napkin. He paused for what seemed like an eternity and then looked up to meet my gaze. "I think I need some space."

"Oh, no. Oh, Sweetie." I hadn't seen this coming. I knew he wasn't ready for a long-term commitment, but I had no idea our relationship was so tenuous. How could I have been so blind? My stomach tightened into a knot, and I wished I hadn't just stuffed myself to the gills.

"I don't want to hurt you, but I'm worried that if I don't date other women, I'll spend the rest of my life worrying that I jumped into this relationship too quickly."

I held my breath as I watched my dreams evaporate. "Are you saying you want a temporary break, or are you saying you want to end our relationship?"

"I don't know what I want. Right now, I just need some space." The sun had slipped down behind the Flatirons as we were eating. Under normal circumstances, the darkening dining room might have felt romantic, but at that moment, the darkness felt like a blanket of gloom.

I kicked myself for pushing him too hard when he was still raw from his second wife leaving for another man, just as his first wife had done fifteen years earlier. My rational mind understood his skittishness, but my inner child hated it. I wanted to scream, *No! No! No! You're making a horrible mistake! You'll be sorry someday!*

But I knew a temper tantrum wouldn't help, and I knew you couldn't talk someone into being in a relationship they didn't want to be in.

Alan got up from the table and deposited his plate in the kitchen sink, while I remained at the table, too stunned to move. He must have said, "I'm really sorry," at least a dozen times as he backed out my front door, leaving me with a kitchen full of dirty dishes and what felt like a rock lodged in my gut.

I didn't sleep for the rest of the week. I don't mean I didn't sleep *well*. I didn't sleep *at all*. For a whole week. It was *not* my first experience with heartbreak, but it *was* my first experience with insomnia. I dragged through the week in a fog, unable to think straight, unable to concentrate on my work.

On the Saturday afternoon before the party, my friend Connie came over to do my hair and makeup. I was out of my element with anything more than a mascara wand. I didn't even wear lipstick most of the time.

"I don't want to go to this stupid party," I whined when she arrived at my door. "And I don't want to wear this stupid costume."

"Nonsense! You are not going to let Alan ruin this evening for you. We are going to make you look so hot that Alan is going to kick himself from here to Christmas when he sees the pictures," she said as she laid out her supplies on the bathroom counter. Connie's husband had divorced her and taken off with his secretary after Connie had worked long hours to put him through law school, and as a result, she had honed a keen appreciation of subtle and not-so-subtle ways to extract revenge. Or at least to lick her wounds.

Connie applied layers of concealer to hide the dark circles under my eyes. After smoothing foundation over my face, she wanted to know where she should put my beauty mark.

"I've never understood why people wear fake beauty marks. Is it necessary?"

"Madonna has a beauty mark," Connie assured me. "Along with a long list of other celebrities who are considered beautiful: Elizabeth Taylor, Dolly Parton, Marilyn Monroe, and Sophia Loren, for example."

How could I argue with that lineup? I shrugged and let her draw a big, black beauty mark on my right cheek.

Connie moved on to eye liner and mascara, "to give you that come-hither look Madonna wears," she said. I felt like a raccoon when she was done with my eyes.

Then she tackled my hair using gobs of styling gel and copious quantities of hair spray.

"With hair as thin and fine as yours, I think our best bet is to aim for a 'naughty' look," Connie proclaimed. *How on earth does she know all this stuff about makeup and hair styles and celebrities?* I wondered. She might have said "knotty" instead of "naughty," based on all the teasing and back-combing she did. But she did achieve a level of wanton abandon my hair had never seen before, nor has it seen since. Basically, when Connie was done with me, I looked like a slut.

I rode to the party with Connie and her date: Alan's roommate, Chris. Chris was at least fifteen years younger than Connie, but they shared a Midwestern sensibility—Connie was from Indiana, and Chris grew up in Wisconsin—and laughed a lot when they were together. As a third wheel, I felt awkward and lonely and conspicuous all tarted up in my ridiculous costume.

"I'm not sure I can go in there dressed like this," I said as Chris pulled the car into the crowded stable parking lot.

"It's too late to change your mind," Connie said as she grabbed my arm and ushered me out of the car. Connie was a kindergarten teacher. You could tell she was good at dealing with little kids. She was firm and direct and didn't accept "no" for an answer. Chris took my other arm, and the two escorted me into the stables as if they were my security detail. Which they were, in a way.

Daryl and his wife had transformed the cavernous indoor riding arena into a magical haunted house populated with gossamer ghosts and goblins, complete with hay bales for seating, pumpkins scattered everywhere, and a wooden dance floor laid over the pea-gravel surface beneath. Guests arrived bedecked in all manner of sartorial splendor. Daryl, dressed as Merlin in a sparkly black robe and a wizard hat, cast spells with his magic wand, while Abraham Lincoln and Mary Todd Lincoln worked the fringes of the room. The band's loud and frenetic music inspired an undulating crowd of gypsies and pirates, flappers, scarecrows, hula dancers, and mermaids on the dance floor and made it impossible to carry on a conversation.

I hung out by the beer kegs for most of the evening, making it easy to top off my big red Solo cup as I drank away my sorrows and tried to erase my self-consciousness. By the time the band took its second break, I was sloshed. But I didn't stop topping off my cup. The next thing I knew, I was sitting on a cold concrete floor, leaning against the wall in a brightly lit hallway that led to the stable's office and rest rooms. Chris, who was dressed as a pirate, had his arm around my shoulder, and the curved blade of his plastic cutlass poked my side. I was weeping, ruining all the meticulous work Connie had done on my eye makeup, the remains of my beauty mark streaked down my cheek.

"Why does he want to date other women?" I sobbed. "What is he thinking? What can I do to make him change his mind?" Chris did his best to comfort me, but he didn't have any more insight than I had, or if he did, he wasn't going to betray Alan's confidence by sharing the answers with me. He disappeared for a minute to find Connie, and the two of them helped me into the back seat of Chris's car. They drove me home and poured me into bed.

I finally slept. Not the peaceful, restorative slumber required to rejuvenate a sleep-deprived insomniac, but the fretful, sweaty sleep of a drunk, punctuated with sudden, stumbling trips to the bathroom to pee and retch.

The phone's insistent ring woke me way too early on Sunday morning. I couldn't let it keep ringing because the shrill sound felt like a dentist's drill piercing my skull, cleaving it in two. I rolled over and picked up the receiver from my bedside table. A wave of nausea swept over me. Rolling over had not been a good idea. I grunted. It was the best I could do.

"Hi, Joanne," Alan said.

Oh, God! I cannot retch in Alan's ear.

"I'd like to talk with you," Alan said. "Can I come over?"

"No, I can't talk right now." I was relieved I could actually form words and articulate them in a way that made sense to another human being. Even though they were not the words I would have liked to have said.

"Please?" Alan said.

"No. I'm sorry." I heaved myself into a sitting a position, dropped the phone back in the cradle, and lurched into the bathroom, retching as I went. I was forty-three, and I hadn't been this hungover since I was in college. I grabbed some aspirin and a glass of water and went back to bed.

Two hours later my phone rang, waking me again, piercing my throbbing head once more. I groaned. Was it better to put my pillow over my head and wait for the ringing to stop, or to pick up the call and survive another mortifying experience of being too hungover to talk? *What if one of my kids needs help? I'd better answer it.* Both of my kids were living on their own near their dad's house in Pennsylvania, so it wasn't likely they would call *me* for help, but I didn't want to take any chances. Caller ID was not yet available in those days.

It was Alan again. And the second conversation sounded much like the first, but his voice betrayed a hint of nervousness this time. Or maybe I was imagining it.

"I'm sorry, Alan, but I can't talk right now." I was too embarrassed by my own stupidity to tell him why. I knew I needed several more hours of sleep and something to settle my stomach before I could face a conversation with anybody. But especially Alan. I wanted to have my act together if I were going to talk with him.

By late afternoon, I finally felt a bit more human. I managed to keep down two glasses of ginger ale and a piece of toast. I dragged myself into the shower and washed away the remainder of my raccoon makeup, erasing the haunted look that clung to my eyes. I used a half bottle of conditioner trying to get all the tangles out of my naughty knotty hair, and even though I was not entirely successful, it was close enough. I felt like I had successfully unsullied myself. I was back to unglamorous Joanne.

When Alan called a third time in the early evening, I finally said, "Yes, Madonna is accepting visitors this evening." I was nervous about seeing him, unsure what he wanted to say to me, worried he'd be disgusted that I'd gotten so drunk.

When Alan walked in the door, he gave me a perfunctory hug. I didn't know if that halfhearted greeting signaled good news or bad. I made us cups of herbal tea, and we sat at opposite ends of the couch in my living room. Soft strains of the Bach classical guitar music I'd inserted in my CD player took the edge off the awkwardness between us.

I went first. I hung my head. "I got roaring drunk last night at Daryl's party," I confessed. "I was trying to drown my sorrows, but all I did was give myself a massive hangover. I am so mortified by my out-of-control stupidity. When you called this morning, I was way too sick to talk."

Alan took a long, deep breath and blew it out his mouth in a gust. He scooted over to sit next to me and took my hand in his. "I'm so relieved." He was smiling, but his eyes brimmed with tears. "I assumed you couldn't talk to me because you had another man in your bed. And that thought made me crazy. I want to be the man in your bed. The *only* man in your bed. I don't want you falling in love with someone else while I'm getting my head on straight."

I wrapped my arms around him and held on tight as I sobbed. Not dainty little tears slipping down my cheeks, but big gulping sobs accompanied by large quantities of snot. Alan untangled himself and hurried to the bathroom for a box of Kleenex.

As my waves of sobs subsided, Alan gently brushed the hair back from my forehead and looked me in the eyes. "Are you sad that I want to be the only man in your bed?" He sounded puzzled and concerned.

"Oh no! Is that what you thought?" I laughed through my tears. "I always do whatever it takes to get through a crisis, and then I fall apart when the crisis is over. This is me letting go of all the tension and terror of the last week."

"Terror?"

"I was terrified that the man I love was jitterbugging down the road without me, and petrified I'd be dancing alone again."

Alan pulled me to my feet and wrapped his arms around me. We swayed gently and shuffled our feet to the rest of the Bach sonata.

July 1995

Even though Alan had decided he was ready to be in an exclusive relationship, it took almost a year before he was ready to move in with me. I invited my parents out to visit so they could meet him before he became my official roommate. As a forty-something adult, I knew it wasn't necessary for them to meet him first, but I decided it would be polite.

My father and I had had a fraught relationship ever since I married my first husband, Marc, against his wishes, when I was only twenty. When I announced my engagement, my father roared, "No daughter of mine is getting married before she turns twenty-one and has her college degree!" It was the first I'd heard of this rule, after I'd already made a commitment to break it.

With the impetuousness of youth, I roared back, "Oh yeah? Watch me!" as I stomped up the stairs to my room. The age of consent in New York was eighteen, so I knew he couldn't stop me. That was the beginning of my father not speaking to me for fourteen years, which was how long my marriage to Marc lasted.

So I wanted to be thoughtful with how I introduced Alan to my parents, not because I needed their approval, but because I wanted to avoid any hard feelings, especially long-term hard feelings. I knew Alan would charm them with his wit and kindness, and indeed he did. He listened patiently and asked pertinent questions as my dad told him the entire story of his life. During the recitation, my mother and I escaped to the back yard and puttered in the flower beds together. We told ourselves we were giving the guys some time to bond, but in reality, we'd both heard my father's stories too many times to count, and neither of us had the patience to sit through them yet again.

On the last night of my parents' visit, as Alan was saying his goodbyes and preparing to go home to his apartment, Father's parting comment to him was, "Take good care of our daughter," which raised the hackles on my neck so swiftly and surely I couldn't keep my mouth shut.

"Father, I don't need anyone to take care of me. I am a self-supporting, home-owning, independent woman, with a retirement account and a stock portfolio. I am perfectly capable of taking care of myself." I didn't say it with venom, but it was clear I was unhappy. After experiencing his underhanded put-downs for decades, maybe I was overly sensitive, but I was hurt by his suggestion that I needed a caretaker. Father stood in the middle of the living room staring at me and shaking his head. Alan and I had been standing next to the front door when this exchange occurred, and he quickly pulled me out onto the porch, into the cool evening air, and closed the door behind us. He hugged me, gently rubbing my back until I had calmed down, at which point, the front door burst open.

"Alan, I want you to know who you're getting involved with," Father barked. "If you tell Joanne to have a nice day, she'll say 'Don't tell *me* to have a nice day!'" He slammed the door shut. Through the open windows I could hear my mother trying to calm him down in the living room. She hated conflict even more than I did. I was glad they were leaving first thing in the morning.

Father's outburst didn't deter Alan from moving in, and "Don't tell *me* to have a nice day!" became one of our inside jokes.

Now, looking back at Father's comment urging Alan to take good care of me, I can imagine he might have meant something different but was incapable of articulating it: "Alan, I like you. I am glad you and Joanne found each other. May your relationship blossom into something beautiful." It's a stretch perhaps, but I will give him the posthumous benefit of the doubt.

When Alan finally made the move, I watched him claiming space in my house. I was willing to relinquish the space in order to wake up with him next to me every morning, yet I was aware of what I was giving up too. My ceilings lost the luster of purpleness that had sustained me for my single years.

That night before bed, I stood behind him watching in the bathroom mirror as he brushed his teeth. There wasn't room for me to stand next to him in front of the sink so we could brush our teeth together because he dominated the sink and surrounding counter space. He moved confidently, as if the space belonged to him alone and always had.

The day after Alan moved in, I hummed as I unpacked a box of his compact discs and alphabetized them with mine in the bookshelf next to my fireplace.

"Wait a minute!" Alan said when he saw what I was doing. "Don't you think we should mark mine with a sticker or a piece of colored tape?"

"Why do we need to do that?" I was genuinely puzzled.

"In case we need to sort them back out from each other someday."

"Oh. That hadn't occurred to me. I guess I assumed you were here to stay."

"I don't think we can assume anything until we've tried it for a while."

I was operating under different assumptions than he was, based more on wishful thinking than any concrete discussions we had had about our expectations. "I need some time to adjust to that reality," I said. "I'm going to let you finish unpacking your CDs. You can mark them any way you choose. I'm going for a walk."

I wasn't at all concerned about separating the CDs. Mine were all the Mozart, Bach, and Beethoven, the Handel and Vivaldi. His were all the Willie Nelson, Garth Brooks, Dolly Parton and John Denver. The only overlap was in some Beatles classics, an Eric Clapton album or two, and some James Taylor CDs. Surely, we could sort those out if the necessity arose.

What startled me was how easily I had fooled myself into an assumption of permanence.

The box of Alan's CDs sat on the floor in front of the bookshelf for more than a month. We both skirted it as we walked in and out of the living room. I stopped noticing it, until one day when I was vacuuming, it struck me that something was missing. Alan had finished the job of integrating his CDs with mine. None of them were marked with tape or a sticker.

Summer 1997

We decided to get married in a church. We'd already had four weddings between the two of us, and none of them had taken place in a church. And none of the marriages had lasted. With the litter of so many dashed hopes trailing behind us, it took courage on both of our parts to step up to another 'til-death-do-us-part commitment, but we trusted that living together happily for two years ahead of time and having the ceremony in a sacred space would bode well for a marriage that would stand the test of time.

Figuring out *which* church took some compromising, though. There were two Unity churches in town. I belonged to the big one in central Boulder that was led by a charismatic, street-smart New Yorker whom Alan couldn't stand. Alan belonged to a tiny start-up Unity church that had broken away from the larger congregation three years earlier and was meeting in a middle-school auditorium on the outskirts of town. I had visited his church often enough to know his minister's sermons put me to sleep, which was why I hadn't joined the exodus.

"Sweetie, I am not the least bit interested in getting married in a middle-school auditorium." I crossed my fingers that Alan would understand. "First of all, it doesn't feel like a sacred space, but the worst part is that the place smells like sweaty sneakers." With my second husband, I had refused to get married at a dude ranch, his first choice, because it smelled of horse manure. We had had such a big fight about the venue that we almost called off the wedding. I knew Alan would be more flexible.

I reminded Alan that *my* Unity had just finished building a beautiful new church, complete with a huge stained-glass window and elegant maple pews. It smelled faintly of furniture polish and the patchouli incense burned during meditation services.

"Well, I am not the least bit interested in being married by your minister," Alan huffed. "I'd vote for eloping to Las Vegas before I'd vote for having him officiate."

"Do you think they'd let us have the service at my church with your minister as the officiant? I could live with that if your minister promises to keep the homily short."

"That would work for me."

It turned out to be a good solution.

Alan asked his friend Andy to be his best man. He and Andy had participated in a men's group together for several years and had come to understand each other's deepest pains and vulnerabilities. Alan was a diehard Boston Red Sox fan, and Andy rooted with passion for the New York Yankees. They teased each other endlessly about the teams' screw-ups, shortcomings, and losing seasons, but always their friendship flourished.

Connie agreed to be my matron of honor. We had met at a divorce recovery workshop when I first moved to Boulder after divorcing my second husband. When I bought my purple-ceilinged house, I had to rebuild the fence surrounding the backyard before I could move in, because the spaces between the pickets were too wide to contain Jasmine, my miniature schnauzer. Connie volunteered to help, and we forged a close friendship as we pried off pickets, pounded nails, and shared the stories of our lives. Connie was the one who dragged me to church at Unity of Boulder for the first time, as I'd been decidedly church averse since earning my last Sunday School pin at the age of twelve. The singles' group at Unity of Boulder became the center of my social life for a while, and I met many men and women there who became longtime friends, including Beverly, who agreed to play her cello at Alan's and my wedding.

With the busyness of planning a wedding, reception, and honeymoon in addition to our full-time jobs, Alan and I were struggling to find the time to sit down and write our vows. As our wedding date loomed, we decided to take a long weekend in Steamboat Springs specifically for vow writing. We booked a room in a chalet that was tucked into a stand of pines nestled close to the ski slopes, which were blanketed in summer greenery. The spacious room was dominated by a king-size bed, piled high with goose-down pillows. We parked ourselves among the pillows and stayed there, pretty much around the clock, ordering from the room service menu when we needed sustenance and negotiating our vows.

"Wait a minute. You're not going to promise to love, honor, and obey me?" Alan asked with mock surprise.

"I'm fine with loving and honoring you to the moon and back, Sweetie, but the thought of *obeying* makes me break out in hives."

"Actually, I knew that about you," Alan said as he massaged my feet with lavender-scented massage oil. "But I always thought you looked kind of sexy with those splotches of hives blooming across your chest."

I stuck my tongue out at him. In response, he lifted my foot to his mouth and planted slow, voluptuous kisses on each of my toes, without taking his eyes off mine.

"Mmmmm. You keep that up, and we're not going to get very far with our vows."

"You're right. I'm sorry. I promise to behave." He tucked my feet under the sheet and closed the lid on the massage oil.

"I'll take a rain check, though."

"You got it," Alan agreed without a moment's hesitation.

"Is there anything else we need to add to the list before we get down to working on the exact wording?" I was the one keeping track of what we decided.

"Yep, I'd like to say something about not trying to change each other," Alan offered.

"What do you mean by that?"

"Well, I don't want you nagging me to be someone I'm not."

"Have I been doing that?"

"No, not at all. But I'm worried once we're hitched you might start. One of my previous wives did that."

"Good thing you're not married to *her* anymore. How about we each promise to accept the other just the way we are? Would that cover it for you?"

"Baggage and all?"

"Yep, baggage and all."

"Sounds perfect."

We finished our negotiations and finalized the wording of our vows early enough on Sunday that we had time to redeem the raincheck and go for a hike before we returned home. We headed up Rabbit Ears Pass, outside Steamboat, where a hiking trail followed the Continental Divide. The rain and snow that fell on the east side of the ridge drained into the Atlantic Ocean, while the basin on the west side drained into the Pacific. I pictured the ridge as a symbol of our upcoming wedding, marking the divide of our lives: before on one side and happily-ever-after on the other.

Splashes of columbine and Indian paintbrush decorated the meadows along the trail, and the raucous caws of Steller's jays accompanied our footsteps.

August 2, 1997

Before the service, as I waited nervously in the bride's dressing room, Alan's younger daughter, Megan, poked her head in the door. Blond, blue-eyed Megan was twenty-three at the time and was just starting out in her career in corporate finance at a firm in Denver. Both of Alan's daughters were busy with their own lives and careers and boyfriends and didn't seem very invested in spending time with their father and his soon-to-be-wife, so I didn't have a close relationship with either of them, but Megan in particular had felt wary over the past three years. I chalked it up to the hard time she'd had with her previous stepmother and tried not to take it personally.

"Can I come in a minute?" Megan asked, as her eyes darted around the messy room that served dual duty as the sound booth for the sanctuary.

"Of course."

"I wanted to make sure you had your bases covered with 'something old, something new, something borrowed, something blue.' I was pretty sure you had 'something new' taken care of, since your dress is new, so I only brought the other three."

"How sweet of you! I do have the 'new' and the 'blue' under control, but not the rest." I hoisted my skirt to show off the pale blue garter hugging my thigh beneath my dress. She giggled and pocketed the dainty blue handkerchief she'd brought in case I needed it.

"This bracelet was my Grandmother Kelly's," she said as she held it out to me. "I'm not giving it to you, I'm just offering to lend it to you. That way it covers both the 'old' and 'borrowed' categories."

"Perfect! Look at how well it goes with my pearl earrings!" I held the bracelet, with its three strands of tiny pearls, next to my earrings and admired it in the full-length mirror. Megan stood behind me, and our reflections smiled at each other. Even if the bracelet had clashed with my outfit, I would have worn it gladly anyway.

I slipped the bracelet over my wrist and held out my arm for Megan to fasten the clasp. It took her several tries before the antique closure cooperated, but she eventually managed to secure it. She gave my hand a quick squeeze when she was done. I pulled Megan to me in a bear hug and whispered in her ear, "Thank you, Megan. I'm touched by your thoughtfulness." Then she slipped back out the door to join our other guests in the padded maple pews.

The folder containing all my wedding to-do lists, the guest list, the contracts and invoices for the photographer, the reception, the DJ, and even the receipt for Alan's wedding band hung in the three-drawer file cabinet in the corner of my home office, almost a quarter of a century after the ceremony. The only thing missing from the folder was a copy of our vows, for which I would gladly have traded all the other documents. *How could I have allowed that precious piece of paper to escape my grasp?*

August 3, 1997

I had found us the perfect honeymoon cottage perched on the banks of the Russian River, on the outskirts of Healdsburg in California's wine country. Looking back, I wonder how I found that spot. The Internet was still in its infancy then, and while I was definitely an early adopter, perhaps even an early evangelist, I don't recall finding our cottage online. I'm sure I didn't call a travel agent. Maybe I had a copy of a Frommer's guide from the library. In any case, it turned out to be an inspired find, a lovely hideaway.

A redwood tree growing up through the middle of the kitchen was the most notable feature of our cottage. We'd read about it in the brochure they'd sent us, so it wasn't a surprise, but we found it more charming than either of us had expected.

"I love it!" I exclaimed as I walked in the door. The redwood's wide trunk emerged through the floor, bifurcating the room, and exited through the roof. "It feels rustic and smells like we're in the woods, but it's got all the comforts of home. This is my kind of roughing it!"

"Wow! I wonder how they engineered the floor and the roof to allow for the tree's expansion as it grows." Alan always wanted to know how things were made, how they worked. He pulled a chair over to stand on so he could get a closer look at the ceiling.

While Alan was examining the cottage's kitchen ceiling, I was falling in love with the bedroom. Large French doors stood opposite the bed, and they opened onto a deck that looked out over rolling hills planted with row upon row of grapevines and framed by distant pines, firs, and redwoods. That first evening, we threw the French doors wide open and lay back on our pillows.

"It's magical," Alan whispered as we watched the swallows

swoop though the twilight, scribing arcs through the air as the stars appeared.

"Do you mean the swallows or my negligee?" I whispered back.

Alan guffawed. "Both, of course." He turned his attention away from the swallows and nibbled my earlobe between bouts of laughter.

After breakfast each morning, we headed out for wine tasting. We meandered from winery to winery without much of an agenda. At our first winery, Alan had said to the tasting room host, "We know you make the best zinfandel in the valley, but who would you recommend for the second-place prize?" That line had worked so well he used it repeatedly, so we always had a list of good candidates to try next. We crisscrossed the valley on back roads, visiting tiny wineries like Limerick Lane Cellars and Hop Kiln Estates, as well as more corporate establishments like Rodney Strong and Alexander Valley. We took turns on different days being the designated spitter and the person allowed to swallow the samples. By lunchtime, one of us would be tipsy.

We'd stop at the grocery store in Healdsburg to buy a crusty loaf of French bread, some cheese and fruit, some decadent chocolates, and head back to our cottage for a picnic on the riverbank. As the sun climbed high overhead and the heat lulled us into indolence, we'd pull on our bathing suits and slip into the river.

"Yikes! Help!" I squealed as I lost my footing navigating the slippery stone steps leading down to the water. Instead of offering me a hand, Alan gave me a playful shove and I flopped clumsily into the river. I came up sputtering and giggling and grabbed the largest of the innertubes—one from an oversize truck tire that gave me lots of room to lounge—from its perch on the bank.

Alan entered the water more gracefully but had to settle for the smaller innertube since I'd draped myself into the deluxe model. He hooked his feet through the bottom of my tube so we floated together. The current was sluggish at that time of year, and we drifted lazily, barely moving, the sun melting the stress from our faces.

"Do you think we'd get bored if we did this every day for the rest of our lives?" Alan asked me as we drifted.

"I don't know, but I'd be willing to try," I said as I listened to the birds' giddy twittering in the trees along the riverbank.

"Listen! Did you hear that?" Alan sat up straight in his innertube, which made us both tip precariously, and cocked his ear.

"Hear what?"

"The bird that's saying, 'Hi, Sweetie.'"

I listened for a few seconds until the voice of a single bird differentiated itself from the background babble of bird calls. "That one?"

"Yep, that one."

"I heard him earlier but I thought he was saying, 'Cheeseburger,'" I said with a laugh.

"Boy, do you need to brush up on your birdcall vocabulary," Alan answered, working hard to keep a straight face. "He's definitely saying, 'Hi, Sweetie,' and I'm pretty sure he's speaking to you. It's chickadees who talk like that. We have them at home too."

"Hmm. Thanks for the birdy language lesson." I settled back into my tube.

Alan trailed his hand in the water and flicked droplets on my face. "That feels divine," I whispered, too lazy to add volume to my voice.

After we'd drifted for a while—perhaps an hour—Alan announced, "My fingers are starting to look like prunes. What would you say to a nap?" I knew what would follow the nap, and both the nap and the after party sounded like fine ideas to me. This time, he offered me his hand on the steps.

In the early evening, we showered and headed out for a dinner at a farm-to-table restaurant we had stumbled across on our travels earlier in the day.

And the next day, we did the same all over again.

1998

Shortly before we were married, the plastics company where Alan worked was bought by a nationwide company that was on a spree, buying up small companies with expertise in molding precision plastic parts for the medical industry. At first, it seemed like good news, since the larger company offered a more robust benefits package. But it wasn't long before Alan got the bad news: The large company had its own national sales and marketing teams, so Alan's job was being eliminated.

Alan quickly discovered the entire injection molding industry was consolidating, and many plastics jobs were being outsourced to distant parts of the world. A couple of companies offered Alan sales positions, but he was smart enough to turn them down. He viewed sales as having to ask people for something, which made him uncomfortable. He did much better in positions where he viewed himself as helping customers solve problems, where he was offering something rather than asking for something. He picked up a few contract jobs, managing individual projects for various manufacturers, but all of them were short-term positions by design.

After a couple years, Alan felt worn out from trying to string together a steady flow of short-term gigs and battered by the uncertainly of what to do next. He hunkered down and played house husband intensely for months on end, taking over many of my household chores so I could work longer hours at my freelance marketing and writing jobs to make up for his lost income. He devoted endless hours to shopping for food and cooking extravagant meals.

"What are you making for dinner tonight, Sweetie?" I asked as I grabbed a cup of coffee on my way to my office three steps down the hall.

"I found a fabulous-looking recipe in *Bon Appetit* for an Italian fish stew with fresh fennel. I thought I'd make it with either mahi-mahi or halibut and serve it over polenta. How does that sound?"

"Heavenly!" I answered. "But haven't we had fresh fennel three times this week already?"

"Yeah. I guess I'm on a fennel bender. Is that a problem?"

"I could use a break from it." It was a luxury having a live-in personal chef, and I knew Alan was still feeling fragile from all the turmoil in his career, so I didn't want to be too critical.

"If I make you one of my famous chocolate tarts with the walnut crust, will you forgive the fennel overdose for one more night?"

"It's a deal! But you have to promise me a whole week off from fennel next week." I loved his chocolate tart.

The problem was that Alan wasn't working very hard at finding a new job. I bought him a copy of *What Color Is Your Parachute*, but I don't think he ever read it. I'm not sure he even opened it. He talked about maybe going back to school to become a massage therapist or a psychotherapist, but he was in his early fifties and felt like he was too old to go back to school.

I urged him to find a therapist who could help him figure out a path that felt right for him. But he didn't do that, either.

I started getting cranky.

"Alan, I love my work." I tried to keep my voice neutral, but I could hear myself slipping into crabbiness. "I've always been willing to put in long hours to meet urgent deadlines or squeeze in a last-minute job for a desperate client, but I can't keep doing this nonstop. I need a break and don't feel like I can afford to take one." We had just finished a major remodel of a new home, and with Alan not bringing in any income, we had ended up with a much bigger mortgage than we had anticipated. And the money he was spending on lift tickets in the winter and greens fees the rest of the year irked me.

"I'm sorry, Sweetie." Alan was contrite. He was always contrite when I brought up the subject of finding work, but it wasn't leading to action.

"How about we go up to the mountains for a long weekend to give you a break?" he suggested.

"We can't afford a long weekend in the mountains!" I slammed the rolled-up newspaper on the edge of the dining room table, partly out of frustration and partly for emphasis. The breakfast dishes rattled, and Alan jumped up quickly, scanning the room as if he were looking for the closest exit.

"It was not part of the plan for me to support you so you could enjoy an early retirement," I fumed. "Why aren't you working harder at finding a job?"

Alan sat back down at the table and hung his head. "I don't want to go back to the plastics industry," he confessed. "All the other jobs I've looked at don't pay squat." He heaved a big sigh and paused before continuing. "What I really want to do is become a handyman, doing fix-it jobs, helping people maintain their homes, and working on small remodeling projects. But I'm pretty nervous about doing that."

"Because you don't have the right skills?"

"No. That's not it." He fidgeted with a spoon that was resting in a cereal bowl, and I could see the muscles under his left eye twitching.

"What's the problem, then?"

He sighed again and kept his eyes glued to the spoon. "I'm afraid you'll leave me if I make my living doing something so menial."

My anger evaporated. "Sweetie, it took me years to find the man I wanted to spend the rest of my life with. If you think I'd leave you after all that work, you're not as smart as you look."

"Are you sure?" Alan sounded incredulous.

"If being a handyman would give you joy, I would support you in doing that," I answered, taking the spoon from him and giving his hand a squeeze.

"I'm sure I wouldn't make much money, especially at first."

"I'd much rather see you doing something you love and not making much money than have you doing a job you hate just to make more money or have more prestige." I knew we could downsize to a more compact house with a smaller mortgage if we needed to. "If becoming a handyman is what you want to do, go for it!"

And so he did. And he ended up loving it. Helping people with home repair and maintenance fed his soul like nothing he had done before. The learning curve was steep, but Alan was good at problem solving and good at finding books, articles, and videos that showed him step-by-step how to do things like fix leaky toilets, replace garbage disposals, install kitchen cabinets, hang doors, and replace screens. He quickly had a backlog of projects to keep him busy and a growing list of clients who were delighted to have a handyman who was reliable, trustworthy, and intelligent, and who made them laugh.

Working as a freelancer or contractor was a good fit for me. I would attend meetings with my clients at their workplaces, where we would discuss the objectives and project parameters, and I would get up to speed on the target audiences, the products involved, the features and benefits, and the relevant technologies. Then I would go back to my desk in my home office and generate drafts of the requested materials. Working this way suited me because I learned over the years that I need quiet, uninterrupted blocks of time to do my best work. I can't concentrate well in noisy office spaces where phones are ringing and people are talking to each other and someone is stopping by to ask if I will sign a card for a coworker who is about to retire. When someone or something interrupts me, I have to start all over on the train of thought I was building, word by word, phrase by phrase, in my head.

Writing in the solitude and quiet of my home office worked well until Alan stopped working at a nine-to-five job and became a self-employed contractor himself. As a handyman, his days had more flexibility than when he worked at his previous desk job. He'd be on his way to pick up plumbing supplies or driving across town from one job site to the next, and he couldn't resist the urge to call me.

"Hi, Sweetie," he would say when I picked up his call. "I was thinking about how happy I am to be married to you and thought I'd call to tell you how very much I love you."

What could I say? Most women would be thrilled to have their husbands calling daily to profess their love and appreciation.

Most of the time, I would thank him in the moment for being so sweet and thoughtful and return the warm fuzzies. But while we were eating dinner that night, I might mention a study I'd read that said it took people an average of twenty-five minutes to return to the original task after an interruption and remind him how hard it is for me to find my groove again once I'm jolted out of it, even by the sweetest of sweet talk.

Alan would hang his head and apologize, but a few days later, he'd call me again to express his overflowing affection. That night at supper, I would mention again how hard it was for me to pick up the thread of my work after he called.

Of course, I considered not answering his calls during my workday, but I couldn't bring myself to actually do it. What if he'd been in a car accident and needed me to come pick him up? What if he'd been shot by someone robbing a gas station where he was filling his van? What if he'd just learned his daughter had a massive brain tumor and he needed me to reassure him everything would be okay? Two of those things had actually happened (he'd never been shot during a gas station robbery), but it didn't stop my mind from making up all sorts of scary stories that distracted me even more than stopping to talk to him would.

Ultimately, we reached a compromise. I stopped complaining as long as he didn't call me more than once a week during the workday. I finally learned to close my eyes and appreciate all the love humming over the telephone network, all the love enfolding me from my sweet, sweet husband.

Not long after we were married, I gave up my resistance to joining Alan's church because I wanted to attend church with my husband, to sit next to him and hold his hand, to discuss the sermons with him, to be friends with his community of church friends. And to be perfectly honest, I also wanted to make sure all the single women in the congregation could plainly see he was happily married.

Once I was firmly integrated into the congregation, Alan and I attended the wedding reception of a mutual friend from church. The bride was a member of the quilting circle that met at our house on Tuesday evenings, and the husband was one of Alan's home-maintenance clients.

During the reception, one of the bride's neighbors, a woman we hadn't met before, sat at the table with us. As she sipped her champagne, she kept glancing over at Alan. I suspected she was trying not to stare, but I couldn't figure out why. His pants were zipped. He didn't have spinach caught in his teeth. I figured he must look like someone she knew from her past.

As Alan got up to dance with the bride, the neighbor leaned over and whispered to me, "Your husband is the most handsome man I've ever laid eyes on."

"He cleans up well, doesn't he?" I responded. He did look handsome in his suit and tie, but I was a bit surprised by the woman's "most handsome man" accolades. That covers a lot of ground, half the human race.

If you looked at the individual elements of Alan's face, they were not perfect. His nose had a beak-like hook and was large for his face. His front teeth were crooked, overlapping. He had a weak chin, but he kept it well hidden with a carefully trimmed beard.

On the other hand, he had beautiful blue eyes that sparkled when he smiled. His lush and wavy hair always looked well groomed. At the time, Alan's body was trim and athletic, with only the barest hint of mid-fifties, age-appropriate pudginess around his belly. When you put all the pieces together, he looked distinguished, striking even, but not in an air-brushed male-model sort of way. More in the way that illustrates the Japanese concept of *wabi-sabi*: the idea that beauty incorporates that which is imperfect or transient.

Teasing out the separate threads that form the weave of attraction between two people is complicated, but I don't think Alan's good looks played more than a passing role in the spark between us back when we first met, when he first hired me. Beyond the initial electricity, what drew me to him was the kindness in his smile, the effervescent goodness that lit his eyes, the aura of good humor and friendliness that emanated from his pores. His joie de vivre.

CHAPTER 3

2009–2012

In 2009 and 2010, I flew back and forth from Boulder to Albany, New York, every other month, trying to figure out how to best support my parents, who were both in their early eighties. My mother's dementia had been creeping forward like a skunk at dusk. My father really didn't want to deal with it. On some level, I think he thought that if he ignored the skunk, it would go away eventually. But instead, the skunk reappeared daily, bringing its extended family along to make a permanent home under the porch.

I tried to arrange everything from doctor appointments to respite care to meal delivery services—anything I could think of to take the burden off my father, who was feeling increasingly stressed and increasingly bewildered, and to make life a bit more pleasant for my mother, who was disappearing by degrees.

But the more I tried to help, the harder Father pushed back. His Depression-era upbringing trumped all the logic I could muster and trashed all the arrangements I labored to research and line up, even when I had gotten his buy-in up front. It wasn't that he didn't have the money to pay for services that would improve the quality of their lives. The problem was he couldn't let go of his need to save it all for a rainier day. Whatever a rainier day looked like at that point.

After my mother incinerated one too many dinners by putting a pan of chicken or pork chops in the oven and forgetting she had done so, after she burned the bottoms out of several saucepans by leaving something simmering and walking away, after she microwaved leftovers covered with aluminum foil, I finally convinced Father it had reached the point where it wasn't safe for her to cook, and it wasn't safe for him to leave her home unsupervised. My dad, who had always expected my mother to cater to his needs and bend her life around his priorities, was at his wits' end. He was having more and more trouble managing the finances and the car and yard maintenance and all the tasks he traditionally handled. The idea of taking on Mother's duties as well seemed daunting to him. Offering Mother the support and nurturing she so desperately needed didn't even make his list.

Whenever I returned from a visit to Albany, I unloaded my fears and frustrations on Alan. He listened well and commiserated copiously.

"Argh! Father keeps undoing all the arrangements I make to get Mother some extra care and attention, even when he has agreed to it beforehand," I complained. "He yells at her for forgetting things—'Margaret, why are you doing this to me?'—and acts like she is doing it just to torture him. I can't stand it when he yells at her. He thinks he is doing a fine job of taking care of her, but he can't even see what she needs."

Alan listened attentively as I vented. I don't think he was surprised when I brought up the possibility of moving them to Boulder to live with us.

"It would be horribly stressful for you," Alan answered. He knew my dad and I had clashed for decades.

"Of course, it would be. But you'll help me get through it, won't you? You'll listen to me bitch and moan, and then I'll feel better. Right?"

Early in our relationship, I had discovered it was best to plant a seed with Alan and then let him ruminate on it for a while before bringing up the question again. I'd learned the hard way that he didn't like to be pushed too hard, too soon. It didn't take him long to start throwing out ideas for remodeling our downstairs to create a pleasant living area for my parents.

"We could turn the laundry room into a kitchenette," he suggested. "But without a stove so your mom isn't tempted to cook. And we can widen the downstairs bathroom door so we can get a wheelchair in when she needs one." At that point, I knew he was on board.

It took a while to convince Father to move halfway across the county. He knew he needed help with my mother, but he couldn't imagine abandoning their neighborhood or their friends or packing up their house, which was quite literally stuffed to the rafters with all the odds and ends they couldn't bear to part with after a lifetime of accumulating twist ties and scraps of wrapping paper and used envelopes, the blank side of which could still be used for making lists and writing reminders. And then there were all the boxes of my maternal grandparents' possessions, which had resided untouched in my parents' attic for several decades. It took a side-by-side comparison of local sales tax rates and state income tax rates, New York versus Colorado, to finally convince Father to move. Meanwhile, Alan and I proceeded with the remodel of our garden-level downstairs.

2011

The first inkling we had that something strange was happening in Alan's brain was nearly a decade before he died—although we didn't realize the significance of the problem at the time—when he started acting out in the middle of the night while he slept. He might flail his arms and yell, or grunt and groan and kick the mattress repeatedly. Not every night and certainly not all night long. He might act out briefly for three nights in a row and then not have another episode for a month. At first we made light of it and didn't worry much, but as his episodes increased in frequency, duration, and intensity, I became more concerned. Alan didn't seem particularly worried, probably because he only heard about the commotion secondhand—he slept soundly through all the antics and didn't remember any of it the next morning. And also because I was the designated worrier of our family.

I did what I always do when faced with a new or confusing situation: I turned to Google. It didn't take me long to uncover a disorder that fit his symptoms: rapid eye movement (REM) sleep behavior disorder, which causes people—mostly men over fifty—to have violent dreams and act them out without waking up. The mechanism that paralyzes the muscles during REM sleep stops functioning properly. Of course, I didn't know for sure that's what he had, but it seemed to fit. I started waking Alan up during the episodes to ask what he was dreaming.

"The buffaloes were stampeding!" he gasped when I woke him one night when he was groaning in distress while his legs jerked and twitched furiously. "I couldn't get out of their way, and I couldn't outrun them. I was about to get trampled to death." After a few deep breaths, he thanked me for saving his life. I was amused to be an unintentional hero, and amazed and jealous when he promptly rolled over and fell back asleep. Being woken abruptly by all the noise and commotion had filled my veins with adrenaline that took hours to dissipate.

I never knew in advance when Alan would battle drunken bikers in a dark alley or throw punches at schoolyard bullies in the middle of the night. Being jolted awake by screams was terrifying. It was the unexpectedness and the violence of the encounters that left me stunned and wide awake.

One summer night in 2011, we were helping my parents sort their possessions in preparation for their move from Albany to Boulder. Alan and I were sleeping in the bedroom where I had slept the summer before I headed off to college. That night, Alan knocked a milk-glass lamp off the bedside table while he scuffled with muggers who were trying to steal his wallet in his dreamscape world, waking me and my aging parents and shattering the lamp.

"That's it!" I declared as I swept up shards of glass at three in the morning. "As soon as we get back home, I am making an appointment for you with a sleep doctor. And I'm going with you so I can tell him how it looks from my side of the bed."

"I guess it's time," Alan answered with a yawn.

It took several months for Alan to get in to see the sleep specialist and a couple more months after that before he could be scheduled for an overnight sleep test. But, finally, the big night arrived in early December. The lab technicians attached electrodes and sensors to his head and chest and instructed him to sleep on a wired bed in the middle of the room. There was no way to plan the timing of the test in advance, and unfortunately, it happened during one of the periods when Alan was not having violent and noisy dreams. Although the sleep test showed two brief periods when Alan's body was not paralyzed during REM sleep, they were so short the doctor dismissed their significance with a wave of his hand. Based on the stories we told, not on the sleep test results, he lumped Alan's sleep problems into the broad category of "parasomnias," a category that includes sleepwalking, bedwetting, and nightmares, and sent us home with a prescription for a drug that would reduce the frequency of the nighttime outbursts.

The sleep test revealed that Alan's sleep latency was 1.8 minutes. In other words, it had taken him less than two minutes to fall asleep, despite the wires protruding from his scalp, the strange bed, and the unfamiliar environment. I was not surprised, because he had always fallen asleep easily. But I *was* filled with envy. *How does he turn off his brain so quickly,* I wondered. *How can I learn that skill?*

While it helped, the prescribed drug didn't eliminate Alan's sleep disturbances. The doctor increased his dosage several times, and each time Alan would sleep more peacefully for a few months before the violent episodes flared up again, stronger than ever. It was the only prescription drug available, but users could develop a tolerance to it if they weren't careful, and a large study showed a strong correlation between long-term use of the drug and the development of Alzheimer's disease later in life. We didn't want to do anything that might jeopardize his brain. So, eventually, he weaned himself off the drug.

After we got my parents sorted out and moved, they settled into their new home in Boulder in our newly refurbished downstairs apartment. But as Father tried to adapt to a new routine, I became increasingly concerned about *his* cognitive abilities. He'd been living with us for two weeks when I asked him to get the mail from the mailbox at the front curb. He walked out the *back* door, thinking he was heading in the right direction, and got lost in the yard.

Every morning and every evening, he would stand at the bottom of the stairs and yell up to me, "Joanne, I can't find my toothbrush. Did we forget to bring it?" He couldn't remember that the mirror on the wall in his bathroom concealed a medicine cabinet where we'd stowed the toothbrushes and toothpaste. Every morning and every evening I'd trot down the stairs and show him the medicine cabinet, and every morning and every evening he was surprised it was there.

"Well, look at that!" he'd say with a chuckle, as if he thought it was a clever place to hide a medicine cabinet. Eventually, I decided it wasn't something he was ever going to remember, and I moved the toothbrushes and toothpaste to the bathroom counter.

I knew caring for my mother had taken a toll on Father and that moving to a new home after so many years in the same location was a major life stressor, so I tried to rationalize away his lapses. But it became increasingly clear that the routine in my parents' lives in New York had made it possible for my dad to hide significant cognitive deficits. Trying to adapt to a new routine exposed them, one by one.

A few months after they moved in, Mother started using the wastebasket in the kitchenette as a toilet. And a few months later, she started having trouble negotiating the stairs.

I would hear her whimpering on the stairs from my office, which was right at the top of the stairs. Knowing my father was not paying attention to her whereabouts, I'd jump up from my desk to rescue her.

"What's wrong, Mother? Do you need help?'

"I'm stuck," she'd say, sounding bewildered.

"Well, that's not very fun. Let me see if I can help you figure this out. Can you turn around and take a step down?" She'd stand there, perched on the step, grasping the railing, struggling to figure out how to take a step down.

"Pick up this foot." I'd bend over and touch her ankle so she knew which foot to move. "Now move it to the next step down." I'd hold her arm as I talked her through each step. When we reached the bottom of the stairs, I'd call out to Father, who usually had his nose glued to a book or to his computer screen in his office. He would heave a big sigh, a "poor me" sigh, to indicate his displeasure at being interrupted. I would suggest he take Mother for a walk around the block. He'd act like it was a big imposition, but he'd do it.

I'd go back up to my office and try to pick up where I'd left off with my work.

When Mother started getting stuck on the stairs regularly, we solved the problem by installing a baby gate across the bottom of the stairs.

Then Mother lost the ability to feed herself, and before long, she refused to eat when Father tried to feed her. She wasn't buying his "You have to do this because I said so" approach. She *would* eat when I fed her. I would smile at her and tell her the same three funny stories, over and over, trying to distract her enough that she didn't even notice she was eating. I would alternate between bites of brownie and bites of chicken, or pudding and green beans, or noodles and salad, until she had had enough.

Much of the time, she didn't recognize me as her daughter. She mostly referred to me as "that really nice lady." I didn't care what she called me; I was just glad to be able to inject a little kindness and comfort in her life.

Mother and Father had lived with us for not quite a year when one night Father woke me shortly after midnight.

"Something is wrong with your mother, and I don't know what to do," he said. He sounded scared. Never before had I heard my father admit he didn't know what to do.

I grabbed my robe and ran down the stairs to find Mother sitting on the edge of their bed in her shabby nightgown, moaning and staring blankly into the middle distance.

"Can you tell me where you hurt?" I asked. She rocked back and forth, grimacing, but she didn't respond.

"Do you want to lie down?" No answer, just more moaning, more rocking.

"Do you need a drink of water?" No response.

Father and I discussed the options. We decided to call 911 in case she had had a stroke. Alan met the ambulance out front and directed them to the driveway beside the house. The EMTs wheeled a gurney down the back sidewalk. It was Mother's fourth trip to the emergency room in as many months.

It didn't take the ER physician long to figure out she had pneumonia.

"What would you like to do about her pneumonia?" the doctor asked my dad. Too shaken to respond, Father flashed me a forlorn, beseeching look, asking for help with his eyes.

"Would you explain to us what the options are?" I asked the doctor.

"Well, we can start her on IV antibiotics and keep her for observation for a couple of days. Or you can decide not to treat her and take her home."

I turned to face my dad. Slouched in his plastic chair, he looked shrunken and wizened, as if he were an apple left too long on the shelf. I could tell he didn't understand the implications of the second option.

"What could we expect if we chose not to treat her?" I asked without taking my eyes off my dad.

"We would make a recommendation for her to have hospice care at home, and hospice would make sure she stays comfortable. Most likely your mother would stop eating and drinking pretty quickly, then it would take her another few days to slip into a coma and perhaps another day or two to die. So maybe a week."

Suddenly alert, Father sat up straight in his chair and growled at the doctor, "Why would we do that?" He did not say, "Why would we do that, *you stupid cretin*?" but his tone of voice made clear that's what he meant.

"Because it would be a very humane way for your wife to die, given her medical history," the doctor answered, his voice full of compassion. "I am not trying to talk you into anything here. I'm merely giving you some options to consider. You take your time thinking about this. I'll stop back in a little while to see if you have any more questions." As he left, the doctor pulled the curtain across the entrance to the emergency room bay, giving us a scrim of privacy. Mother drifted off to sleep in her gurney, and Father and I sat next to her in our rigid plastic chairs, the lights turned off.

"What do you think, Father? Would it be more loving to help Mother live or to allow her to die?"

"I don't want her to die!" Just the thought of it made him weep. He took off his glasses, pulled his handkerchief out of his pocket, mopped his eyes, and blew his nose with loud abandon, a foghorn in the darkness. Mother moaned quietly in her sleep, but she didn't rouse. "We've been married for sixty-three years. How would I live without her?"

"I know it would be really hard for you to let her go," I said. "But I think it might also be really hard for you to watch her continue to deteriorate until there's not a scrap left of the woman you married." Father stared at his hands in his lap, trying to control his tears.

"What do you think Mother would want?" I asked.

"She'd be horrified if she could see herself objectively now. Incontinent. Constantly confused. Unable to recognize her own children. Unable to feed herself or bathe herself or brush her own teeth." He started to weep again.

I reached out and grabbed his hand. We had never been affectionate with each other. I could count on one hand the number of times he had hugged me since I reached puberty. But we'd never had a discussion like this before. Holding his hand seemed like the right thing to do. He didn't extricate his hand from mine until he needed to use his handkerchief again.

Dawn was already lifting the opaque film of night from the edges of the Colorado sky when the same ambulance crew that had taken Mother to the hospital a few hours earlier brought her home to die.

Five days later, Father and I each held one of her hands as she took her last breath.

February 2015

Alan and I stopped sleeping in the same bed, or even the same room, one night in 2015, shortly after Valentine's Day, when I awoke to find him on top of me. He held me down with one hand and punched me in the face with the other, mid-dream.

"Alan, wake up!" I screamed again and again. His fist kept right on pummeling my face. I tried to escape his grasp, but no amount of struggling made a whit of difference. Frantic, I kneed him in the groin. Not hard enough to hurt him badly, but hard enough to get his attention. He released his hold on me and rolled over on his back, finally awake, but groggy and confused.

"What? What?" He sounded angry, as if he might start swinging again.

"You attacked me! You wouldn't stop punching me," I sobbed. I sat up and turned my back to him, turning on the lamp on my bedside table so I could see how badly I was bleeding.

"Oh no! Oh, Sweetie! I am so sorry. I didn't mean to hurt you." He cried too, but when he tried to put his arms around my shoulders to comfort me, I pushed him away. I didn't want him touching me.

"I don't give a rat's ass where you sleep for the rest of the night, but it's not going to be with me. You can grab a blanket from the linen closet." I threw a pillow at him and hurried down the hall to the kitchen for an ice pack and some paper towels. After I mopped up the blood, I crawled back in bed, held the ice pack to my nose and turned the light back off.

I was sure my nose was broken. It turned out it wasn't, but my face was sore and black and blue for days, and then yellow and green as the bruises healed. I was grateful to discover a tray of pancake makeup, leftover from a long-ago Halloween, in the bottom of a bathroom drawer. I carefully hid the bursts of color before we went out shopping for a bed to turn Alan's office into a bedroom. I didn't want anyone to think I was a battered wife. Or that Alan was a batterer.

Over the next week, Alan must have apologized a thousand

times, but I wasn't angry with him any longer. Wary maybe, but not angry. I knew he hadn't injured me intentionally or even knowingly.

I missed sharing a bed with Alan. I missed cuddling him in the middle of the night and waking up with him next to me in the morning. I missed the tender moments and intimate interludes that occur spontaneously in bed. But I didn't miss dodging his fists and elbows or being jolted awake by his screams and curses, groans and grunts. I slept more soundly with Alan in the next room, but my heart was heavy and my skin parched, thirsty for his.

June 2015

As Alan's list of symptoms grew longer and more baffling, his neurologist—a general neurologist who handled patients with everything from migraines to strokes to epilepsy—referred Alan to her team's movement-disorder specialist. As the name implies, a movement-disorder specialist is a neurologist with more specialized training than a general neurologist, specifically in illnesses classified as movement disorders, things like Huntington's disease, restless leg syndrome, dystonia, and all the illnesses under the Parkinsonian umbrella.

On the day of Alan's appointment with the movement-disorder specialist, Dr. Kurtz, I marched into the office and blurted, "I think my husband has multiple system atrophy." My conclusion was based not on any extensive medical background—because I don't have one—but on my compulsive Googling of Alan's symptoms, of all possible illnesses that might fit his history, of all research and observational studies that might be related in some way, tangentially or otherwise.

It was probably the first time in my life I really didn't want to be right.

I suspect doctors hate it when patients or their family members come in with all the answers after scouring the web, but at least Dr. Kurtz was polite about it when I offered my layman's conclusion. I probably wasn't the first opinionated spouse he'd dealt with.

"Well, let's take a look at what's going on here," Dr. Kurtz replied. He pulled his stool up directly opposite Alan's chair and looked Alan in the eyes with an air of compassion and concern. After asking Alan about his medical history and symptoms, he put him through a series of exercises that appeared to test his reflexes, strength, coordination, and agility.

"Alan, can you hold your head still and follow my penlight with your eyes?" Dr. Kurtz asked. He moved the light from left to right and up and down. As far as I could tell from my position to the left of Alan, he followed the light perfectly. But I had no idea what Dr. Kurtz was looking for. Was he just trying to see if Alan could track the movement of the light, or was he looking for involuntary twitches in his eye muscles or something else altogether? Feeling embarrassed by my earlier presumption, I didn't want to intrude, so I didn't ask.

"Okay. Hold your right hand out with your palm facing up, then turn your palm over facing the floor and back facing up as quickly as you can. Don't stop until I tell you to." Alan did as he was instructed, moving without hesitation.

"Good. Now the same with your left hand." Even though Alan was left-handed, there were many activities he did equally well with his right hand. He batted left-handed but golfed right-handed and was ambidextrous when it came to brushing his teeth. When he walked, his right hand swung normally, but his left hand barely moved, probably as a result of his unnamed illness. For this exercise, I couldn't tell if one hand moved with more fluidity than the other. I wanted to ask Dr. Kurtz a hundred questions about the tests and what he was learning from them, but it felt rude for me to interrupt.

"Now I want you to touch my finger with your index finger, then touch the end of your nose. Keep doing it until I tell you to stop." Dr. Kurtz moved his finger constantly, so Alan had to pay attention and react quickly. Again, it seemed to me that Alan executed the moves flawlessly. But what did I know? Dr. Kurtz gave no indication that anything was amiss.

When he was finished with his clinical exam, Dr. Kurtz again sat in front of Alan and spoke directly to him, not to us as a couple. I was taking notes, but I felt invisible. "I suspect you have dementia with Lewy bodies, rather than multiple system atrophy. The two illnesses have overlapping symptoms and are difficult to distinguish from each other in the early stages. Dementia with Lewy bodies usually presents with more problems with cognitive function than MSA. I'd like to see you every six months. As your illness progresses, it will be easier to tell what's really going on." He did not exactly say, "Come back when you are sicker, and then we'll be able to make a diagnosis," but that's what Alan and I heard.

Dr. Kurtz seemed to base his hypothesis of dementia with Lewy bodies—at least in part—on an incident we shared where Alan's memory failed him. Alan had dropped off my father at the bank while he made a quick stop at the grocery store, but then he forgot to return to the bank and pick up my dad before he came home. I was in my office on a conference call with a client and didn't notice that only Alan came home. To be honest, I hadn't even noticed he and Father had left in the first place. Two hours later, with my workday finished, I was putting the final touches on our evening meal.

"I'm ready to put dinner on the table," I said to Alan, who was sous-chef that night. "Would you let Father know, please?"

Alan stood at the top of the stairs and yelled "Fred! Dinner," but didn't get an answer. Seconds later, it dawned on him: "Oh, my God! I left him at the bank. Oh my God! He's going to be furious." He grabbed his keys and ran out the door.

Father was still standing in front of the bank when Alan rushed back to get him, two hours later. My dad had forgotten his wallet, so he didn't have my phone number with him, nor did he have a cell phone because his memory impairment prevented him from mastering the fundamentals of using one. And he was way too proud to ask someone for help. So he stood where he was, on the concrete steps leading to the bank entrance. Under the circumstances, staying put was a good idea.

Alan was mortified by his mistake and the abject failure of his memory, and he apologized for weeks to my dad and to me. I was glad the weather had been decent that day and no irreparable harm had been done, and I hoped Alan's excessive apologizing would make an impression on my dad, that he might notice that adult males are capable of acknowledging their errors and attempting to make amends. But if he noticed, he never mentioned it, and I made a conscious decision not to point it out to him. Bringing it up it would most likely merely annoy a man who was almost constantly irritable already. I knew he wasn't going to learn any new tricks at this point in his life, so why bother?

I was heartbroken when the neurologist proposed dementia with Lewy bodies as Alan's most likely diagnosis. I didn't want Alan to be sick at all, but mostly I did *not* want him to have anything that even vaguely looked like or smelled like or tasted like dementia. I knew from my research that MSA was a nasty illness, but I didn't know it in my bones. Dementia I knew intimately. I'd watched my demented mother disappear gradually until she died in 2012, and I was still taking care of my father, whose dementia bloomed more robustly every day. I couldn't stand the thought of Alan leaving me mentally, of his getting to the point where delusions, hallucinations, and plain old forgetfulness would send him into another dimension where I couldn't reach him, and he didn't recognize me as his wife.

Alan was devastated too, of course, but not so much by the idea of dementia with Lewy bodies. He was beside himself with grief that he was going to die way too soon—no matter which of the two illnesses it turned out to be—many years short of a normal lifespan, that he was not going to see his granddaughters grow up and become adults with careers and husbands and kids of their own. He was going to be disabled, mentally or physically or both, for God knows how long, and then he was going to die young. Alan was in his late sixties at that point, and instead of living for another ten or twenty years, he would be lucky to last another four.

When we got home from the appointment with the neurologist, we lay down on our bed, too stunned to even take off our shoes. We held on to each other for dear, dear life and took turns making round-robin speed trips through several stages of grief, weeping, shaking our fists, bargaining, worrying about each other, comforting, and being comforted. Whether it was MSA or dementia with Lewy bodies didn't really matter. What mattered was the loss of our dreams of growing old together. Of having a long, healthy retirement full of adventures and hikes and picnics with friends, of watching robins and finches frolic in the birdbath and spending long evenings sitting on the porch together, watching the stars come out, the moon rise.

July 2015

One morning in late July, I woke early, when dawn's diffuse light brushed the windowsill with peach fuzz. I listened to the ringed-neck mourning doves cooing to each other, the towhees trilling their distinctive *chip-chip tweee*. I could hear Alan rustling in his room, a few steps down the hall. Suddenly, he stood next to my bed, looking down on me with a strange mixture of emotion on his face: shame mixed with confusion. A little fear smudged the fringes.

"What's up?" I asked, sitting up.

Alan didn't answer right away, which alarmed me. He stared at me and struggled for words. "I . . . I wet my bed." I knew then what his face looked like when he was five.

"Are you talking about a wet dream?"

"Nope. I'm talking about waking up to find my sheets completely soaked."

"Goodness. How bizarre! Do you need a hug?"

"First, I need a shower. Then I'll take the hug."

Later that day, Google revealed that bladder issues were common in people with multiple system atrophy, but also in people who had dementia with Lewy bodies.

November 2015

I checked the government's clinical trials website regularly to see if there were any studies for which Alan might qualify. Because multiple system atrophy was so rare, there were few trials for new drugs, but because Alan didn't have a clinical diagnosis yet, he wouldn't have been eligible to participate in MSA trials anyway.

But one study sounded interesting, and it looked like Alan might qualify.

Approximately two-thirds of people who have REM sleep behavior disorder end up with one of the Parkinsonian illnesses, sometimes as much as a decade after the onset of the sleep disorder. But there was no way to predict which people would end up with regular Parkinson's or an atypical Parkinsonian illness like MSA or progressive supranuclear palsy, and which people would be in the lucky one-third who end up dodging the Parkinsonian bullet. Researchers at the University of Texas in Houston were studying volunteers who had been diagnosed with REM sleep behavior disorder to see if they could discover any blood markers, brain changes, or other physical signs that would indicate the likelihood of future illness.

Alan's violent behavior while he slept left no doubt in my mind that he had REM sleep behavior disorder, even though his sleep test in 2011 had been borderline. Alan contacted the researchers to discuss his possible participation in the study. After he sent them the results of his earlier sleep test, they urged him to come to Houston for further testing. Alan agreed for two reasons: because he genuinely wanted to help advance the science around diagnosing Parkinsonian illnesses, and because he hoped we might learn more about his individual prognosis by participating. We were both anxious to know what was happening inside Alan's brain.

We drove from Boulder to Houston in November 2015. That's the royal *we*. Actually, Alan drove the whole way there and the whole way back, more than two thousand miles altogether, because I was recovering from breaking my right ankle in two places—the result of a fall in a dark and unfamiliar stairway—and there was something about the angle of my foot on the gas pedal that made driving painful. I wore an orthopedic boot that let me walk without discomfort as long as I didn't overdo it. We each had retired in October, and we decided to make a vacation of it, taking the scenic route and stopping on the way down to explore Stephenville, Texas, where many of my father's ancestors had lived and died, and stopping on the way home in Santa Fe for a few days of R&R. I lined up people to come in and take care of my dad while we were gone, and we headed south.

We avoided the interstate highways because we wanted to see the real Texas. After hours of staring out the window at the seemingly endless emptiness, flecked sporadically with cotton, cattle, windmills, oil derricks, and small towns in various stages of decay, I gained a new appreciation for the state's vastness. Driving a Subaru in the small towns of rural Texas marked us immediately as outsiders. Pickup trucks dominated the roads, and their drivers thought nothing of going 95 mph on two-lane roads.

On our first evening in Houston, the researchers hooked an impressive array of wires and electrodes to Alan's chest and head for another sleep test. As I prepared for bed by myself in our hotel room, Alan texted me a selfie of his get-up at the university medical facility. He looked like an actor in a low-budget sci-fi movie, but he grinned from ear to ear. I was glad he could see the humor in his outfit.

Alan's sleep test confirmed our suspicions that his violent nocturnal outbursts were caused by REM sleep behavior disorder. So the next day the researchers put him through an extensive battery of tests: blood tests, different kinds of brain scans, and a variety of clinical examinations.

It was difficult to find gluten-free food at restaurants in Texas. (I had observed a strict gluten-free diet since 2008, when several health issues that had nagged me for decades were miraculously cured when I stopped eating gluten.) We were grateful to finally discover a restaurant at the hotel attached to the MD Anderson Cancer Center that catered to people's dietary restrictions. The food was uninspiring but safe. After three days in Houston, we were itching to get back on the open road, back to the emptiness.

February 11, 2016

We were huddled in the back corner of Rite-Aid where they keep the incontinence supplies—with Alan having just turned sixty-eight and me on the cusp of sixty-five—trying to figure out what kind of adult diapers we should get for Alan to wear on our upcoming trip to Mexico.

Should we buy the extra-absorbent kind, or is regular absorbency good enough for the plane flight? Are the extra-absorbent pullups going to be either too noticeable or too bulky to be comfortable? The pads were a lot cheaper than the pull-ups, but did they work as well? Can you wear them with boxer shorts, or would Alan need to get a new wardrobe of tighty-whities for the trip? We hadn't found answers online. We couldn't ask our friends—in person or on Facebook—what their experience had been, because as far as we knew, nobody we knew was incontinent. As Alan said, if any of our friends had problems with incontinence, they wouldn't "leak" the news by answering a question about Depends, would they? Nor would Alan want the world to discover his bladder problems by asking the question in the first place.

After discussing the pros and cons at length, we finally decided to buy one package of pads and one package of regular-absorbency pullups so Alan could try them out before we headed for the airport.

With our arms wrapped tightly around the bulky, plastic-wrapped unmentionables, we passed the rows of greeting cards, the aisles of makeup, the shelves full of ear wax remover and Epsom salts. As we approached the check-out counter, Alan whispered, “If you see anyone we know, pretend we’re buying these for your dad.” My dad was eighty-nine years old at the time, and despite his dementia-pocked brain, he was not incontinent. Not yet. But it was certainly more believable that he would need adult diapers rather than my handsome, fun-loving husband.

We stood in the checkout line behind three middle-school boys who were trying just as hard to look inconspicuous as we were. They had obviously cut school in the middle of the day. They laughed too loudly and avoided eye contact as they waited to pay for their chips, pop, and candy bars. Alan, whose inner eleven-year-old self loves to poke his head up whenever possible, nudged the shortest of the three and asked him, “Do you know why a nose can’t be twelve inches long?” The boy looked at Alan quizzically and shook his head. “Because then it would be a foot,” Alan told him, chuckling. The boy rolled his eyes, as if he were used to hearing dumb dad jokes, but he laughed. He had never spent a single minute thinking about incontinence supplies. Whereas we’d been agonizing about this purchase for weeks.

In addition to his incontinence, when Alan stood up, his already-low blood pressure dropped another thirty points, leaving him dizzy, lightheaded, and disoriented—a condition known as orthostatic hypotension. What’s more, his ears rang, the bottoms of his feet burned, and his fingers turned purple and felt like icicles when everyone else’s hands were toasty warm. He had trouble with previously simple tasks like figuring out which dish you have to start cooking first to get your whole meal on the table by six thirty. His confusion was compounded when he was stressed. He had sleep apnea, meaning he stopped breathing for several seconds many times per night, and his sleep-disorder outbursts disrupted my sleep with alarming frequency, even though we slept apart.

Alan's incontinence was the most troublesome feature of his illness at that point. He never knew when he was going to have to urinate or defecate. It might be five minutes after he last peed or pooped, but when he had to go, he had to go *right then*. It was manageable when we were hanging around the house, because there was always a toilet a few steps away. It was the trips out in public that were problematic. Alan had accidents—not mere dribbles, but full pants-soaking, shoe-drenching floods—in the nuts-and-bolts department at the hardware store, in the customs line at the airport, and after his third trip to the men's room at the movie theater. The idea of sitting on a plane with a seat belt sign dictating his ability to get up and go filled Alan with dread. Hence the shopping trip for adult diapers.

The other hard part about his illness was not knowing what it was. If it was MSA, we knew his prognosis was poor. There was a good chance he would be in a wheelchair within three years, confined to bed in five and gone from this earth in seven. Alan was worried his granddaughters wouldn't remember him by the time they were adults. That's why we had invited his daughters and their families to join us for a week at a resort in Mexico—to create some fun grandpa memories for his four granddaughters, aged two to twelve.

If it was dementia with Lewy bodies, in a few years he was not likely to know who his granddaughters were. Or his daughters. Or me.

In her book *A Short Guide to a Happy Life*, Anna Quindlen says that knowledge of our own mortality is the greatest gift from God. If that's the case, Alan and I were well blessed. The knowledge of Alan's emerging disability permeated the air we breathed, and the specter of his likely too-soon death hung over our heads like a permanent thought bubble in a decidedly unfunny cartoon. And it made the challenge of choosing the best incontinence supplies suddenly seem like a hangnail in the grand scheme of things. This, at least, was a solvable problem.

October 2016

Even though Alan didn't have an official diagnosis, I felt a sense of urgency about getting our house ready to accommodate a wheelchair. It didn't matter whether the doctor eventually decided Alan had MSA or some other degenerative illness, there was no doubt Alan would end up in a wheelchair. I urged Alan to build a ramp to our front porch while he was still able to.

"It's too soon," Alan had protested. "It would be like putting up a big billboard on the front of our house that flashes in neon lights, 'Alan's got an illness that's going to put him in a wheelchair.' I'm not ready for the world to know."

"If we wait, you're not going to be able to build it yourself. We can tell the world it's for my dad and my sister," I countered. My sister, Carol, had suffered a stroke that left her unable to walk, and my father's dementia had consigned him to a wheelchair as well. While Carol seldom visited, I picked up Father, who was living in a nearby memory-care facility at the time, and brought him to our house for occasional meals and family gatherings. The four steps from the driveway to the porch made his visits difficult.

Eventually, Alan warmed to the idea of building the ramp. Together, we designed it, and Alan hired a friend who had been his assistant on many handyman projects over the years to help him with one last project. Blessed by balmy Indian-summer days, the two men worked well together, digging postholes for cement footings, cutting beams and railing supports and floorboards, and screwing everything together. Alan was stunned by how exhausted he was at the end of each day, and how difficult it was for him to complete tasks that required dexterity or mental acuity.

We ended up with a beautiful ramp at a fraction of what it would have cost to have professionals build it. And Alan had the satisfaction of completing one last, lovely project that he would appreciate for all his remaining days.

June 2017

After a cold, wet spring—including a sloppy six inches of snow on May 18, three days *after* Boulder's typical last frost date—the weather finally warmed at the beginning of June. We decided it was time to get the evaporative cooler, or swamp cooler, on our roof ready to go for the summer. Alan had put it to bed for the season the previous fall, which involved climbing to the roof, shutting off the water valve, closing off the air shaft, unplugging the motor and the pump, and wrapping the metal box in its canvas cover. It was his last trip up an extension ladder. He managed the process successfully, but his increasing clumsiness and lack of coordination were scaring us both.

Despite my lifelong fear of heights, I thought I should at least attempt the climb to the roof before trying to find someone else to get the swamp cooler ready to go. *How hard can it be?* I wondered. Before I married Alan, I had my own hand tools and a few power tools and knew how to use them. I had watched the workers scrambling around on the roof like mountain goats two years earlier when we had the shingles replaced. I told myself that if they could do it with such ease, surely I could manage.

The last time I had tried to climb a ladder to a roof had been more than thirty years earlier. I had wanted to rotate the antenna on the roof of my rental house to see if I could improve my TV reception. The stepladder I owned was not quite tall enough for the job, so there was a gap of several feet between the top of the ladder and the edge of the roof. I climbed that ladder at least a half-dozen times, but I could not talk myself into making the last giant step to the roof. When I shared that story with Alan, he assured me we would use an extension ladder that would extend higher than the edge of the roof, which would make getting off the ladder and onto the roof much easier and safer.

I decided to try it. The pitch of our roof was not steep, and I trusted Alan to help me.

We retrieved the extension ladder from the garage and set it up on the front corner of the house, where the structure is only one story tall. Our house sits on a slope and has a walkout lower level, so the house is two stories tall in the back.

Alan shoved a screwdriver and a heavy pipe wrench into the back pockets of my jeans. As I mentally prepared myself, he cautioned me: "Take it slow, and don't look down."

I took a deep breath and started up. I paused on each rung to make sure my footing was solid and to give myself a silent pep talk: *You can do this, Joanne. People climb ladders every day and don't get hurt. You are going to be okay. Alan is holding the ladder. It is not going to tip over. You can do this.*

Step by slow step, I made it to the top of the ladder and took the first tentative step onto the roof, the step that had stymied me so many years earlier. Feeling quite proud of myself, I took another step. The rough texture of the shingles gave me more confidence in my footing than I had expected. Careful not to look down at the ground, I took small steps and slowly traversed the length of the house to the swamp cooler. Alan hurried around the house to the back deck where he could see me on the roof and I could hear his words of advice and encouragement.

Following Alan's step-by-step instructions from the deck below, I knelt on the shingles next to the swamp cooler and removed the bungee cords that held the canvas cover over the swamp cooler housing. Focusing intently on the task, I removed the aluminum panel from the front of the unit, then pulled the wrench out of my back pocket to open the water valve. The next step, sliding out the metal tray that blocks the air shaft, proved difficult. I couldn't budge it. As I practiced deep breathing on the roof, Alan rummaged in the garage until he found a piece of dowel and handed it up to me from the deck below. I used it as a handle to pull against the sharp lip of the tray and finally managed to dislodge it.

As I finished the job and gathered up my tools, I felt like a five-year-old who had just ridden a bike without training wheels for the first time. I slowly retraced my steps to the other end of the roof. Before I started down the ladder, I stood tall and dared to look out at the majestic panorama of the mountains to the west. All these years of living in this house, and I hadn't known what a great view we had from the roof. I was glad Alan had coaxed me into tackling the climb to the roof, but I was also acutely aware that I would not have attempted this challenge without Alan's guidance and encouragement, his repeated reassurance that I *could* accomplish this task.

It suddenly struck me: *What will I do when he is gone?*

June 25, 2017

The sad truth is that there is nothing available to prevent or cure MSA or dementia with Lewy bodies, or even to slow down their progression. I continued to believe Alan had MSA. His symptoms seemed to fit the MSA profile better than anything else.

According to some experts, MSA sufferers live for six to nine years after symptoms start. But we had never been able to figure out when to start counting. Should we start counting when Alan's REM sleep behavior disorder symptoms erupted—seven years earlier in 2010? Or when he first started experiencing erectile dysfunction—four years earlier? Or when he first started getting dizzy when he stood up—three years earlier? Or when his bladder stopped functioning properly—two years ago? Or do we not count at all, since his doctor has not given him an official diagnosis yet? Nobody seemed to know for sure. And even if they did, each person with MSA declines at his or her own rate. Even though I *believed* Alan had MSA, not dementia with Lewy bodies, we didn't know for sure, and we had even less of an idea what his rate of decline would be.

But knowing that Alan's life was likely to be much shorter than we had originally envisioned, I vowed to make the most of the time he had left. As a result, I started watching TV with him in the evenings. For years, he would retire to the couch after dinner and turn on the TV, and I would retire to my office to catch up on work or head off to bed with a book. We'd occasionally sit on the porch or watch a movie together instead, but not very often. Once we realized Alan's life would be cut short, I chose to spend my evenings with him, even if it *was* in front of the television. I'd hold his hand or snuggle my head against his shoulder, content to feel his warmth while we communed side by side in the glow of the TV.

One Sunday evening, we watched two *Grey's Anatomy* episodes and one *West Wing* episode before we turned off the TV and stood up. Alan headed to his room while I bustled around locking doors and turning off lights. I heard him calling me from the dining room. He stood gripping the slate counter that forms the pass-through to the kitchen. He looked a little pale and wobbly.

"I've been meaning to tell you all week that if I start to go down, don't try to catch me, just guide me down," he said.

"What do you mean? What would that look like?" I asked.

In response, his eyes rolled back in his head and his knees buckled. For an instant, I thought he was answering my question, doing a great imitation of what it would look like if he started to "go down." A split second later, I realized he was truly falling down and that he had lost consciousness. There was no way I could catch him, but I managed to slow his fall so he didn't hit his head when he landed on the floor. His head missed the edge of the dining room table by a fraction of an inch. I immediately and instinctually understood what he was trying to tell me a few seconds earlier.

"Are you okay?" I asked as I knelt on the floor next to him. Some part of my brain realized it was a dumb question. He would not be lying on the floor if he were okay. But it was the best I could do in the moment.

"No," was all he could muster. At least he was conscious

again. Flitting like a manic moth in a spotlight at the edge of my brain was a study I had read that said 38 percent of people with MSA—more than a third—die suddenly of unexpected heart problems. I swatted away the thought.

"Are you in pain? What do you need? How can I help?" I was almost begging. Typically, I am calm in emergencies and fall apart later, but that evening, I was frantic in the moment.

Alan was too out of it to respond to my panicky questions.

Even though he outweighed me by forty pounds at that point, I managed to get him sitting up on the pine bench next to the dining room wall. He didn't seem to understand what I was saying to him, and his speech was slurred. After getting him propped up, I took his blood pressure. It was a startlingly low at 60 over 45. But it had been lower before—down to 58 over 38—and he hadn't passed out then.

Was this happening because he sat on the couch for a couple hours and then stood up, triggering his orthostatic hypotension? Was it an exacerbation of his MSA symptoms, a glimpse into the future at what would soon become the next "new normal"? Was he having a heart attack or stroke? Alan's father had died of a heart attack at fifty-eight. Alan was sixty-nine at that point. My sister had suffered a major stroke two years earlier, at the age of sixty-six. Everything seemed possible.

I racked my brain trying to remember the stroke tests. I knew the acronym was FAST. Face, arms, smile, and talking? I wasn't sure, but I didn't want to take the time to look it up. I had him smile, and both corners of his mouth curved upwards. I asked him to raise his arms. They went up evenly. He could talk, but his words still sounded blurry. I decided it was unlikely to be a stroke. I needed to talk to someone who could assess the situation better than I could.

Alan asked for water, and I got him a glass while I dialed his provider's advice line on my cell phone. I tried to hand him the glass of water but discovered he couldn't make his hands work to hold it. I held the glass for him and helped him drink with my right hand while I held the phone to my ear with my left. While I was waiting my turn to speak with the nurse, he told me he couldn't move his feet. At that point, I was sure it *was* a stroke.

I was pretty sure my blood pressure was as far off the high end of the chart as his was off the low end. My pulse was rapid, and I was hyperfocused.

When the nurse finally picked up the line, I stammered out the story. In the back of my brain, I wondered how much she knew about MSA. The illness is so rare that many medical professionals have never encountered it before. I told the nurse it was possible this whole episode could be related to the orthostatic hypotension that is a hallmark of MSA, which is what we thought he had but were not sure. She peppered me with questions and then said she needed to consult with the on-call emergency doctor.

The nurse called back two minutes later: the doctor wanted Alan to be transported to the emergency room by ambulance. She wanted me to decide whether the ambulance needed to come immediately with lights and sirens. If you ask for no lights and sirens, the ambulance can take up to a half hour to arrive. Alan was starting to look a little less green around the gills, and his speech was clearer. His blood pressure had recovered by a few points, so we decided not to wake the neighbors at ten thirty at night.

I left Alan propped against the wall and threw a sweater, a

book, my iPad, and some food into a tote bag. I had no idea how long we would be gone.

Alan looked perkier by the time the ambulance arrived minutes later. The ambulance attendants attempted to a do an EKG before they even left the driveway, but they couldn't get the electrodes to stick to Alan's hairy chest. They gave up and ripped the hair-encrusted electrodes back off, which made Alan yelp with pain. The attendants shaved clear patches in his chest fur and nicked his skin in the process. Blood dripped down his chest as they applied new electrodes to the abraded spots. He waved wanly as the ambulance pulled out of the driveway. I followed the ambulance in our car.

When Alan arrived at the hospital, the first thing the ER nurses did was rip off the electrodes applied by the ambulance technicians and apply a new set. Apparently the EMT-supplied electrodes were not compatible with the hospital EKG equipment. All the chest-hair yanking had left Alan wide awake and alert. His blood pressure had returned to normal and the color had returned to his face. He turned on the charm and in no time had the nurses smiling and pouring out their life histories to him.

After we'd spent a couple of hours in the ER, the doctor decided the fainting episode was most likely related to Alan's orthostatic hypotension, and she sent him home with instructions to eat more salt and wear support hose. I had already bought him support hose, and he adamantly refused to even try them on.

Later, I shared the episode with a woman in our support group whose husband had had MSA for years. She told me a similar story about her husband's trip to the emergency room after he lost consciousness and fell for the first time.

"Now I just grab the blood pressure cuff and two pillows, one for him and one for me. I make him comfortable and join him on the floor. I don't let him even sit up until his systolic pressure gets back up to one hundred. And I get a rest at the same time."

That sounded like much more practical advice than what we got from the ER doctor.

July 2017

I had never been good with limbo. Not the Jamaican dance kind where you bend backwards at the knees and shimmy your way under a horizontal bar, and not the kind of limbo that is an in-between place, neither here nor there, drifting oarless and untethered in the middle of a choppy lake with no knowledge of where you'd come ashore or when. That's where we had been with Alan's illness for more than two years.

Even if the news were bad, I would rather know.

Alan had seen Dr. Kurtz, the movement-disorder specialist, every six months for the two years since our initial visit. Dr. Kurtz had ordered a variety of brain scans and tests and requested a second opinion from one of his colleagues. As input accumulated, the verdict evolved: Yes, it looks like multiple system atrophy (MSA), but you don't yet meet all the diagnostic criteria, so we can't give you a firm diagnosis yet.

A year earlier, Alan had easily met all the diagnostic criteria for one category of MSA symptoms, the autonomic dysfunction category. The autonomic nervous system controls bodily functions like changes in blood pressure, urination, sweating—functions that take care of themselves without our having to think about them. When those functions stop working properly, it's pretty obvious. The other classes of symptoms, motor and cerebellar symptoms, came later and were more elusive in Alan. The cerebellum controls coordination, so symptoms of cerebellar dysfunction include clumsy movements, stumbling, an unsteady gait. When you drink alcohol, it impairs your cerebellum, so many people with cerebellar dysfunction appear to be drunk when they are not.

Two years after we first met Dr. Kurtz, his answer changed. This time, he said, "There doesn't appear to be anything else it could be besides MSA." Since he had been polite two years earlier when I told him I thought my husband had MSA based on my Internet research, I chose not to say "See, I told you so." But I thought it.

If the doctor had said, "I am delighted to tell you I am giving Alan a diagnosis of ________" (insert the name of a curable illness), I would have been overjoyed. But I didn't expect to feel much emotion around a diagnosis of MSA because we had anticipated it for so long. So despite the sigh of relief I breathed to finally move beyond the limbo stage, I was surprised to feel as sad as I did. I realized the diagnosis erased that microscopic splinter, that magical iota of hope I carried, that Alan would ultimately be diagnosed with something—anything—curable.

Alan and I held hands and avoided eye contact as we left Dr. Kurtz's office and crossed the cavernous lobby of the medical facility. As we stepped out the door into the dazzling July sunshine, I was flooded with tenderness for Alan. "Sweetie, I'll be here for you to the end, no matter what it looks like," I said as I finally dared to meet his eyes.

Alan pulled me to him in a bear hug on the sidewalk in front of the towering building. "Thank God I married you," he whispered in my ear. Swarms of people bustled around us as we stood there wrapped in each other's arms, swaying almost imperceptibly, oblivious to everything but each other and the knots of grief that clogged our throats, our hearts.

CHAPTER 4

August 10, 2017

I watched Alan lurch down the crowded concourse in the Seattle airport in search of a men's room where he could empty his bladder. His self-catheterization supplies were stowed in his "murse," a manly-looking army-green purse, slung casually over his shoulder and across his chest. Alan had finally gotten used to the idea of carrying a murse and was no longer self-conscious about it. But his stride didn't convey self-confidence. His gait was wide and tentative. His shoulders slouched forward, and he stumbled slightly every few steps, like a lush who had consumed one too many shots of tequila.

Casual observers might not have noticed his clumsy stride, but I did because I remembered him in his prime, at home in his body, fluid and sure. My eyes filled with tears as he made his halting way down the concourse. I allowed my sadness to surface briefly, knowing I would have several minutes before he returned to get it put back in place, packed safely away in a private vault in the center of my chest. I had to let small sips of sadness out occasionally, or it erupted on its own at unpredictable times. I tried not to cry in front of Alan because he already felt so bad that he was "putting me through the ordeal" of being his caretaker.

I assured him I was choosing to be his caretaker because I loved him, but that didn't stop him from apologizing. The apologies wore me down faster than the constant caregiving.

We were on our way to Anchorage to begin our week-long cruise down the Inside Passage of Alaska to celebrate our twentieth wedding anniversary. Both of us were thankful we had taken the chance on another marriage. We each felt blessed to be in this relationship.

Alan returned to his seat next to me in the boarding area and told me that while he was catheterizing himself, which involved threading a narrow plastic tube through his urethra, he discovered blood in his urine. He was almost finished taking an antibiotic prescribed a week earlier for a urinary tract infection, so finding blood in his urine could mean he needed a stronger—or different—antibiotic. Alan called his Colorado urologist and left a message asking for advice. Before we caught our connecting flight, we searched his provider's website and discovered they had no facilities in Anchorage, nor in all of Alaska. We figured if we didn't hear back from Alan's Colorado doctor by the time we landed in Anchorage, we'd head for an urgent care facility. When Alan had a UTI, his MSA symptoms intensified: his walking became clumsier, his fatigue intensified, and his cognitive processes slowed to a glacial pace. We didn't want to be dealing with a recurrence while we were on vacation and far from expert medical care.

When we finally arrived at our hotel in Anchorage, it was late afternoon. We would be spending a single night before taking a scenic train ride to Seward, on the coast, first thing in the morning, to start our cruise. I had been up since three in the morning, and my too-short night was starting to sap my energy. Alan had slept a little later but then couldn't seem to gather his wits enough to get out the door. As I loaded the last of our bags into the car—a half hour later than we had intended to leave for the airport—he tripped on the bottom step of our porch stairs and almost landed on the concrete driveway face first. I breathed a quick prayer of gratitude that he hadn't injured himself and made a mental note to allow more time for last-minute packing for our next trip. We took the toll road to shave ten minutes off our drive time, and I drove 85 mph most of the way to the airport. By the time we pulled into long-term parking, my hands were cramped from gripping the steering wheel so tightly. The airline had almost finished boarding our flight when we arrived at our gate, but I was relieved we made it before they closed the door. That's how the day had started.

Without unpacking our bags in Anchorage, we searched the web for an urgent care facility close to our hotel. The website of the closest facility said they took Medicare and welcomed walk-ins, so we called a cab and, twenty minutes later, found ourselves in the almost-empty lobby of a new-looking building just south of downtown Anchorage. The receptionist asked Alan a few questions and quickly determined he could not get medical care at their facility because he had insurance through a Medicare Advantage plan.

"No problem," Alan said. "We'll pay out of pocket and get reimbursed when we get home."

"Nope," replied the receptionist, who clearly hated turning down the business. "If you don't have plain Medicare, we can't treat you. It would be against the law. But there is an urgent care center on the other side of town that can treat you. I'm sure of it because I've sent other patients there."

She gave us the address and called a cab for us.

When the cab arrived twenty minutes later, the driver started the meter running and then took the time to brush crumbs from the seats and dust his dashboard. I was in a hurry to accomplish our mission, and the delaying tactic annoyed me. Rush-hour traffic clogged the main arteries, and it seemed to take forever to get to the east side of Anchorage. When we finally arrived at the small urgent care facility tucked into the end of a strip mall, we quickly learned they couldn't treat Alan because he didn't have his Medicare card with him. Knowing the number was not sufficient, nor was having a photo of the card on my phone. Again, we offered to pay out of pocket, but the receptionist could not be swayed. The only place Alan could get care without his Medicare card was at the hospital emergency room, she told us. My patience was nearly gone.

Alan called for a cab, and this time, it was forty-five minutes before the cab arrived. Forty-five minutes of standing on the pavement at the end of the strip mall, both of us getting crabbier and crabbier. Alan fatigued easily, and that much time on his feet left him wobbly. He couldn't go back inside the urgent care facility to rest because the staff had locked the doors and gone home for the day.

After our third cab ride of the day, Alan was seen promptly at the hospital ER, but their tests showed few bacteria in his urine. To be safe, the doctor wrote a prescription for an antibiotic we could take with us on the ship in case things got worse. But the closest pharmacy that was still open was down the highway near the first urgent care facility we had visited earlier that day. Once again, we called a cab, waited for it to arrive, and rode across town.

We certainly didn't want to wait forty-five minutes again for a different cab to pick us up to take us back to the hotel, so Alan waited in the cab while I ran into the pharmacy hoping for a quick turnaround on filling the prescription. There were several people in front of me in line to get prescriptions filled; I waited impatiently, conscious of the taxi's meter ticking away out in the parking lot. Right as it was finally my turn to speak with the pharmacist, the assistant who was staffing the pharmacy's drive-through window announced she was going on break, so the pharmacist took over her duties at the window until she returned. Grumbling to myself, I shifted from foot to foot, trying to stay awake, trying to be patient. I couldn't remember the last time I had been this tired. Finally, twenty minutes later, the assistant returned from her break, reeking of cigarette smoke, and the pharmacist returned to the line of customers at the counter.

I slid the prescription across the counter to her. "How long will it be before this is ready?"

"Lady, I have thirty prescriptions to fill ahead of yours," she replied with an air of exasperation, as if I had asked a question she had already answered a hundred times that day. Dark circles stained the skin under her eyes and made her look as exhausted as I felt.

Caught off guard by her crabby tone, I burst into tears. "I have a cab and a sick husband waiting for me in the parking lot," I blubbered. The pharmacist paused, then laid her hand on top of mine and gave it a gentle squeeze.

"Just give me a minute," she said, her eyes full of empathy. She disappeared into the back room and filled the prescription on the spot. "Now don't you tell a soul I did this," she whispered as she handed me the bag.

"Thank you, thank you, thank you," I whispered back, then turned and hurried out to the parking lot.

By the time we got back to our hotel, it was nine thirty at night, and we had spent close to $150 on cab fares. We hadn't eaten since lunch in Seattle, but I was too exhausted for food. I flopped on the bed and couldn't move. Alan took my shoes off for me and joked about how relaxing it was to be on vacation. I laughed for a few seconds before my laughter morphed into sobs. All my reserves were used up, and I couldn't keep the sadness locked down any longer. Alan joined me on top of the covers and held me in his arms until I fell asleep, fully clothed, teeth unbrushed.

We decided that day didn't count as a vacation day.

September 13, 2017

On a warm, sunny September afternoon, Alan was on his way home from his exercise class when he decided to stop at our local farm stand to buy sweet corn for dinner. As he pulled into the parking lot, he made a left turn directly in front of an oncoming car. The woman driving the oncoming vehicle slammed on her brakes and caught the rear quarter panel of Alan's car.

Alan called me from the farm-stand parking lot. His voice sounded shaky as he painted a quick picture of what had happened.

"Sweetie, would you drive over here and help me fill out the paperwork for the accident report? Please?" Alan's handwriting had deteriorated to point where it was barely legible. He didn't stand a chance of writing anything decipherable in the tiny spaces allotted on the form provided by the Colorado State patrolwoman who had responded to the accident call.

Five minutes after he called me, I was at his side. Alan stood next to the dented car in the dappled shade of a towering cottonwood tree, a gentle breeze shushing the leaves overhead. He studied the shifting patterns of sun and shadow on his shoes. He looked like an eight-year-old who was sure he was about to get spanked for breaking yet another window with his baseball. I certainly wasn't planning to punish him or even deliver a lecture. I was relieved nobody had been injured and that both cars involved were still drivable. I wanted to gather Alan in my arms and hum a lullaby in his ear, but I settled for a quick hug. We had a job to do.

Alan stood leaning against the car door and dictated while I sat in the passenger seat and filled out the triplicate form for him. As he recounted the details, it became clear that Alan hadn't seen the oncoming car.

His driving had been worrying me for at least a year. His inability to multitask, his tendency to get distracted easily, and his brain's glacial processing speed made me nervous when I sat in the passenger seat. For the past few months, I had been doing all of the driving when we went somewhere together. But Alan continued to drive to his exercise classes and physical therapy appointments—all relatively short hops during daylight hours. Alan thought his driving was still safe enough, and I wasn't ready to force the issue. I was still traumatized from the experience of wresting my father's car keys from his iron grasp two years earlier. Even with significant dementia, my father was able to hold a grudge for a long time. Over the course of his long life, he'd had lots of practice.

Alan wouldn't react with the venom my father had, I knew, but I hadn't been able to face the stress involved in insisting Alan stop driving altogether. As I sat in the shade of the cottonwood finishing up the accident report, my stomach tightened into a knot. We could no longer postpone the conversation.

After handing the paperwork to the officer, Alan drove his

car home from the farm stand, and I followed him. As we left the garage together, he reached over and handed me his car keys.

"I hate to admit it, but it's time for me to call it quits," he said. "I was lucky this time, but I know it was my fault, and I don't want to take any more chances."

He didn't make excuses or try to blame someone else or try to minimize the magnitude of his error. He simply decided it was time to stop driving. I was flooded with relief and gratitude. *I am so lucky to be married to this amazing man,* I thought.

Being the only driver in the family changed my life significantly. Always on call to drive somewhere, my days were chopped into smaller pieces. And relying on me for transportation changed Alan's life too. It is not about who sits in the driver's seat and who sits in the passenger seat. As any teenager can tell you, the inability to drive severely limits your life and curtails important activities.

For example, for several years Alan had done almost all the grocery shopping. I hated the chore, but Alan was in his element. An extrovert, he turned shopping into a social event. As he stood in line at the meat counter, he would ask the other customers—all strangers—what they were making for dinner and discuss their menus and recipes with them. At the seafood counter, he would ask the fishmonger for advice on the best preparation method for tilapia or trout or whatever the day's special might be. When we shopped together, Alan introduced me to the store's assistant manager as if she were his best friend. Alan would frequently be gone for hours on end when he left to buy groceries. When it became my chore instead of his, I could get what we needed at two grocery stores, drive home, and bring the bags of groceries into the kitchen in an hour and a quarter. But I suspected he had more fun when he did it.

Before he stopped driving, I could count on at least two hours of precious alone time while Alan was at his Parkinson's exercise classes. While multiple system atrophy is in the Parkinson's family based on the underlying pathology, Alan's rate of degeneration was galloping at a reckless pace compared to people who had regular Parkinson's disease. The two illnesses share many attributes, though, so Alan attended Parkinson's exercise classes at the YMCA.

The class itself didn't last long enough for me to drive home after I dropped him off, so I usually delivered Alan to the Y and then headed to do errands at the drugstore, hardware store, or bank—whatever errands were required to keep our lives on an even keel. I might try to find a quiet corner at the Y to read or write, but quiet spots were in short supply. When the weather was nice, I would sit in my car, roll down the windows, and balance my laptop on the steering wheel so I could write. One time when I did that, I forgot to turn off the seat warmer, and by the time Alan emerged from his exercise class, our electric car's battery was dead.

We were both convinced of the importance of Alan exercising regularly with expert supervision, so we were determined to do whatever it took to get Alan to the YMCA at least three times a week. When I dropped him off at the Y and watched him join the parade of hunched and wizened seniors shuffling up the sidewalk, I wondered how my vibrant, agile husband blended so quickly and seamlessly into this crowd.

October 2017

With tears streaming down my face, I read short bios of the fifty-eight people killed by a gunman at a Las Vegas musical festival. Single mothers, husbands, grandfathers, recent graduates just starting out on their careers, school secretaries, Little League coaches. They sounded like people who were kind and loving and adored by their families and friends.

How could God allow a mass murderer to wreak this kind of mayhem on the lives of unsuspecting, ordinary people gathered outdoors to enjoy some music? How could a loving God allow children to be abused or neglected or born with life-threatening deformities? What about plagues, massive earthquakes in heavily populated locales, genocides, and terrorist attacks that kill people indiscriminately? What about people struck down in their prime by cancer or heart disease or unrelenting neurological diseases like MSA?

Our minister reminded us every single Sunday that everything is working out for our highest good. Before Alan became ill, I accepted that statement without examining it too closely. But once Alan's MSA barged into our lives, every single Sunday it clawed at my heart.

In our church's annual fall program, we were studying a book called *I of the Storm*, by Reverend Doctor Gary Simmons, the premise of which is that nothing and no one in our lives is against us. When the class started, I was not convinced this premise was true, but I was willing to open my mind to the possibility.

That October, Simmons served as the guest speaker at one of our Sunday services. He declared unequivocally that we should be thankful for people or circumstances we perceive to be against us because they provide us with opportunities to learn the lessons we need to learn. He told of his former wife, who was dying from a brain tumor at the time, hurling his book across the room and declaring it rubbish when she read that statement in his book. I had the same reaction, although the book hurling was a mental exercise in my case. I could have sworn I saw a slight smirk flit across Reverend Simmons's face when he relayed the story. That fleeting smirk annoyed me. The idea that I could ever be thankful for Alan's illness outraged me.

My best friend, the love of my life, was dying from a horrible disease that was slowly robbing him of his ability to walk, talk, swallow, think, write, and breathe. It had already stolen his ability to run, ski, dance, control his bladder, make love, climb a ladder, and stand up without holding on to something. In the future, he would be unable to stand up at all, to sit up, or even turn over in bed. And I was supposed to be grateful? Alan was supposed to be grateful? I couldn't picture it. I *could* imagine being grateful for the good people who stepped forward to help, for the gift of deepened intimacy and love for each other engendered by our intense journey together, for the wisdom and compassion we gained as a result of our struggles. But I could not for a moment picture being grateful for the disease itself.

The best I could hope for was that someday I might achieve the equanimity of my friend Barbara, who was living with Stage 4, triple-negative, inflammatory breast cancer. In a blog post, she wrote: "I don't want to look ahead; I just want to feel gratitude for this perfect moment, for all of the blessings in my life."

It took her thirty-five years of daily meditation to achieve her grace-filled state. To adopt her attitude, I suspected I would need an intervention from a fairy with a magic wand.

October 16, 2017

Earlier, as Alan's symptoms intensified, but before the doctor gave him an official diagnosis, I had resumed my obsessive Web searches on multiple system atrophy and related neurological disorders, hoping to find either a *curable* disease that fit Alan's symptoms or promising research results. I discovered no curable diseases and little noteworthy news, but I did stumble on contact information for two support groups in Colorado, one about a fifty-minute drive north in Johnstown, and another about a fifty-minute drive south in Englewood. The support groups cater to people with MSA, progressive supranuclear palsy (PSP), and corticobasal degeneration (CBD), all rare atypical-Parkinsonian diseases characterized by unstoppable deterioration of different areas of the brain.

Alan and I had agreed it would be helpful to talk with others who were on similar journeys. Studies of different populations vary slightly, but the incidence (the number of new cases per year) for MSA is typically 0.6 to 0.7 cases per 100,000 population per year. MSA prevalence (the number of people currently living with the disease) is typically four to five people per 100,000 population. So in a city the size of Boulder, there might be five people with MSA, but because diagnosing it is so difficult, there's a good chance that several of them think they have a different disease. It's no wonder there is no support group here.

We decided to try the support group in Johnstown first, mostly because I could avoid driving in Denver traffic to get there. When we arrived, the room was full of people from northern Colorado and southern Wyoming, all living with or caring for someone with PSP. While the facilitator assured us it was not always the case, not a single MSA patient or caregiver attended.

The following month, May, we braved the city traffic and tried the support group in Englewood, a southern suburb of Denver. When it was our turn to share, the facilitator tried to prompt Alan to talk about his experience. She asked him earnestly if he had trouble with falling. "Heck no," Alan said, totally deadpan. "I do it all the time. I'm quite good at it, actually."

We were delighted to meet several other husband-and-wife couples, one of whom lived with MSA and the other of whom was the caregiver. The rest were PSP couples, except for one man with CBD and his sister, who was his primary caregiver. The people welcomed us and freely shared details of ongoing clinical trials, the quirks and strengths of local medical professionals, helpful assistive devices, and the best companies to call for help making bathrooms more wheelchair friendly. Even better, they shared the compassion and understanding of people walking the same path. There was way more laughter than I expected.

This was exactly what we had hoped to find.

We met Phil, a man who had been diagnosed with MSA eleven years earlier, and his wife and caregiver, Barb. My late-night forays on the web had led me to believe it was rare for an MSA patient to survive ten years past diagnosis. But here was Phil to prove it was possible. I was elated. His very survival sparked a new bubble of hope for both Alan and me. We immediately set to work quizzing Phil and Barb. *To what do you attribute Phil's long survival after diagnosis? What types of exercise works well for him? How often? How long? What medications does he take? Any special diet? Supplements? What else? What else? What else? Please, please tell us the secret to living a long and happy life with this cruel illness.*

Two months after we met Phil, Barb moved him to an assisted-living facility. Exhausted from a decade of caregiving, Barb could no longer care for him at home as his condition deteriorated. A week after he moved in, Phil ate breakfast in the facility's dining room, returned in his wheelchair to his room, and died from his disease.

Tears streamed down my cheeks when I got the email announcing his death. Even though I barely knew the man, he had become a symbol to me, a shimmering thread of hope. And now that thread was broken, the hope dashed. I had rooted for him to live at least another decade.

In October, Barb brought Phil's brain autopsy report to a support group meeting to share with us. A brain autopsy is the only way to get a definitive diagnosis for atypical Parkinsonian diseases. We were stunned to learn Phil did not have MSA after all. According to the neuropathology report, he suffered from dementia with Lewy bodies—the illness Alan's neurologist had initially suspected, the atypical-Parkinsonian illness that shares some of the symptoms of MSA. When Barb finished her report, she made an impassioned plea for all of us to consider donating our brains to the Mayo Clinic in Jacksonville, Florida, to help researchers discover causes, treatments, and cures for neurodegenerative illnesses.

It turns out Phil was not alone in being misdiagnosed. My web searches uncovered an online article about a study published by the Mayo Clinic in 2015. Researchers autopsied 134 brains of people clinically diagnosed with MSA and discovered only 62 percent of the clinical diagnoses were correct. I was floored. Fewer than two-thirds of MSA patients were correctly diagnosed! Of those incorrectly diagnosed with MSA, 37 percent had dementia with Lewy bodies, 29 percent had PSP, 15 percent had standard Parkinson's disease, and 18 percent had other illnesses.

How were researchers going to find a cure for MSA if doctors couldn't even diagnose it properly? The outcome of clinical trials depends on having a test pool of individuals accurately diagnosed with the disease in question, half of whom will be treated with the intervention under study and half of whom will be treated with a placebo. If you don't know for sure whether the people you are studying have been accurately diagnosed, you cannot draw accurate conclusions about the efficacy of the intervention. The article suggested the current diagnostic criteria needed to be revised. I heartily agreed, but the experts would need to figure what changes were required. I didn't have a clue.

October 23, 2017

My father died on March 5, 2017, after falling and fracturing his pelvis in multiple places when he tried to get out of bed in the night at the memory care facility where he'd been living for a few months. That fall was only four months after he had fallen and broken his right hip. He'd broken his left hip a year earlier, when he was still living with Alan and me. He could not remember he was not supposed to stand up from his wheelchair without help. His bones were fragile, and his memory was even more porous than his bones.

I had been his primary caretaker for more than six years, and I was exhausted.

Knowing I had another huge caregiving project looming, I gave myself the gift of a summer in the garden. After arranging Father's memorial service and taking care of the main chores required for settling his estate, I gave my flowers and vegetables priority over most other activities.

It had been a glorious summer.

There was something healing about having my hands in dirt. About planting seeds and nurturing them, watching the shoots push their way up through the soil and turn their faces toward the heavens. Even weeding, a chore some gardeners dread, offered solace. I turned off the chatter in my brain and luxuriated in the feel of the sun warming my back, my ears tuned to the choir of birds gossiping in the tangle of bushes along the yard's edge. As I listened to their chatter and communed with Mother Earth, the stress I'd carried in my shoulders softened, sublimated by degrees.

My daughter gave me a refrigerator magnet that proclaimed, "Gardening is cheaper than therapy, and you get tomatoes." It was true, although the list of delightful garden produce was dramatically abridged. "Gardening is cheaper than therapy, and you get tomatoes, snow peas, asparagus, green beans, cucumbers, zucchinis, winter squash, pumpkins, peppers, beets, basil, dill, oregano, chives, chard, kale, and lettuce," would be a better list for that year's garden, but of course it wouldn't fit on a refrigerator magnet. I found it annoying that the magnet extolled the virtues of only the edible fruits of gardening, as if feeding the body counts more than feeding the soul. Perhaps my magnet should have said, "Gardening is cheaper than therapy, and you get peonies." Or iris or roses.

On October 23, 2017, which would have been my father's ninety-first birthday, I was delighted to discover several pockets of miniature black-eyed Susans that had survived our early frost. I picked a small bouquet to grace our dining room table and felt a flicker of joy every time I walked by and noticed their sunny faces.

The next morning, when I sat down to breakfast, the black-eyed Susans in the vase had called it quits. Their petals were brown and desiccated, despite the water in the vase. The remaining leaves were shriveled, curled into themselves. "How can they be dead already?" I whined indignantly out loud. "I just picked them yesterday."

It took me only a minute to realize how ridiculous my

indignation was. Mother Nature had bestowed an unexpected gift—an extra day of floriferous cheer—and here I was complaining about the gift's ephemerality. How much better it would be to offer gratitude for the fleeting gift instead of complaining about its rapid demise.

And two minutes after that, an analogous thought ripped through my brain with the force of an earthquake. After two stressful marriages that ended badly, the universe had offered me the perfect partner: a kind and loving man who shared my values and dreams, who challenged me gently to continue to grow, who taught me by example that being happy was more important than being right. A man who laughed easily, celebrated my successes, held me when I hurt, and brought me coffee in bed every single morning.

At that point, we had been together for twenty-three years. Instead of being heartbroken that I wouldn't get to spend another two decades with him, I could choose to be grateful he had given me so much joy and for so long.

Even though the thought had ambushed me, I realized it was not an original idea. I remembered Marilyn, a friend from church, who adopted a Russian orphan many years ago, a sweet sixteen-month-old girl named Dina. As Dina grew, church members enfolded her with love and acted as her extended family, cheering her on at the annual Easter egg hunts and buying Girl Scout cookies from her each year. One night during the winter of her senior year in high school, Dina went to bed like she normally did, after talking on the phone with a friend and watching a little TV. But she didn't wake up the next morning like she normally did. Her heart had stopped beating in the wee hours of the morning for no apparent reason. Marilyn was devastated, and our whole congregation mourned with her. As I went through the receiving line at Dina's memorial service, I hugged Marilyn and told her how sorry I was. Marilyn responded, "I'm so grateful to have had Dina in my life for the past sixteen years."

That sentence left an indelible tattoo on my brain. I could imagine a mother reaching that state of grace after decades of mourning and reflection, but I could not fathom how Marilyn could ascend to that place of saintly gratitude within weeks of her daughter's unexpected death. I was pretty sure she was more evolved than I.

I had coffee with Marilyn shortly after my father died, and I mentioned her comment that day at the memorial service. She did not remember saying it. Four years after Dina's service, she was still grieving her death. I doubt that Marilyn's gratitude was fleeting. I suspect it was buried by a grief she could not yet face when her wound was so fresh.

I left the vase of dead flowers on the dining room table to remind myself to dig deep and find the gratitude for Alan's presence in my life whenever I felt suffocated by the pain of losing him in slow motion.

October 2017

Some nights, Alan had trouble standing up from the couch after we watched TV in the evening. Even if we took breaks throughout the evening for him to march around the living room. Even if he consumed extra salt at dinner and drank extra water all evening long. Even if he had remembered to take all of his medications that day.

On nights when Alan couldn't stand up, I typically took his blood pressure, and it was typically, but not always, lower than it should be. We would sit back down and try again a few minutes later, as many times as it took. His blood pressure eventually recovered, and then he used his cane to get to the bathroom so he could take his supplements, brush his teeth, and empty his bladder before bed.

One night in October, he had a particularly hard time gaining enough equilibrium to walk from the living room to the bathroom. His blood pressure was only slightly low. He stood up from the couch and sat back down several times before he felt steady enough to walk to the bathroom. I thought he was going to be fine, so I left him to go put on my nightgown and brush my own teeth in the other bathroom. I had just managed to get undressed when I heard him call my name, followed by a big thud and the sound of small, hard objects skittering on tile. I threw my nightgown over my head and ran down the hall. I found Alan lying on the bathroom floor surrounded by his nighttime allotment of prescription medications and supplements.

I helped him sit up with his back leaning against the bathroom wall, and I slid down the wall to sit next to him on the floor. “You okay?” I asked.

“Yeah, the only thing I injured was my pride.” It was his typical response, but I don’t think he was trying to be funny. He hated that his body would not cooperate.

I kissed his cheek and snuggled my head against his shoulder. He grabbed my hand, squeezed it, and sat for a minute with his eyes closed, as if he were praying or gathering his strength.

When Alan sighed and opened his eyes, I picked up the pills I could reach from where I was sitting and cupped them in my hand. Alan attempted to do the same with the pills he could reach, but no matter how hard he concentrated, he couldn’t make his fingers work to pick them up.

"Shit, shit, shit," he grumped. Unlike me, Alan didn't use foul language often.

"Don't worry about the pills, Sweetie. I'll get them. Let's figure out how we're going to get you to your bedroom." I was glad to switch into problem-solving mode. I didn't want to pull him up to standing, only to have him fall again. Based on how poorly his fingers were functioning, I didn't trust his legs or feet to cooperate.

"We still have your mother's old walker someplace, don't we?" Alan asked. "The one with the wheels and seat?"

"That's a good idea. I think it's out in the garage. I'll go look. Don't move." I left Alan propped against the wall and rummaged in the garage until I found the walker hiding under a shelf stacked with scraps of lumber left over from various projects. I grabbed a broom and brushed the cobwebs and sawdust from the walker's frame.

We quickly discovered the walker was too wide to fit through the narrow bathroom door. Using Alan's cane and the bathroom door for support, we managed to get him up off the floor and maneuver him onto the walker seat on the outside of the doorframe, not an easy task when his limbs were ignoring his commands for action. Even pushing him down the hall with his body draped over the walker was difficult. Alan listed hard to the left and couldn't pull his torso into an upright posture. The off-balance load made it hard to steer. But we made it to his bedroom.

Little did I know, we had completed the easiest part of the evening's tasks. I wheeled him through the bedroom door, untied his shoes, and pulled them off his feet. Next, I had to figure out how to get a pair of jeans off a seated man who outweighed me considerably. He could not stand without my using both hands to support him, and if I was supporting him, my hands were not available to pull down his pants. I was able to unbuckle his belt and pull down his zipper while he was still seated on the walker seat. Using all my strength, I managed to pivot him from sitting on the walker to sitting on the edge of his bed. From there, it was easy to get him horizontal. We giggled like teenagers wrestling out of their clothes in the back seat of a Volkswagen.

"I bet that's the most trouble you've had getting a man into bed in decades," Alan laughed.

Sleep eluded me that night. But by morning, Alan's body had regained most of the skills it had lost the night before.

Alexis and Megan had been in their twenties when I first met them. Alexis was dark haired and looked a bit like her dad, with a high forehead, thick, wavy hair, and intensely blue-green eyes. Megan, with her blond hair and rounder face, looked more like her mom. The elder of the two, Alexis had moved with her husband and daughters in 2012 from a Denver suburb to San Diego when she was offered a job that moved her several rungs up the career ladder. Other than college, it was the first time either of Alan's daughters had lived more than an hour's drive away from him. It was a hard adjustment for Alan, for Alexis, and for Alexis's daughters, Olivia and Kayla, who were four and two when the family moved. The little girls missed their Colorado cousins and their four sets of Colorado grandparents.

Online tools allowed us to stay well connected. Alan and I oohed and aahed remotely as the San Diego granddaughters showed off the gaps where their baby teeth had been, modeled their Halloween costumes, performed improvised dance routines, and did fancy tricks on the jungle bars at the local park. We also watched long-distance as Alexis's marriage fell apart.

Once we shared our worries with Alexis and Megan about the likelihood of Alan having a progressive, incurable illness, Alexis was anxious to move back to Colorado so she could spend more time with her dad. But being in the middle of an acrimonious divorce complicated everything. Every little detail of her life and her daughters' lives became bargaining chips that required her soon-to-be ex-husband to give his consent. It took Alexis three years to negotiate the move.

During those San Diego years, we still saw Alexis and her girls in the flesh fairly regularly because Alexis couldn't stay away for long. On one of Alexis's Colorado visits, Alan and I met Alexis and Megan for lunch at a sidewalk café in Golden, which is approximately halfway between Megan's house in Littleton and our house in Boulder.

It was one of those luminous Colorado days with an achingly blue sky and a gentle breeze ruffling little tufts of clouds above the mountain peaks. A perfect day for sitting outdoors. As we waited for our burgers and salads to arrive, we handed each of his daughters a thick folder containing copies of our wills, Alan's general durable power of attorney, his healthcare proxy form, and his advance directives.

"These documents describe how I want to be treated when I reach the end of the line," he told them. "If I am unable to make my own decisions, Joanne will step in and make decisions for me, and she already knows I don't want any ventilators or feeding tubes—no extraordinary measures or heroic interventions—to keep me alive. I want the two of you to support her in making decisions that align with my wishes when the time comes."

Both daughters nodded, their eyes filling with tears.

"Please read these documents carefully, and call me if you

have questions. I want us all to be on the same page so we don't have any last-minute drama."

"We get it, Daddy," Alexis reassured him.

"Yep, we're good," Megan said.

"Also, you know I'm a weenie when it comes to pain, right?" Both girls nodded again. "So, I want you to know that if I'm suffering when the end is near and if I qualify, I plan to use Colorado's medical-aid-in-dying law to end my life with dignity. I've already discussed it with my doctors. Joanne is on board, and I hope you both will support me in this too."

Both girls had heard their dad's "we treat our pets better than we treat our elders" spiel numerous times over the years, so they were not surprised by his pronouncement.

During the drive home, I thanked Alan for being thoughtful and deliberate about making sure we all knew his wishes. At times, my relationships with his daughters had been less fluid than I would have liked.

We all had baggage to overcome when Alan and I married. My experience with stepparenting in my second marriage had left me traumatized. Megan and Alexis were also scarred by their experiences being in a stepfamily with Alan's second wife. Alan had had sole custody of his girls since they were four and two years old, and Alexis, as the eldest, had grown accustomed to being the "woman" of the house. According to Alan, it was not easy for her to give up her alpha-female position, and it sounded like wife number two didn't have much flexibility or compassion for Alexis as she struggled with the adjustment. As teenagers, Megan and Alexis gave up trying to make things work within the stepfamily and moved in with their mom, with whom they hadn't lived for more than a decade. Alan was beside himself. Being a parent to his girls was such an important part of his identity that he didn't know who he was anymore without them.

By the time Alan and I were married, both girls had graduated from college and had good jobs and boyfriends. It was clear from the beginning his girls wouldn't be living with us, nor would my kids, who were both living on their own in Upstate New York at that point. But our earlier experiences with stepfamilies had left us all skittish.

I recognized both daughters loved their daddy dearly, and they recognized that he and I loved each other dearly. And that had been good enough.

Which was why I appreciated Alan's attempts to be clear with his daughters about his end-of-life wishes. There was no guarantee it would keep fault lines from cracking open, but it was a step in the right direction, an act of love for all of us.

November 2017

In early November we made our third annual visit to Houston for Alan to participate in the study of early signs of Parkinsonian illnesses. By our third trip, we had figured out the routine well enough to plan our clinic visit and imaging tests around our flight schedule, so we could spend a single night in Houston. Lyft and Uber rides took the terror out of getting around the city. We tried for two hours to find a restaurant in the vicinity of our hotel that would deliver a gluten-free supper to us, but we ultimately gave up and ate the emergency gluten-free peanut butter and jelly sandwiches we'd brought along as a backup.

When I looked back at our first trip to Houston, just two years earlier, I was saddened by all the capabilities Alan had lost in the interim. He had driven two thousand miles in 2015, and by 2017 he was not driving at all. During our 2015 road trip, Alan and I hiked all over Los Alamos in a walking tour and then spent another couple of hours at the Los Alamos National Laboratories museum. I was the one who slowed us down as I plodded along in my orthopedic boot. In 2017, Alan was exhausted by the trek from our gate to baggage claim. I kept finding myself worrying about what the 2018 trip to Houston would look like. Would Alan be able to walk at all? Would we be able to travel?

April 2018

My grocery cart was almost full. I was cruising the canned goods aisle when my phone rang. My caller ID told me it was Alan. This was not a good sign, since I had dropped him off at the YMCA for his exercise class thirty minutes earlier. He should have been marching and balancing and stretching with his classmates with his phone tucked safely away in his locker. Red flags slapped furiously in the gale-force winds howling through my brain as I answered the call.

"Doing anything important?" Alan asked.

The red flags turned into emergency flares fired from the bow of a sinking ship. His question meant he was injured and on his way to the emergency room or perhaps already there. How did I know? He was actually poking gentle fun at me and telling me he was injured simultaneously in one of those little Morse-code messages married couples use to convey massive quantities of information in few words. Those were the words I had said to him three years earlier when I broke my right ankle in two places. As I was driving home from my sister's house in the mountains, using my brakes as little as possible because my brake foot hurt like hell, I called Alan on my cell phone to see if he would research where my insurance company wanted me to go for X-rays. I figured I would do it myself when I got home if he was in the middle of something important. That's why I had asked the question he was now asking me: "Doing anything important?"

"Uh-oh. What's up?" I asked him, holding my breath.

Alan told me his exercise class had been playing a game of "horse," when he instinctually galloped after an errant basketball. He still thought of himself as a natural athlete and expected his feet to cooperate when he decided to run. He took only a few steps before he fell face-first on the gym floor, and the impact burst open the skin above his right eye. The YMCA staff had sent him to the emergency room in an ambulance. He told me he was waiting for a CT scan, after which they would stitch his wound.

Should I abandon my grocery cart and rush to the ER? Alan was in a safe place, I told myself, and he was already getting the expert care he needed, so I decided to pay for my groceries instead of abandoning my cart and having to redo the shopping later. It would take me only a few extra minutes, I rationalized. Fortunately, I had an insulated bag in the back of my car, a Christmas present from my daughter, to keep my groceries cold until I got home. I chose the shortest checkout line and unpacked my cart onto the conveyor belt. Unfortunately, it was the clerk's first day on the job, and he needed assistance from his trainer on almost every item. I kicked myself for choosing this line. I couldn't believe how long it was taking him to ring up each item. I wanted to jump over the counter and strangle the poor guy. He scrunched his face as he looked up the code for my Bartlett pears, then punched in the numbers, one slow digit at a time. Tears slid down my cheeks.

"Look, I just got a call. My husband's in the emergency room. Could you hurry up, please?" Mercifully, his trainer guided him out of the way and scanned the rest of my items in no time flat. I finally got my purchases to the car, repacked my meat and frozen foods in the insulated bag and headed for the hospital.

"It is just stitches. Calm down, Joanne," whispered the voice of reason on my right shoulder as I drove. But the voice of calamity on my left shoulder hissed urgently in my ear, "Alan is falling apart. There is nothing you can do to stop it or even slow it down." I knew both voices spoke the truth.

I spent the next three-and-a-half hours holding Alan's hand, fetching glasses of water, filling out hospital paperwork, and commiserating. He was kicking himself for forgetting he couldn't run, but other than that, he was his usual good-natured self. After the ER technician cleaned up his wound and gave us the results of the CT scan—no broken bones, no signs of concussion—I took photos of his face and texted them to his daughters. We tried to decide if his three-pronged wound looked more like a peace symbol or a Mercedes Benz hood ornament. The doctor sewed him up with a latticework of stitches and warned us this scar would be more visible than the one from his previous fall—when he'd slipped on ice on our driveway four months earlier—because of the way the skin had torn and the wound's location above his eye. We got our home-wound-care instructions and headed out.

The frozen peas in the insulated bag were still frozen solid. I was grateful for the insulated bag. I was grateful that Alan's injuries were relatively minor. And I was terrified that I had no way to keep him safe.

CHAPTER 5

Alan had been turning down all requests from his clients for a couple of years, but he still did small jobs for me that didn't require a ladder or step stool.

Giving up what he loved doing was hard for Alan, but he found solace in teaching me skills I would need when he was no longer capable of handling home maintenance chores himself. So, while Alan was still reasonably able—he could still walk safely with a cane and talk clearly most of the time—he felt compelled to teach me how to perform the home maintenance chores he had dealt with for years. I had mixed feelings about this.

Being married to a handyman entailed a fair number of inconveniences. For example, we'd be on our way to a party on a Friday night, and his phone would ring. A client with a single bathroom and a houseful of out-of-town company would beg for help with a plumbing emergency. Alan was unable to say no, despite the fact he wasn't dressed appropriately to be dealing with sewage.

"I'm really sorry to do this to you, Sweetie," he would say, "but I can't leave them without a functioning toilet while their in-laws are in town. This will only take a half hour, I promise." He would grab his bucket of emergency tools from the trunk and leave me waiting at the curb. After a while, I learned to keep emergency magazines alongside the emergency tools in the trunk, so at least I had something to read while I waited. Those little jobs always took at least twice as long as he had promised.

Another of the inconveniences associated with being married to a handyman occurred Sunday mornings at church. We'd walk in the front doors and immediately a line would form, people wanting to talk to Alan about a little remodeling project they were considering, or people looking for advice on fixing a crack in the dining room ceiling or the best sealer to use on their deck or what to do about a bathtub that drained too slowly. Alan enjoyed giving advice and couldn't bear to tell people it was his day off. He chatted with all comers, while I stood waiting, not very patiently at times, thinking I probably had a lot in common with the spouses of physicians who were besieged for advice everywhere they went.

In recompense for the inconveniences, I had decided early on that I needed to take full advantage of the brighter side of being married to a handyman: Alan not only knew how to do all the annoying little chores associated with home ownership, but he did them willingly, as if it were his duty and his right. I didn't have to nag or insist. I gave up even thinking about things like deck staining and chimney cleaning. And I was fine with that.

So I admit to a bit of reluctance when Alan wanted to start teaching me how to take over these chores. On some level, I knew it would be wise for me to learn, but there was a part of me that was angry at God for making this knowledge transfer necessary. But, eventually, I came around and paid attention without too much complaining.

"Let me walk you through baiting mousetraps," Alan said one night as we were locking doors and turning off lights before heading to bed.

"Now? I'm tired. Let's do it in the morning."

"We need to do it now, Sweetie. The mice come in and raid the kitchen at *night*," Alan replied. He'd seen mouse turds on the counter that morning when he arrived to fill my coffee cup.

"You do it and I'll watch, then."

"I'll do the first one, but then you can do the other two. I'm going to show you the Alan Kelly sure-fire method for catching mice," he said as if he were about to impart the location of a secret treasure. "You need to bait three traps and line them up side by side perpendicular to the wall."

"Why three? And why do they need to go against the wall?" I'd seen his three-trap setup before but had never given it much thought.

"It's all about the middle trap. The mouse can reach the bait on the two outside traps from the sides, which means he can get the goodies without tripping the trap if he's careful. But to reach the bait on the middle trap, he has to climb over one of the outside traps, and when he does that, bam! The trap springs shut, and we got him."

"Well, who knew there was strategy involved?"

"I have a few other tricks up my sleeve too," Alan said. "Grab a pack of traps from the pantry and the sports section of this morning's newspaper, please."

"Why the sports section? You trying to bore the poor mouse to death?"

"Because I was done with it, and I knew you weren't going to read it." Alan smiled, pleased with himself. "We're going to put the newspaper down on the counter and put the traps on top, so when you have a dead mouse, you can just wrap him in the newspaper and drop him in the garbage without getting your hands dirty."

"Good thinking."

I handed Alan the traps and the newspaper. "Okay, what kind of cheese do these little critters prefer?"

"I think they like brie best, but if we're out, peanut butter is their second choice."

"You don't really bait mousetraps with brie, do you?" I asked, not knowing if he was kidding. Alan chuckled at my gullibility and kissed the tip of my nose.

He showed me how to put a dab of peanut butter on the business end of the trap, pull back the spring, and notch the wire arm under the shallow ledge attached to the bait receptacle. He made it look easy. But when I tried it the first time, I didn't get the wire arm hooked securely enough in the ledge. As I set the trap down, the spring snapped open, and it shot slivers of peanut butter all over the tiles of our kitchen backsplash. I shrieked and combed a few spatters from my hair with my fingers. I did better on my second attempt.

In the morning, Alan left the dead mouse for me to clean up. Looking at that poor mouse, limp and lifeless, was the hardest part of the job. I sniffled as I carried him out to the trash bin and vowed not to leave any food on the countertops that might attract the little rodents.

Alan also attempted to teach me to attach the utility trailer to the trailer hitch on the back of our Subaru wagon and hook up the electrical system so the trailer lights worked. He envisioned my needing it for hauling loads of branches to the composting facility after big storms. Despite my newly acquired skills, it turned out to be useless information because I was a total failure at backing up a vehicle with a trailer attached. I tried for an entire morning before I finally gave up and vowed silently to get rid of the trailer at my earliest opportunity. I'd find another way to dispose of yard debris.

I gleaned many smaller nuggets that were more manageable, things like where to find the box of lug nuts for the snow tires for each of our cars and how to replace the filter for the whole-house humidifier.

Alan rested easier knowing he had taught me what I needed to know to carry on in his absence. I was comforted by the knowledge that Alan had a phone full of contacts, contacts I could copy to my phone should the need arise, people I could hire to help me with the bigger chores.

June 2018

I can't tell you exactly when Alan lost the ability to walk independently because it happened in such small increments I barely noticed. I *do* know that in the fall of 2017, he occasionally used trekking poles to help him keep his balance. That was all the help he needed. You wouldn't have mistaken him for an energetic college freshman on his way up Long's Peak, but you could have missed the wobble in his step, the extra width of his gait. Trekking poles made him feel safer when he walked, but without the connotation of disability that other assistive equipment carried.

But a few months later, Alan realized he felt steadier using a cane, and having a single item to hang on to left him free to hold my hand or use his free hand on a railing. By early 2018, he regularly used my mother's wheeled walker for trips to the bathroom at night, but he refused to use it in public.

One day in June, we stopped at the grocery store on our way home from a doctor's appointment. I grabbed one of the compact carts as we walked in the door and headed for the fresh produce section.

"Hey, wait up. I want to push the cart," Alan said from behind me. I ceded the cart handle without thinking much about it. Alan hung his cane off the side of the cart basket as I wandered off looking for organic broccoli. When we hit the canned-goods aisle, Alan stopped to read a can label to make sure the contents were gluten-free. Without thinking, I slipped behind the cart and pushed it farther down the aisle.

"Hey, come back here with my cart!" Alan sounded annoyed.

"I'm sorry, Sweetie. I was off in la-la land. I didn't mean to strand you." I backed up and returned the cart to him. It was second nature to push the cart myself when I shopped, but I worked to keep my brain in gear so I wouldn't repeat my mistake.

When we got to the car, I stowed the bags of groceries in the trunk while Alan eased himself into the passenger seat. When I got behind the wheel, I teased Alan about pushing the cart. "You know those carts are just glorified walkers with extra-large baskets, don't you? I bet they're even made by the same company. How come you don't mind pushing a cart in public but refuse to push a walker in public?"

"Okay. Okay. I admit I feel safer using a walker, but emotionally, it's hard." He turned his head to look out the passenger-side window. "I don't want people to think of me as disabled," he said quietly, as if he were talking to himself.

"Oh, Sweetie! I'll still love you if you use a walker. Your daughters and friends will still love you if you use a walker. And nobody else matters one iota." I patted his knee, hoping it felt reassuring to him.

"I know you're right. But I reserve the right to be crabby about it." He crossed his arms over his chest in an exaggerated gesture, but his eyes still smiled.

"You got it. I'd rather have you crabby than in a heap on the sidewalk. How ’bout we stop for ice cream on the way home to see if we can make a dent in that crabbiness?”

It was a big step for Alan, a statement to the world that he was no longer the man he used to be, but using a walker quickly became a necessity. Soon after, he risked falling if he attempted to take the three steps from one kitchen counter to the next without holding on to his walker.

We were constantly adjusting.

A year earlier, we could still cook a meal together. Now I had to carry the burgers to the deck and place them on the grill for him. He could tend them while they were cooking, but he called me to take them off the grill when they were done.

The whole time we had been together, we had each cooked our own breakfast. As Alan struggled more in the kitchen, I started taking all the breakfast ingredients out of the refrigerator—the fruit, yogurt, eggs—and lining them up on the kitchen counter, interspersed with the cups and plates and required utensils, to make it easier for Alan to cook his breakfast. That helped for a short while. But it wasn’t long before he couldn’t crack the eggshells without breaking the yolks. Alan asked me to crack his eggshells and put the raw eggs in a cup for him to poach. I started doing it regularly for him, each egg an incremental sign of loss.

When my mother lived with us in her final year with Alzheimer’s, we realized it was important for her to feel like she was helping with the household chores. She was happy to sit on a stool in the kitchen snapping green beans from the garden or peeling a carrot, whatever it took for her to be part of the action, the camaraderie of meal preparation, an activity that had been part of her daily routine for decades. When those chores became too much for her, we would fill the sink with warm sudsy water and let her wash a few dishes, even if we had to pull them straight from the stacks of already clean plates in the cupboard. She would swish the suds around the sink and pour water from one cup to another, like a two-year-old in a bathtub, not stopping until we told her it was time to eat. Even though she could no longer articulate the thought, we could tell how important it was to her to feel useful and included.

As Alan's losses piled up, I continued to do whatever he asked me to do on his behalf. I tried hard not to do things for him that he could still do for himself. Some days it was hard to tell which was which.

July 2018

Showering, dressing, and eating breakfast left Alan exhausted. He needed to rest before he could tackle other activities. To recuperate, he parked himself on the sofa and fired up his laptop. For a while, he watched reruns of Johnny Carson's late-night TV shows. Before that it was performances and interviews of Robin Williams and other comedians—anything that would make him laugh. Before the comedians, it was videos involving big trucks (usually big *red* trucks), cranes, bulldozers, and other heavy equipment, sometimes knocking over buildings, sometimes getting stuck in ditches. That phase lasted several weeks. He also went through a phase of watching videos of people doing clumsy things like falling off bicycles, falling into swimming pools, tripping over their own two feet. Maybe they made him feel better about his own clumsiness.

I knew I should be glad he had found restful activities that made him happy. I was ashamed to admit it wasn't so. I tried to figure out why his video watching annoyed me so much. At first,

I thought it was the constant noise that was grating on me. I have always needed big stretches of quietness to gentle my nerves. I never turn on the radio and seldom listen to music. Quiet is the balm my soul craves.

So I suggested Alan use his headphones when he watched videos. But the headphones drove me nuts because he couldn't hear me when I yelled to him from another room that lunch was ready or we needed to get ready to leave for a doctor's appointment.

Even when he wore his headphones, when I sat next to him on the sofa, his constant, almost-silent, wheezy laughter irritated me. I felt it in the vibration of the sofa more than I heard it. I kicked myself for not being more tolerant. If I were truly a good person, I told myself, I would be delighted he was laughing. So what was really going on for me? Was it some childhood trauma rearing its head? Was his behavior reminding me of something I disliked about myself? Was I jealous he was having fun, and I was not included? Or that I was closed out of his world, and he was not paying attention to me? I hoped not. It sounded so petty. Was it my overdeveloped Protestant work ethic kicking in, judging him as deficient because he was not doing something productive? Again, I sure hoped that was not the case.

It was not the resting that annoyed me, because I didn't have the same reaction when he closed his eyes or napped.

Usually when Alan was in video-watching mode, I was working, taking care of the house and yard, managing our house-remodel project, cooking, planning, cleaning, paying bills. I missed the days when I had a partner to help me with the chores, but I didn't usually feel resentful about the added responsibility I carried. I sometimes wished I had more time for the activities I enjoyed, like gardening, reading, writing, and working on creative projects. But I was glad to be taking care of Alan and all that it entailed. I was glad I had the capability to take care of chores he formerly handled, to rise to the occasion. I didn't think it was about the workload.

Alan spent so many hours a day online, I wondered if he suffered from an Internet addiction. If he was not online with his computer, he was using his phone, reading news alerts, weather alerts, keeping track of the latest natural disasters and political bombshells. Maybe it was that addictive quality that irritated me.

Maybe I needed a vacation.

August 2018

As I settled into bed, just down the hall from Alan doing the same in his room, he called to me: "Joanne, please come here." It sounded more like a command than a request, and a note of alarm lurked at the edge of his voice.

As I reached his doorway, he pointed to a splotch of brown on the inside of his window frame. At first glance, I thought it was a large moth, perhaps a cecropia. But I realized almost instantly it was too big and the wrong shape to be a moth. Before I had a chance to come up with another hypothesis, Alan announced, "It's a bat."

The morning paper had featured an article about a local woman who was bitten by a rabid bat, an experience I was anxious to avoid. I shoved Alan's walker in front of him and pulled on his arm to help him stand up.

"Let's get out of here! Now!" I yelled. I pushed firmly on the small of Alan's back, trying to get him to hurry, but hurrying was no longer in his repertoire. Adrenaline pumped through my veins until I got him safely into the hall and pulled his bedroom door closed behind us.

We stood in the dining room debating how to get the bat out of the house.

"Someplace I have an old butterfly net," I offered. "But I have no idea where."

"We need to open the sliding door onto the deck and chase him out," Alan declared.

"I'll get you a broom," I answered.

"You know I can't help you chase him, right?" Alan said.

Half of my brain knew it was true, but the other half was outraged at the thought. "There's no way I can do it myself," I sputtered. Alan had always been my savior when it came to spiders, mice, and snakes, all of which filled me with irrational, heart-pounding panic. And bats were ten times worse because they could fly, which the bat promptly demonstrated after he slipped out from under Alan's bedroom door. I kicked myself for not stuffing a towel in the crack under the door.

The bat swooped over our heads as he circled the house—dining room, kitchen, living room, front hall—repeatedly, occasionally alighting in the dark living room before resuming his circuit of terror. I did a quick Internet search to see what advice others had to offer, but found nothing useful. Truth be told, I didn't really want advice on how to get the bat out of the house myself; I wanted someone to magically appear and take care of the problem.

We tried to think of someone we could call to help us, but it was too late at night to bother our friends and neighbors. I knew the animal control team would not be answering calls until morning. I finally swallowed hard and tiptoed to the pantry, as if tiptoeing would keep me safe from the marauding rodent. I grabbed a broom, hoping I could use it to gently guide the animal out the door. The bat was too fast for that strategy to work, and I did not want to injure him. I may have tired him out, though, because he took a rest on the floor between the kitchen and living room.

I noticed the tent-like mesh cover on the kitchen counter—the kind you take to a picnic to keep the flies off your pie. We used it to keep fruit flies off a pile of newly picked tomatoes from the garden. Breathing hard, I grabbed the mesh tent and snuck around the wall that divides the kitchen from the living room, gingerly reaching around the corner and plopping the tent over the bat. Using my broom, I slid the contraption across the hardwood floor to the still-open sliding-glass door. The shallow hard-rubber ramp we used to make it easier for Alan to take his walker out the door also made it easier for me to get the bat-containing tent up and over the door frame and out onto the deck, where I used my broom to upend the tent. We watched the bat soar free into the night.

As I lay in bed waiting for the adrenaline to dissipate and mulling the evening's events, I reached two conclusions: Alan was no longer going to be my savior. I was it. And even when I was petrified and positive I could not do something, I had a reservoir of courage I could tap.

Maybe I would be able to reach deep into that reservoir to find the courage to go on after Alan died. I couldn't imagine it, but I decided to remain open to the possibility.

In a magazine for people with neurological illnesses, I read a first-person story about a woman who was devastated by her Parkinson's disease diagnosis, so much so that she had to pull over on her way home from her doctor's appointment to have a good cry before she could continue driving.

I was not proud of this fact, but I could muster little sympathy for her. We would have been overjoyed if Alan had received a diagnosis of Parkinson's instead of multiple system atrophy.

We had a good friend, Ann, who lived with Parkinson's disease for more than twenty-five years, more than a quarter of a century. She sometimes found her illness to be an inconvenience, yet she was less disabled by her illness than Alan was by his—and he was newly diagnosed. They both used walkers, although Ann could sometimes leave hers behind when she was having a good day. Alan did not have good days—at least not good enough for him to abandon his walker. Ann was one of the first people to have deep-brain stimulation surgery, which suppressed her symptoms for years. Ann's medications sometimes gave her times when you could hardly tell she was ill. Deep-brain stimulation surgery is not helpful for people with MSA, and medications provide no relief. There was nothing that helped with Alan's illness.

But I wondered if people who had illnesses like Stage 4 pancreatic cancer—illnesses where likely longevity was measured in months, not years—might be jealous of people with MSA, who were likely to live for a handful of years following diagnosis. And if people whose loved ones died suddenly, without warning, were terribly jealous of people who had Stage 4 pancreatic cancer. Even though they may only have had months to live, at least they had enough time to say their goodbyes and get their affairs in order.

When I discussed this line of thinking with my friend Connie, she reminded me that there are plenty of people in my own circle of friends who would be delighted to have a loving partner at all, even if he or she were to die suddenly or otherwise. Of course, she was right.

I *was* grateful Alan had been my partner for twenty-four years, and even though his illness changed the trajectory of our lives, I was grateful he was still with me, that he could still communicate, still get from one place to another using his walker, still feed himself.

I sent blessings to the woman newly diagnosed with Parkinson's disease who wrote the article for the magazine.

"How can I help?" Friends started asking long before I thought we needed help, and they didn't stop asking. For months, my response was, "Right now I can't think of anything we need, but I'm sure opportunities will arise as Alan's illness progresses."

Part of the problem, I suspect, was my upbringing. My siblings and I were taught from an early age not to expect help from others, not to seek help from others, not to rely on anyone else. If we wanted to be seen as competent individuals, we needed to solve our own problems and get the job done ourselves. Watching my father, I learned through osmosis that asking for help was a close cousin to admitting failure, which was something I should avoid at all costs.

As Alan's caregiver, I knew I was going to need to overcome my proclivity to avoid asking for help, but most of the time, I honestly couldn't think of a thing people could do for us. For all but the smallest handful of trusted friends, cooking meals for us was out of the question. Despite their best intentions, most people don't have enough knowledge or awareness to create dishes that are reliably gluten-free. They might neglect to check the ingredients list on the chicken stock they used in their soup, or they might not know that soy sauce contains gluten. I could not afford to get sick, so it felt much safer to do the cooking myself.

But there *was* the problem of the fish tank. Alan had lovingly tended his forty-gallon aquarium from the very beginning of our relationship. Mostly the fish were small and well-behaved, but more than once he'd had one so intent on escaping the confines of the tank that it jumped out and thrashed around on the floor, gasping for oxygen, its gills utterly useless.

Alan's tank occasionally housed a couple of fluttery-finned angel fish or a sleek little shark, but mostly his tank was populated by dainty little mollies and tetras. Like most animals, Alan's fish pooped regularly and abundantly, but the gross part was that they did it in the water in which they swam. Alan's tank always had a healthy population of little snails to hoover up the debris, and usually a prehistoric-looking Plecostomus, which is actually a type of algae-eating catfish, that Alan would trade in for a smaller model when it grew too large for his tank. But despite the assistance from these little tank-dwelling janitors, the tank needed to be cleaned regularly. Over the years, Alan had cleaned his aquarium faithfully every two or three weeks in a production that took the better part of an hour.

First, he would siphon off three quarters of the water, which sounds simple enough on the surface, but here's the issue: he started the siphon by sucking on the plastic tubing, which has to be one of the most disgusting things a person could possibly do with his or her mouth, when you consider what is in the water that flows through the tubing. There was no way in hell *I* was going to do that. After that stomach-churning start, he would carry the buckets of disgusting, foul-smelling water to the kitchen sink to empty them. Next, he thinned out the aquatic plants and removed the big rocks, the "furniture" that gave the fish places to hide and made the tank more interesting to look at. He loaded the rocks into a bucket and hauled them to the sink where he scrubbed the slime off them, soaked them in a bleach solution, and rinsed them well. Then he used a vacuum contraption to clean the fish poop out of the fine gravel that lined the bottom of the tank, all the while talking gently to his fish, which remained swimming in the murk at the bottom of the tank. He then prepared fresh water to use for refilling the tank, fussing over the temperature and adding conditioner to balance the pH or remove any traces of chlorine or whatever the heck it does. Then he had to reassemble the tank. Before calling the job done, I would insist that he scrub the kitchen sink because I didn't want fish poop contaminating our food-preparation area.

As Alan's symptoms worsened, it became harder for him to clean his tank himself. Carrying buckets of water when your balance is shaky is hard enough. But it's next to impossible if you're using a walker that requires two hands—unless, of course, you are using a wheeled walker that has a seat, and then you can transport buckets on the seat as long as you are careful not to slosh water around as you move. As Alan's balance and coordination degenerated, he asked me to help him clean his tank. I assured him there was nothing about that whole process that appealed to me. I am a dirt person, not a slimy-water/fish-poop person. I am fine with mud up to my elbows and clay caked between my toes. I am even okay handling the composted cow manure I spread on my garden periodically. But don't ask me to put my hands, much less my mouth, anywhere near fish feces.

One day, Pat Foss, a friend from church, stopped by to visit Alan, and she asked the million-dollar question: "How can I help?" Her timing was impeccable because that morning Alan had spilled his first bucket of slimy fish water on the kitchen floor, which I mopped up while trying to suppress my disgust. I finally had a good answer to her question: "You could help me find someone to clean Alan's fish tank every two weeks." As a founder and pillar of our church, Pat knew everyone. I figured she'd scroll through her mental Rolodex and come up with the perfect young person who was looking for a way to be of service to our community. Instead, she said, "If you teach me how, I'd be glad to take that on myself."

Pat was in her mid-seventies and was almost painfully thin. She suffered from heart problems and insomnia, but despite her afflictions and the dark circles rimming her eyes, she remained ever cheerful and positive. I worried about her ability to hoist around heavy buckets of water and rocks, but once she got an idea in her head, she didn't let go. Her tenacity had carried our church through its rocky early years.

Pat took notes as Alan explained the steps to her. Two weeks later, she showed up with her own water-proof apron and her notes typed up neatly on a card. She got the hang of the job quickly and did better than I expected at jockeying heavy buckets. When she came again two weeks after her initial attempt, she had laminated her note card, which she kept in her apron pocket. She was set for the duration. She was delighted to have a reason to stop by and visit with Alan regularly. And I was overjoyed not to have to deal with the slime.

It was a good first step for me in asking for help. I didn't have to admit *I* needed help. I had asked for help for *Alan*. Alan needed help, that was easy to see. But it cracked open a door for me, a door that would eventually be blown off its hinges by all the kind people who crowded in to lend a hand when I was finally ready to admit I couldn't do it all myself.

September 2018

At our support group meeting, Julia, a woman who had suffered from progressive supranuclear palsy (PSP) for several years, asked to be the last person in the room to speak. She didn't actually make the request herself. Catherine, her Jamaican caregiver, a beautiful woman whose English tickled my ears and reminded me of a tropical breeze, asked on her behalf. Julia could speak only in a barely audible whisper. She sat in her wheelchair looking regal, back straight, chin held high, peering down through the slits in her eyelids. Many people with advanced PSP can no longer voluntarily open their eyes unless they pry them open with their fingers, but that wasn't Julia's problem. The room's bright lights caused her too much pain to open her eyes more than a crack. She couldn't walk or feed herself. She needed help using the toilet, showering, getting dressed.

When we started attending the support group almost a year and a half earlier, I was drawn to Julia immediately. Her gusto, her sparkle intrigued me. Despite her increasing disabilities, she loved to make people laugh. She regaled us with stories of her antics and adventures with visiting family members and friends, some of whom accompanied her to support group meetings. She was obviously well loved.

When the other thirty or so people in the room had finished the updates on their lives, we passed the microphone to Catherine. She stood next to Julia with one hand on her shoulder. Catherine paused for a moment, looking around the room, gathering her courage.

"Julia asked me to tell you that she plans to take advantage of Colorado's medical-aid-in-dying law in six weeks," Catherine said with her enchanting lilt. "You are all invited to a party to celebrate Julia on October 20. And the next day, Julia will end her life. We have party invitations here with details, so please take one before you leave. Julia also asked me to say thank you to each of you. Your support has been a lifeline for her."

When Catherine sat down, silence filled the room to overflowing. I had a sense that something holy had entered the room, that it sat with us and blessed us.

I don't know if Julia's announcement truly came as a surprise to anyone, because the group's facilitator had warned the caregivers in advance that Julia wanted to share with us her plans for dying. I had mentioned it to Alan before the meeting, and I imagine most of the caregivers had shared the news with their spouses. A few couples who normally attended the support group meetings were conspicuously absent that day, and it's certainly possible they stayed away because they didn't want their loved one to be exposed to Julia's plan, fearing the seeds it might plant.

Like most of the people in the room, I hugged Julia, thanked her for sharing her plans with us, and told her how much I admired her courage.

Would I make the same decision if I were in Julia's shoes? I think so, but I don't know for sure. I don't think we can really predict how we will react until we reach the crossroads ourselves.

When Alan first moved in with me in 1995, our household included Jasmine, my sweet, if somewhat yappy, miniature schnauzer. As Jasmine aged, her brain started malfunctioning, and then, without warning, her body grew weak. She had always loved going for walks with me, but suddenly she would lie down after half a block, refusing to go one step farther. I would carry her home. After a while, she stopped even wanting to go outside. I called the vet the day she walked into a closet and couldn't figure out how to get back out when I called her. After he examined Jasmine, the vet said he suspected a brain tumor. We could take her to the School of Veterinary Medicine at Colorado State University, the vet said, but he was doubtful there was much they could do to help her, and she had already reached the end of her expected lifetime. Alan and I took Jasmine home and caressed her and cried, but we took her back to the vet's office the next day and held her while the vet injected her with a poison that made her heart stop beating almost instantly. It was emotionally painful, but I had no doubt we had treated her humanely by ending her suffering. We did not get another dog.

Theoretically, I agreed with Alan that people should have the right to end their lives when their suffering becomes too much to bear. But in the real world, the world of warm flesh and juicy, ripe peaches, of tender kisses and dark chocolate, of shared adventures, shared secrets, shared mornings tangled in sheets—how could I possibly let him go? And what choice did I really have? Only this: Would I accept his death—whether at a time determined by biological processes or at a time of his own choosing—with grace and dignity? Or would I rail against the universe, shaking my fist at God?

October 2018

It was a Monday morning, and Alan lay in a heap on the hardwood floor of our living room. His legs had given out when he tried to stand up from sitting on the couch. Instead of falling back onto the couch, he had fallen forward, and, unable to catch himself with his walker, he'd ended up on the floor. He wasn't hurt, but he couldn't get up, and he weighed too much for me to help him up by myself. I stuffed a throw pillow under his head to make him more comfortable while we figured out what to do. I parked myself next to him on the floor.

"Do you want to call Sue and Ron to see if one of them can give us a hand?" Alan asked. Ron and Sue lived across the street.

"They're out of town this week," I answered. "And I just saw Tommy pull out of his driveway and take off down the street. Got any other ideas?"

"I'm sure Paul's working. That pretty well takes care of the able-bodied males on the block."

"Our support group buddies always recommend calling the fire department when someone falls. What do you think about that?" I wasn't crazy about the idea, but it was all I could think of.

Alan was quiet for a few seconds. "I don't think so. We'd be telling the world that a disabled person lives here. I'm not ready for that. Let's see if we can't find a way to get me upright."

I suspected it would be safer to call the fire department for help, but I understood Alan's reluctance to get them involved. I was fine with saving that for a last resort. "Okay. Let's see if we can break this job down into tiny steps. First, I'm going to gather some supplies. Sit tight."

I grabbed the low stepstool from the kitchen and the gait belt we'd recently bought, a seatbelt-like strap with handles on the back that allowed me to hold onto him firmly. We rolled Alan so he was lying on his side. From there, with a fair amount of grunting, we got him up on his hands and knees. Alan sat back on his haunches and pushed against the coffee table with his arms. I pulled up with all my strength, using the gait belt wrapped around his middle. Together, we managed to get Alan sitting upright on the stepstool, about a foot off the floor.

"Phew," Alan said as he caught his breath. "Who knew it would be such hard work just to get up off the floor?" Getting him from the step stool onto the seat of his walker was easier. The whole process had taken a half hour, which put us behind schedule to get Alan to the YMCA in time for his exercise class.

I pulled the car into the loading zone in front of the Y, turned off the ignition and hurried around to the back of the car. Alan and I had done it so many times that the process was almost rote. I knew that as I grabbed the walker out of the back, he would be opening the passenger door, unlatching his seatbelt, and positioning himself on the edge of his seat, ready to get out. I brought the walker around to the passenger door and positioned the handles so they faced Alan. I let go of the walker too quickly, unaware that Alan didn't have a firm grip on it yet. I shrieked as he toppled over onto the concrete.

"Oh, Sweetie! I'm so sorry. Are you hurt?" I knelt next to him on the rough pavement and brushed dirt off the sleeve of his jacket. I was closer to tears than he was. His fall hit me hard, partly because it was his second fall of the day, and partly because I felt like I might have been able to prevent it if I had moved more deliberately. How could I have been so careless?

"I'm fine, I'm fine," Alan said, brimming with impatience. "Help me up." The words were barely out of his mouth before several bystanders rushed over to help him to his feet and into the Y's lobby.

Alan had two abrasions, one on the heel of his right hand and one on the knuckle of his right index finger. Both were oozing small drips of blood. The young woman staffing the front desk handed us two miniscule antibacterial wipes, individually wrapped, and two small Band-Aids. My hands shook as I tried to unwrap the first antibacterial wipe.

"Careful! You're dripping blood on my counter," she snapped.

I stared at her in disbelief, stunned by her lack of compassion. I was tempted to grab the ring in her nostril and yank hard. Would she react differently if it were her own blood dripping on the counter?

"Do you have something bigger than these tiny wipes—a

paper towel maybe?" I asked, working hard to keep my voice on an even keel.

"No, I don't. And I need you to step aside so the person behind you can check in."

Can't you see what's going on here? I screamed at the clerk, only not out loud. *My husband, the man I love, is falling apart, and there is nothing I can do to make it stop. My husband is dying, and you're worried about a few drops of blood?*

Alan seemed unruffled by the fall, his minor injuries, or the snotty desk clerk. He reached into his murse and pulled out a tissue, which I used to mop up the drops of blood from the counter. I realized I had left my purse in my unlocked car, which was parked illegally in the loading zone out front. If I'd had my purse with me, I could have retrieved some larger Band-Aids, at least. I made do with the supplies on hand and gave Alan a kiss on the cheek before he took off down the hall to join his class. I returned to my car, relieved there was no ticket on the windshield, and my purse was still on the floor. I pulled into a parking spot at the far end of the lot and gave in to the tears that I'd been working hard to hold back.

We didn't know it at the time, but it was the last time Alan would attempt to attend his exercise class using his walker instead of a wheelchair.

Alan fell twice more that week. Because of the frequent falls, Alan's doctor approved our request to have physical therapy (PT) and occupational therapy (OT) professionals deliver services at our home. Several times a week, two young, vivacious women showed up to help Alan conquer his everyday struggles. They taught him strategies for safe transfers (for example, getting from his bed to his wheelchair) and taught us both good ways to get him up safely when he was on the floor. The PT/OT team also made suggestions for ways to make our house work better for someone in a wheelchair; for example, adding grab bars in closets and adding extender blocks to the legs of our dining room table so the wheelchair fit under it more easily.

Susan, the physical therapist, suggested Alan's frequent falls could be the result of a urinary tract infection (UTI). He was prone to UTIs because he inserted a catheter into his urethra every time he emptied his bladder, and we live in a germy world. I wanted to believe Susan's theory, but part of me remained skeptical. After all, Alan took a daily prophylactic antibiotic to prevent UTIs. But we wanted to make sure. So, with the tiniest glimmer of hope, we spent Friday morning at the doctor's office, then the lab, getting Alan's blood and urine tested. Unfortunately, the tests revealed no blood or urine abnormalities. It would have been a relief if Alan's steep decline were due to a solvable problem like a UTI. But it turned out to be the inexorable, irreversible progress of his illness.

The ramp Alan had built solved the problem of getting him into the house when he was wheelchair-bound, but the remaining big question was how to fit a wheelchair-accessible bathroom into our compact floor plan.

One of the women in our support group advised us to wait on tackling the bathroom. She suggested we use our time and resources to enjoy life while Alan still had the capability for adventures and deal with the remodeling later. But I had a sense that Alan's illness was progressing faster than average, and that we needed to get started right away. I decided to trust my instincts.

I pulled out some graph paper and took a stab at rearranging our existing floor space to accommodate a roll-in shower and sufficient room by the toilet to allow a wheelchair to turn around.

I quickly reached the conclusion that I would have to give up my bathtub to come even close. But how could I give up my tub? One of the ways I take care of myself in the winter months is by soaking in a tub of steaming water scented with lavender oil while reading a good book, perhaps with a glass of wine at hand and candles flickering nearby. My therapist had been urging me to *add* self-care routines to my repertoire. I knew from my experience taking care of my parents as they deteriorated that caregiving for Alan was going to intensify in the coming years, and taking care of my own needs would be crucial to managing the demands. Foregoing one of my favorite self-care methods was not my first choice.

Since my amateur efforts didn't produce any workable solutions that included a bathtub, we hired an architect. The architect did her best to accommodate our list of must-haves within our existing floor space, but each of her designs had a major drawback. We decided we should look at bumping out the bathroom wall three or four feet.

Ha!

By cracking open the door to the possibility of expanding our house's footprint, we unknowingly unleashed a monster, a remodeling project that reminded me of the rapacious plant in the musical *Little Shop of Horrors*. It kept getting bigger and demanding more and more of our resources.

The Boulder County Land Use Department is notorious for making life difficult for residents who want to remodel houses. The county wouldn't let us bump out the bathroom wall three or four feet. They had increased the setback requirements in our neighborhood after all the homes were built, and because of the layout of our house, bumping out the short bathroom wall would violate the revised setbacks. So instead, we had to build a much bigger addition that required many pipes and walls to be moved.

The remodeling project turned out to be long, messy, loud, intrusive, and expensive. But we had a great contractor and some wonderful subs (not counting one member of the framing crew, a very strong man with anger-management issues) to help us get the work completed.

Because of his background in home repair, Alan would have been the logical person to manage the project from the client side. But his disabilities precluded that possibility. So I stepped up. I had plenty of experience with project management—shortly before I retired, I had managed a chunk of a massive worldwide rebranding project for one of my clients—but I knew little about construction. I asked a lot of questions, made a few mistakes, and learned all sorts of fascinating facts about things like soffits, joists, wall-hung toilets, and trench drains. And I wrote a lot of checks.

The addition/remodel project required us to move out of our main-floor bedrooms and rip out the existing main bathroom. Fortunately, we had remodeled our walk-out basement for my parents when they came to live with us in 2011. We couldn't use any of the downstairs bedrooms because all of the ceilings in those rooms needed to be torn out to accommodate the plumbing changes we were about to make. But the lower-level family room was big enough for two single beds in addition to the couch and lounge chair that normally populated the room. However, there was no kitchen to speak of downstairs, only a small kitchenette that was adequate for my parents when they lived with us, because Alan and I cooked for them upstairs.

If we could get Alan up and down the stairs safely, we could come upstairs after showering each morning, spend our day, and return downstairs after supper to watch TV and sleep. But could we get Alan up and down the stairs safely? His feet were not responding well to the signals from his brain. He walked as if each foot were encased in a concrete-block boot.

Alan's ability to navigate the stairs declined steadily as the project progressed. We installed a second handrail and always used the gait belt, but I still worried we both would tumble to the bottom of the steps in a tangle of arms and legs. We kept one walker at the top of the steps and a second walker at the bottom to make the process easier.

We were several months into the remodeling project when I realized maybe it was time to start working on getting Alan a motorized wheelchair. I had no idea how long it took to get a motorized wheelchair and no clear idea of when Alan would be ready for one. But my gut was telling me it was time to start the process. When my dad broke his hip, we bought him a wheelchair out of our own funds rather than have Medicare pay for it, because we learned it would take several months for Medicare to approve the request and obtain the wheelchair for us from one of its approved suppliers. And because my dad's dementia prevented him from remembering to set the brakes before he stood up, we wanted a wheelchair with brakes that engaged automatically when he stood up. We learned this special request was likely to delay the wheelchair delivery even further. So I knew I couldn't wait until Alan needed a motorized wheelchair to request one.

We started the process of requesting the wheelchair through his insurance company in April. After an insurance company physician examined Alan and quizzed him about his capabilities, he approved our request in June, and then it had to go through several more rounds of review in various departments before we got a final blessing. We paid our copay, more than $1,000, and the wheelchair was delivered in September, about the same time we moved back upstairs into our newly remodeled wheelchair-accessible home.

Within a couple weeks of the wheelchair's arrival, Alan was falling so frequently with his walker that he retired it and moved full-time into his chair.

So, here's my question: What led me to ignore the advice I got to delay the remodeling project? What compelled me to start the wheelchair process when I did? I am not claiming any special wisdom or insight of my own. At our church, we use a process of discernment. We get centered and focus on our breath. We ask for guidance, and then we listen. We don't always get an answer right away, and we don't necessarily get an answer in the way we were hoping. But for these questions, my answer came as a knowing, deep down inside, that it was time to move forward with plans to make Alan's remaining days as comfortable as possible.

In early October, I loaded Alan's power wheelchair onto the rack on the back of our Subaru, and the two of us headed out for a hike on the South Boulder Creek trail. The motorized wheelchair weighed almost three hundred pounds, and the rack, by design, was sturdy, but using it was cumbersome. Securing the wheelchair to the rack with ratchet straps was more complicated than I expected, and the rack platform scraped bottom every time we went over the smallest bump or incline in the road. Fortunately, the trailhead was only a half mile from our house, but the maiden trip with the rack made it clear we had some problems to solve before we attempted to transport the power chair to farther-afield locations.

It was a sunny, warm Colorado afternoon, and I was grateful to be drinking in the vistas of snow-capped mountains and feeling the soft autumn breeze caressing my face, the crisp smell of fall enchanting me. The trail skirted the edge of a vast tract of open meadow, part of Boulder County Open Space, which the county has been acquiring and preserving since the mid-1970s. Giant cottonwoods outlined the meandering course of South Boulder Creek, but seldom were the trees dense enough to block our views of the majestic peaks to the west.

Alan hadn't used his power wheelchair outdoors yet, except for a trial run in the driveway. Indoors, he used it only at the lowest speed setting. He welcomed the opportunity to try the higher speed settings outdoors where he had more room.

We quickly discovered that Alan was distracted easily on the trail.

"Is that a hawk at the top of that cottonwood?" he wondered aloud as he stared up at the treetop and veered into the tall grasses at the side of the trail. "It is! It's a red-tailed hawk!" It took me several minutes to get him untangled from the shrubs and grasses and headed in the right direction back on the path. By then, the hawk was long gone.

"Sweetie, if you're going to stare at the birds in the trees, stop first, then look up, okay?"

"Easier said than done," Alan replied.

The second time he veered off the path, he was admiring a pair of mallards dabbling in the creek, tilted forward so far into the water that all you could see was their tails bobbing in the air, like a scene out of a Saturday-morning cartoon. He came dangerously close to the edge of the creek and ended up with globs of mud and rotting organic material oozing from his tire treads.

"I know what you're going to say," Alan said as I used a stick to dislodge the mud from his tires. "Stop first, then look."

"You catch on fast," I said as I winked at him. "But I was also going to say, 'Slow down!' You'll get in less trouble if you're moving slower." I didn't want to ruin his fun, but I also didn't want to have to figure out how to fish him—and his three-hundred-pound wheelchair—out of the creek.

"Okay, okay." He turned the speed control on his wheelchair to the next lower setting.

He veered only a foot off the trail when a dead mouse caught his attention, and he was able to get back on the path without help. But he was completely undone by a pile of scat a little farther on.

"That scat is either from a fox or a coyote," Alan exclaimed with glee as he sideswiped a tree trunk. He missed a full-scale collision by just inches. He wanted to back up and get a closer look at it, but I told him I had had all the exciting adventures I could handle for one day.

"I guess I need more practice," Alan said with a sigh. "At least I didn't knock over any hikers or bikers."

"Maybe you could practice at a slower speed," I suggested. I knew I sounded like my mother.

Alan smiled his ten-year-old-boy grin.

November 4, 2018

We celebrated the end of Daylight Savings Time by spending the extra hour in bed—together, in the queen-sized bed in our master bedroom, which was a treat in itself—with coffee, two newspapers, and gluten-free scones we had bought the previous day from our local bakery. It was easy to forget about Alan's mounting disabilities when we were lounging in bed.

Alan read me snippets from the letters to the editor of our

local paper. I read him his horoscope for the day, and we chuckled at the absurdity of its prediction that he would sing and dance in the evening.

"How much will you pay me if I don't sing?" Alan asked.

"A hundred dollars, and an extra hundred dollars if you don't try to dance," I answered.

"It's a deal!"

I refilled our coffee cups, and we settled into each other's arms, pulling the covers up to our chins. Alan brushed the hair off my forehead and kissed me tenderly. I closed my eyes and soaked in his embrace. It was not our long-ago Sunday-morning ritual, but I felt utterly loved and altogether loving.

When it was time to get up and face the world, Alan practiced what his occupational therapist had taught him for getting out of bed: knees together, roll to the edge of the bed, and pivot to a sitting position. Only he rolled too far and ended up in a heap on the floor. He laughed so hard he could barely breathe.

"Ooh, I needed that," Alan said as he caught his breath.

"What? You needed to fall out of bed?" I asked with incredulity.

He erupted with laughter all over again.

"No, no, no. I needed the good laugh."

Once he recovered, he got to practice the techniques his OT had taught him for getting up from lying in a heap on the floor.

CHAPTER 6

December 2018

Two-and-a-half years earlier, when my friend Barbara was diagnosed with triple-negative, inflammatory breast cancer, which is one of the most aggressive and difficult-to-treat breast cancers, she was convinced her body knew how to heal itself. Barbara's goal was to support the healing process every way she could—through diet, supplements, exercise, and meditation—while at the same time taking advantage of all the radiation and chemotherapy treatments and drug trials offered by the Western medical establishment.

Barbara, who was a retired IBM manager, had a local Boulder oncologist, an oncology team at University of Colorado Hospital in Denver, a naturopathic oncologist in South Denver, and a team at MD Anderson in Houston that specialized in inflammatory breast cancer. She expected all of these specialists to debate the pros and cons of their suggested approaches to treating her illness and present her with their best options—from which she would then choose. That was how she managed her teams at IBM, and she expected nothing less from her medical teams. Because all of the teams worked for different organizations, the reality was not as streamlined as she had hoped, but she coached and cajoled and insisted until she got a semblance of what she wanted.

But Barbara's analytic, left-brain approach to getting the best treatment was only the beginning. During her chemo treatments, when the nurse would bring out each infusion bag, Barbara would hold it lovingly and meditate over it. She also concentrated on the gratitude she had for living in circumstances where all of this technology is available and even paid for, mostly, by Medicare.

In addition to her analytic and spiritual approaches to treatment, Barbara also threw in the whimsical. For good luck, she and Michael, her husband, bought matching lucky socks—black with red cherries—and wore them on the first day of each drug trial to ensure success. None of her approaches cured her.

In early December, Barbara was still convinced her cancer was survivable. She'd been admitted to the hospital because her kidneys were shutting down and the pain was intense. The hospitalist and social worker assigned to her case tried to convince her to enroll in hospice and go home. Barbara told them she wasn't ready to give up treatments that would help her survive long enough for her body to be able to heal itself. The next day, the hospitalist came back with a stronger message: "You are going to live only a few more weeks, at best. Hospice will help you have a better quality of life for the time you have left." Barbara relented, called hospice and went home the following day, a Friday.

On Sunday, two days later, Michael called me. I was out with Alan, his daughter Megan, and his youngest granddaughter, selecting a Christmas tree. I had promised Barbara I would come when she needed me and would hold her hand as she made her transition. I felt honored she had asked me, but worried I would melt into a puddle when the time came. Would I be able to be strong for her when she needed me, to provide comfort and support? Could I separate out and shelve my anxiety about Alan's waltz toward death during Barbara's exit dance?

Choking back tears, Michael said Barbara was ready to use the prescription she'd requested under Colorado's End-of-Life Options Act, and he needed to go to Denver to pick up the drugs. Would I come over to keep Barbara company while he was gone?

"I'm on my way," I said as my gut tied itself into a knot.

Deciding on a Christmas tree suddenly seemed frivolous. How could I waste another millisecond worrying about something so insignificant when my dear friend was inching along a high wire strung taut between life and death? We settled quickly on the smallest Christmas tree I'd ever bought—a tree I could transport and set up without Alan's help. I dropped him and the tree at home and hurried over to Barbara and Michael's house.

When I arrived, Michael showed me how to give Barbara another dose of morphine, then disappeared to make phone calls to arrange to get the medical-aid-in-dying drugs. I curled up on the bed next to Barbara, wondering how long it would be before I was in Michael's shoes and Alan was in Barbara's.

I held Barbara's hand and listened as she vented. She was sure Michael was purposely dragging his heels on getting the drugs because he didn't want her to die. How sad, I thought, to be so caught up in anger at your spouse this close to the end. Especially at a spouse who had worked as hard as Michael in trying to make all of Barbara's wishes come true. Despite his misgivings, Michael had helped Barbara fulfill her dream of traveling to Africa only a couple of months earlier, when Barbara was already on supplemental oxygen.

I assured Barbara that Michael was working as fast as he could, because he hated seeing her in such pain. I speculated that a Sunday evening was not the best time to try to reach the right people at the hospital pharmacy.

To distract her, I reminded her of the story about how we'd met. Barbara had been a housemate for a while in the 1980s with a woman whom Alan had later married—his second wife. When Barbara married Michael, Alan attended the ceremony and ended up becoming good friends with Michael. Alan liked to say that when he and his second wife divorced, Barbara and Michael got custody of him. But I knew better. When Alan and his second wife divorced, *I* got custody of Alan, and Barbara and Michael were the frosting on the cake. Barbara and I shared a love for good books, organic gardening, healthy eating, and hiking. I reminded Barbara about the fun we'd had on our excursions to the Denver Botanical Garden and our adventures exploring local artists' studios during Boulder's annual Open Studios events.

Finally, the morphine trumped Barbara's pain, and she fell asleep. The soft puffs of her oxygen-delivery machine punctuated the quiet evening with commas and question marks. Michael returned to say he couldn't reach the people he needed in order to get Barbara's end-of-life drugs. I was relieved to have more time to prepare myself for her dying. I wasn't sure what I had to do to make myself ready, but I knew I wasn't there yet. At the same time, I knew Barbara was ready. How did she make the leap from being sure she would heal to being ready to die just two days later? Pain must be a powerful persuader.

None of us knew at that point that the delay with Barbara's medical-aid-in-dying prescription was caused by a nationwide shortage of Seconal, the main ingredient in the drug cocktail, a problem that would take two weeks to resolve. Two weeks of intense suffering for Barbara—exactly what she had been trying to avoid when she'd applied for the prescription the previous

August. Two weeks of a morphine-laced fog where Barbara could not find a comfortable position.

I don't know why Barbara's physician didn't write a new prescription for a different potion that would end her life, but I suspect it had something to do with the state's medical-aid-in-dying regulations. Michael sought help from a friend who was a retired physician, who, in turn, enlisted the help of a pharmacist he knew. Together, they canvassed pharmacies all over the state and finally located a single dose of the scarce life-ending drug at a pharmacy in Glenwood Springs, on the other side of the Continental Divide. Apparently, the pharmacy would release the drug only to a licensed pharmacist, so this kind friend-of-a-friend set off from Longmont, Colorado, where he lived, to retrieve the drug. He was halfway to Glenwood Springs, a four-hour drive, when a blizzard closed Interstate 70, and he had to turn around and come back. He tried again the next day, finally making it through on the snow-packed interstate to the pharmacy in Glenwood and arriving home late that night with the drug. The next day, Michael drove to Longmont to pick up the drug from the pharmacist.

While Michael was gone, two friends and I kept Barbara company and tried to keep her as comfortable as we could. Barbara would sit on the edge of her bed with her feet on the floor for a few minutes, until she needed to lie down. It took three of us to help her lie down and find a position that was comfortable. "Rotate my hip to the left," Barbara would instruct us, her voice so quiet I had to strain to hear her. Or "pull my right shoulder toward the wall." After a few minutes of adjustments, she would settle into her fog and rest, if not comfortably, at least without complaint. Twenty minutes later, she would need to sit up, and the process would begin again.

"Where's Michael?" she asked repeatedly. "Where's the cocktail?"

We assured her again and again that Michael was working as fast he could to get her the drugs.

When Michael finally had the prescription medication in hand, he discovered it consisted of hundreds of capsules. He and his retired physician friend spent more than two hours in the kitchen, slitting open and emptying each of the capsules to release the powder. When they were finished with the task, Barbara's meditation group formed a circle outside her bedroom door and chanted *Om Mani Padme Hum*, the Buddhist prayer for compassion. Michael gave Barbara the preliminary medication to keep her from throwing up the life-ending cocktail. Then Michael and Barbara's closest friends, including me, sat on the bed with her, taking turns blessing her on her journey. Barbara's cat, Bubba, curled up next to her.

When we'd waited the requisite time for the antiemetic drug to kick in, Michael dissolved the Seconal powder in grain alcohol. With the toxic beverage in hand, Michael asked Barbara if she was ready. Sitting doubled over on the edge of the bed, she shook her head no. We sat some more, the soft chanting holding us in suspension. Every few minutes, Michael asked Barbara again if she was ready, and each time Barbara shook her head no. It finally dawned on me that Barbara didn't understand the question. The next time Barbara answered no to Michael's question, I whispered to her that it was the cocktail Michael was offering her. Her eyes flew open, her head jerked up.

"It is?" Her voice was strong and clear. She grabbed the cocktail from Michael's hand and slurped it greedily like a thirsty desert wanderer who hasn't had a drop to drink in days.

A little while later—I don't know if it was five minutes or

twenty minutes—she asked for help lying down for the last time. Her breathing became shallower and slower until we couldn't tell if she was still breathing or not. Her skin turned waxy, and she slipped away almost imperceptibly.

December 21, 2018

I woke up the next morning with my eyes puffy and swollen from all the crying I had done during Barbara's death. In my next life, I would like to come back as someone whose eyes do not look like a frog's the day after a good cry. I'm thankful it is almost always sunny in Colorado, so sunglasses never look too out of place, at least during the day.

As I took breaks from tending to Alan's needs, I went through the photos on my phone, transferring all the good pictures of Barbara to my computer. Barbara smelling the lilacs on our bushes, her hair dyed the same shade of purple as the blossoms. Surrounded by roses on Barbara's deck, me shaving Barbara's head when her hair started to fall out. Barbara playing dominos with her granddaughter at her kitchen table. In our wedding album, I found a picture of Barbara blowing bubbles as Alan and I left the church, an impish grin on her face. My plan was to send the photos to Michael for a slide show of her life he could use at her memorial service. But Michael seemed stunned. He walked around in a bewildered daze, unable to pull his thoughts together, unable to make decisions without his wife at his side. My heart broke for him, and I wanted to do what I could to help. I would be standing in his shoes before long.

Michael ended up sending me *his* photos of Barbara, which I curated, scanned, cropped and edited, pixel by pixel, until each one was perfect. I put together the slide show, learning how to use iMovie software in the process, figuring out how to add a sound track, how to fade from one slide to the next. YouTube tutorials saved me whenever I got stuck.

I wrote Barbara's obituary and sent it to Michael and Barbara's sister for review. When everyone in the family was satisfied with it, I placed a short version in the newspaper and sent the longer version to the mortuary for posting online. I helped Michael plan Barbara's service at the church Alan and I attended. Being Buddhists, Barbara and Michael didn't have a church of their own, and our church welcomed people of all faiths. As the date for the service approached, Michael was frantic because he couldn't find anyone to give a eulogy. So I wrote and delivered the eulogy too. And created and printed the programs for the service.

Each of these tasks was a gift of love for Barbara, an act of kindness for Michael, and a chance to rehearse skills I would need much sooner than I expected.

In late December 2018, my friend Beverly moved into the downstairs apartment we had refurbished for my parents, and which we had recently finished refurbishing again after we had to replace all the ceilings on the lower level during our remodel to make our house's main level wheelchair accessible.

I had met Beverly at the Unity of Boulder singles' group shortly after I moved to Boulder in 1990. We were the same age, and she was smart and sassy, just like me. We hit it off. We hiked together, including an infamous trek up McHenry's Peak, a 13,327-foot mountain I can see from my back deck, where we got caught in a lightning storm above tree line. Obviously, we lived to tell about it, but it was a harrowing experience that made my hair stand up on end, exactly like it does in cartoons, and made me leery of all but short, below-tree-line hikes with Beverly from then on. I knew the lightning wasn't her fault, nor the fact that I fell on an ice-covered slope, and the slide I took removed a huge patch of skin from my leg. I didn't break any bones, at least, but I decided it would be wise to forego any more of Beverly's ambitious treks.

I think it was the year we both turned forty that we attended a Halloween party together dressed as matching bags of jelly-beans. We got lots of laughs, but we had to stand up the whole time. Neither of us could sit without popping some of the small balloons that comprised the jellybeans stuffed into the clear plastic garbage bags we wore to contain them.

Beverly had moved to California for several years, so we saw each other infrequently, but we never lost touch. When she returned to Colorado, she ran a nursing program for a college in western Colorado, which was a solid five-hour drive away, so we continued to see each other infrequently.

When Beverly retired and returned to Boulder, she needed a temporary place to live. She had rented out her townhome to tenants, and kicking them out early would have been messy. So when I offered our downstairs apartment, she jumped at the opportunity and offered to help with Alan in return. We were happy to have live-in help, especially from a nurse, and especially from someone as cheerful and thoughtful as Beverly. Frequently, I could hear her whistling downstairs as she went about her day, and the sound comforted me, reminded me to smile.

It wasn't long before Alan and Beverly established a weekly "date night." On Wednesday evenings, they watched episodes of *The Blacklist*, a crime thriller, while I made myself scarce. I refused to watch thrillers in the evening, because the adrenaline they sent shooting through my veins made sleeping even harder than usual. Having Beverly join him was a treat for Alan, and the two of them would dissect each episode for days afterward. I was delighted to have a couple of hours to curl up with a good book and a cup of tea, far from the drone of the television.

January 1, 2019

Our family tradition was to take down the tree and put away the ornaments on New Year's Day, a chore nobody really enjoys, but it always felt good to have the house back to normal.

"I'll give you a hand," Beverly volunteered when I told her what was on our agenda. "As long as we can listen to Christmas carols one last time while we're working."

"It's a deal! How about you take all the flying Santas off the tree and hand them to Alan. He can wrap them in tissue and pack them in the Santa box. How does that sound to you, Sweetie?" Alan had brought a collection of Santa ornaments into our marriage, which created a dilemma because my tradition was to hang only ornaments depicting flying creatures on my tree, mostly birds, butterflies, and angels. To solve the problem, I bought him a flying Santa ornament every year. Some years, finding a flying Santa took days of searching. But after twenty-some-odd years, his collection was impressive.

"I'm game," Alan replied. But he wrapped only three Santa ornaments before he changed his mind.

"I'm feeling awfully worn out," he said as he set the third Santa in the box. "Don't know why I'm so tired, because I haven't done a thing today, but I need to close my eyes for a few minutes. Would you help me transfer to my lounge chair in my bedroom?"

"Of course, Sweetie. If you're sure you can tear yourself away from this rip-roaring party."

Strains of "God Rest Ye Merry Gentlemen" filtered in from the living room as I clipped the gait belt around Alan's waist and helped him transfer to his lounge chair. He groaned and grimaced as he settled back into the deep seat.

"Are you in pain?" I asked. He had mentioned being tired, but he hadn't said anything about being in pain.

"Yeah, my lower back is aching, and it hurts to take a deep breath."

"Why didn't you tell me earlier?"

"It wasn't that bad until just now."

I stuck my head out the bedroom door and yelled, "Nurse Beverly, we need you STAT." I learned that jargon from *Grey's Anatomy*. It had the desired result.

Beverly swung into action gathering data—blood oxygen level, blood pressure, pulse rate, temperature—and listening to Alan's lung sounds with her stethoscope. I called the advice line and shared Beverly's report with the nurse. Alarmed that Alan's blood oxygen level was so low, the nurse wanted Alan to be transported immediately via ambulance to the emergency room. I talked her into letting us bring him to the ER ourselves.

Beverly and I struggled to get Alan transferred from his lounge chair back to his wheelchair, and from his wheelchair to the car seat. It wasn't easy because Alan's legs had turned to noodles. As we struggled, I kicked myself for declining the ambulance. When we arrived at the hospital's emergency entrance, Beverly ran inside and recruited a burly attendant to help us transfer Alan from the front passenger seat into a wheelchair. I tossed the keys to Beverly so she could move the car, and I followed Alan and the attendant into the ER. The medical team immediately performed a series of tests, including blood and urine tests and a chest X-ray, then returned a bit later to take Alan down the hall for a CT scan of his lungs.

By late afternoon, the doctor decided Alan had multiple pulmonary emboli, or blood clots, in both of his lungs. They admitted him to the hospital and started him on blood thinners, including warfarin pills—which take a few days to kick in—and heparin shots in his stomach, which act immediately.

I was relieved the ER team had found and addressed Alan's problem so quickly, but I was mightily disappointed that the blood thinners precluded Alan's surgery to install a suprapubic catheter, which had been scheduled for the following day. A suprapubic catheter is inserted through the skin directly into a person's bladder, where it resides permanently, allowing urine to drip into an external bag. It would save Alan from having to insert a catheter through his penis to empty his bladder, a task that was becoming increasingly difficult for him to perform. But mostly I was worried about Alan's frequent falls when he got up to go to the bathroom at night to catheterize himself. I was concerned for his safety, and a suprapubic catheter would solve the problem. We learned Alan would have to be on blood thinners for four to six months before they would consider taking him off so they could perform the surgery.

By Alan's third day in the hospital, he finally felt human again, and they decided to send him home. But first they had to teach me to administer the heparin shots in his stomach and show me how to remove the Foley catheter that they had installed in the hospital and that they wanted Alan to continue to wear for another day or two at home. A nurse had threaded the Foley catheter tube into Alan's bladder through his urethra, and it was held in place by a small balloon filled with water. It allowed urine to drip into a catheter bag strapped to his leg without his having to think about it. The Foley catheter meant Alan didn't have to get up in the night to empty his bladder manually, which allowed both of us to sleep better, at least temporarily. But a Foley catheter is typically used only for short periods. It is harder on the urethra than a suprapubic catheter and makes the patient more prone to urinary tract infections.

Beverly held down the fort at home while Alan was in the hospital. She shoveled the driveway when it snowed and hauled the trash and recycle bins to the curb on trash day. She figured out what needed to be done and took care of it. She finished taking down the Christmas decorations and packed them away, dragged the desiccated tree to the curb, and swept up the trail of shed needles. On the day Alan was discharged, she made us a mouthwatering fish chowder for dinner. I was grateful Beverly had dropped into our lives.

Alan used a CPAP machine to help with his sleep apnea. We had taken his machine along with us to the hospital, and the staff respiration therapy team apparently made some adjustments to it so they could deliver oxygen directly through the machine while Alan slept. I was busy signing papers when they made the adjustments and did not see exactly what they had changed.

On our first night back home, as I filled the CPAP machine's reservoir with water, it occurred to me that something looked different but I wasn't sure what. I crossed my fingers and hoped it would work the way it always had. As usual, Alan fell asleep immediately, and I knew at once that something was horribly wrong.

The noises emanating from Alan's throat made me think of a dying horse. Not that I have ever heard a horse die, but it sounded like I would *expect* a dying horse to sound, sort of a cross between a whinny and a wail, with a bit of snorting around the edges. Over and over and over again.

I tried adjusting his mask, putting an extra pillow under his head, closing his bedroom door, closing my bedroom door, putting a pillow over my ears—everything I could think of to eliminate or muffle the sound. Nothing worked. In desperation, I called the hospital and eventually made my way through the phone tree to the night nurse on the floor where Alan had stayed. She assured me her team had made no changes to Alan's CPAP machine but promised to have someone from the respiration therapy team call me to troubleshoot the problem. As I waited for the call, I used my phone to make a short video of Alan's disturbing noises.

It was past midnight when Kevin, a kind man from the respiration therapy team, called. I texted him photos of the tubing connected to the CPAP, and he walked me through removing a connector they had added to it that allowed oxygen to be piped though the machine. I was elated until I discovered removing the connector didn't solve the problem. Alan was still making the eerie, piercing sounds. Kevin didn't think the sounds were caused by anything his team had done to Alan's machine. He had no suggestions for next steps to solve the problem.

It looked to me like at least part of the problem was that Alan was breathing through his mouth but his CPAP mask covered only his nose.

After a sleepless night, I did some Internet research and discovered that Apria sold CPAP masks that covered both mouth and nose. I packed up Alan and his machine and headed for the nearest Apria store. When we arrived, we found out we couldn't merely walk in and buy something off the shelf; we needed an appointment. I explained we were desperate and managed to get an appointment for late afternoon.

When we returned later that day, the customer service rep checked the settings on Alan's machine and could find nothing wrong. She gave us the full nose/mouth mask we wanted—it turns out Medicare pays for regular mask replacements, so it was free to us. We tried the new mask before we left, and it seemed to work fine—at least while Alan was awake.

But that night we discovered the new mask didn't entirely prevent the dying-horse noises, and it emitted a high-pitched whistle periodically. In the morning, the water level in the reservoir had not budged. Normally, I had to refill the reservoir every evening to replace the water used the night before. Something was still wrong, but I had my hands full dealing with Alan's medications, his daily blood tests to make sure his warfarin dosage was in the target range, his latest UTI, and his current bout of diarrhea—so I put the CPAP problems on hold. It meant I wasn't sleeping, but at least Alan was. That seemed most important.

After about ten days of almost no sleep, I was so crabby I couldn't stand myself. When I found myself yelling at Alan for spilling his food—a common enough occurrence because of the clumsiness caused by his illness—I knew *I* had a problem, and I had to fix it. I sobbed out my lack-of-sleep story over the phone to the folks at Apria. A kind employee took pity on me and told me to bring in Alan's machine and she would trade it for a new one.

The new CPAP machine transformed our lives. Alan stopped making the dying horse sounds in the night, and I started sleeping again. Life was tolerable once more.

Every six months, Alan met with Dr. Kurtz, his neurologist. At his appointment in January 2019, I showed Dr. Kurtz the video I had made of Alan making the dying-horse noises in his sleep. Dr. Kurtz confirmed what I had suspected. The noise had a name: it's called *stridor*.

Here's why stridor matters: In a 2007 study, six of the twenty-one MSA patients studied had stridor, and of those six patients, five died suddenly. Alan was petrified of spending the last months of his life lying in bed, unable to speak or move. He said many times he did not want to die of bed sores. Actually, people with MSA don't usually die *of* bed sores, but it's not unusual for people with MSA to die *with* bed sores.

Alan was somewhat comforted to know he was more likely to die suddenly, rather than wasting away in misery for a long time.

Dr. Kurtz also confirmed what I had read about the prognosis for people with MSA: Most people live for three to five years after diagnosis. Alan had been diagnosed one-and-a-half years earlier, in August 2017, so he was likely to have one-and-a-half to three-and-a-half years left.

Most researchers agree that people who are older when they are diagnosed with MSA tend to have a faster disease progression and shorter life expectancy. The usual age range for diagnosis is fifty to seventy, and Alan was sixty-nine-and-a-half when Dr. Kurtz diagnosed him. So I needed to make peace with Alan having the lower end of the life expectancy range. That way, every additional day would seem like a gift.

At his January appointment with Dr. Kurtz, Alan asked to be referred to his provider's palliative care team so he could start exploring medical aid in dying. He wanted to discuss his prospects for being approved to end his life with dignity.

To apply for medical aid in dying under Colorado's law, two doctors must agree that the candidate has a terminal condition and that it would be reasonable to expect him to die from his condition within six months. Alan knew he wasn't within the six-month window yet, but he wanted to be prepared when he reached that point. The other two criteria were more concerning: Alan would need to demonstrate decisional capacity (the mental ability to make critical life-and-death decisions himself) and the ability to self-administer the drugs.

Because Alan had exhibited signs of executive function and memory dysfunction well before his official diagnosis, the palliative care team seemed skeptical he would retain enough mental clarity to be able to demonstrate decisional capacity as his disease progressed. And because MSA robs patients of their coordination, the team questioned whether he would be able to hold a glass to his mouth himself when the time came.

When Alan and I talked afterward about his consultation with the team, I found it fascinating that we heard different messages. We both thought Alan had done a good job expressing his unwavering desire to be considered for medical aid in dying. Alan heard the team's response to his request as neutral, something along the lines of, "We'll see where you are when the time comes." I heard a much more negative message. While the team didn't say it would be impossible for Alan to qualify, they sounded to me as if they didn't think it was likely he would be approved.

April 2019

On a Saturday in early April, I had two high school boys, Dylan and Danny, helping me with yard work. It was a chance for them to earn a little spending money and a chance for me to finally get some of my bigger yard projects taken care of all at once, including moving a pile of stones, leftovers from our remodeling project, out of the secondary driveway that led to the back of our property. Alan was out back with us in his power wheelchair, helping to supervise. As lunchtime approached, I decided I'd better feed the boys. Another neighbor had reserved their time for the afternoon, and I knew they'd need fuel. With no teen-ager-appropriate food in the house, I offered to take them to a nearby sub shop. With the boys in the car, I was backing out of the driveway when I heard a loud crunch. I stopped immediately.

"What was that?" I wondered if I'd hit one of the plastic garbage cans piled with yard debris the boys had collected earlier that morning. Dylan suggested the same thing as we both hopped out of the car to check. I was filled with terror when I saw Alan lying in the street, blood oozing from a cut on his forehead. His power chair lay on its side beneath my car's bumper.

"Oh, my God! Are you all right?" I screamed.

"I'm okay," Alan said. "Help me sit up."

"No. What if something is broken that shouldn't be moved? Oh my God! I can't believe I didn't see you in my rearview. I'm so sorry, Sweetie. I had no idea you were out in the street." I was flustered and scared I had caused him serious injury. I felt like I was going to throw up. "Does it hurt anyplace besides your head?" I found a clean handkerchief in Alan's pocket and held it against the wound on his forehead."

"No, I'm fine." His speech was slurred, but no more so than normal. He always thought he was fine, even when it was obvious he wasn't, so I didn't trust his assessment.

Should I ease my car forward so I could attempt to pull his wheelchair out from beneath it? I decided against it, since he wasn't trapped in the chair. Should I call 911? He seemed okay, but did I really want to take any chances? I grabbed a towel out of my trunk and slid it under his head so his cheek wasn't lying against the pebbled surface of the pavement. Even though Alan seemed to have escaped serious injury, I pulled out my phone and called 911. I didn't want to take the chance he had broken something or had a concussion. The 911 dispatcher asked our location and assured me help was on the way. In the eight minutes between my calling and the arrival of the paramedics, she must have told me a dozen times not to move Alan.

"Can you hear me, Joanne?" she kept asking. "Do not move Alan's head. Joanne, do you understand?" It must be part of their training to continually repeat the caller's name.

Fortunately, Alan had stopped taking his warfarin, the blood thinner, five days earlier, or his bleeding might have been a much bigger problem. While we waited for help to arrive, I asked Alan why he was out in the street in his wheelchair. He told me he had heard someone operating a piece of heavy equipment on the empty lot at the end of our street. Once he figured out it was a guy using a Bobcat excavator, his inner ten-year-old boy's curiosity erupted. He had taken off to investigate without paying attention to what was happening around him.

Within minutes, we had a fire truck, two ambulances, the sheriff, and about five hundred neighbors gathered to bear witness to our trauma. I handed the paramedics a list of Alan's emergency medical information. I kept copies in both of our wallets and in the pocket of Alan's wheelchair. I assured them Alan's slurred speech was normal before they whisked Alan away to the ER. The sheriff asked me to stick around and wait for the Colorado State Patrol to arrive. The accident had happened in the roadway, not our driveway, so the State Patrol was required to investigate.

I knew the state patrolman who finally showed up was merely doing his job, but his questions left me feeling soiled.

"So you claim you didn't see your husband out in the street. Is that right?" He bent his head forward and looked at me over the top of his aviator sunglasses.

"Yes, sir." I noticed myself reverting to my Southern roots, calling him "sir." He was probably twenty years younger than me, but the badge he wore made me deferential. "I was unaware he was in the street in his wheelchair, and I didn't see him as I backed out of the driveway."

"Were you mad at him?"

"Good Lord, no! He has a serious neurodegenerative illness, and I have been doing my best to keep him healthy and happy."

"You feeling resentful about that?"

"No, sir! This was an accident."

"You two fight much?"

"No, sir. In our entire twenty-two years of marriage we've had maybe a handful of angry arguments. The most recent one was at least a decade ago."

"Um huh," he said, with a hint of sarcasm, as if he didn't believe a single word I said.

When the patrolman finished grilling me, he sat in his patrol car, filling out forms in triplicate. He ripped off the yellow copy of the form and handed it out the window to me before he took off, driving much too fast for our quiet residential street.

I rushed to the hospital where Alan's medical team was getting ready to put four stitches in his forehead, and the team debated whether the stitches were even really necessary. Besides the gash on his forehead, they found no other injuries. I breathed a huge sigh of relief. I knew it could have been much, much worse.

I took Alan out for sushi on the way home.

Our friend Dave Morden, a kind and handy man who had worked closely with Alan on the building committee for our new church in 2005 and 2006, showed up the next day to straighten the wheel of Alan's power chair, which had been bent in the collision. Alan's stitches and a small dent and scratch in my car's bumper were the only remaining residue of the traumatic day. Except for the jokes.

Perhaps it was evidence of my innate shortcomings in the humor department, but I did not understand all the people who seemed to think the accident was funny. I thought I would explode if one more person said to Alan, "I hear your wife tried to run you down in the driveway." I felt awful enough about it. The pitiful stabs at humor felt like people were rubbing salt in my shame, my wound.

I missed Beverly sorely. She had left for a couple of months of volunteering at her clinic in Uganda a few days before the accident. I knew if she had been here, she would have helped me pamper Alan as he recovered, and she would have dismissed the insensitive jokesters as idiots who should be ignored. I was glad she was tackling drought, hunger, poverty, and a dearth of available medical care in Uganda, but I looked forward to having her return to assist with the relatively small challenges of the Kelly household. But mostly I wanted someone to reassure me that accidents happen, that I was still a good person.

The first few months of 2019 were difficult. Alan had made numerous trips to the hospital for blood clots in his lungs and sepsis that sprang from urinary tract infections. In addition, he had been treated at home for five or six UTIs, depending on how you count, and each of those treatments consisted of a week's worth of antibiotics, each of which caused a week's worth of diarrhea.

Alan always joked that God made only two mistakes when he created the universe. The first was the size of the avocado pit, and the second was locating the body's recreation center in such close proximity to its waste elimination center. I would like to add a corollary to the second of those errors: locating the body's solid waste elimination center so close to the liquid waste elimination center.

When you need to be scrupulously clean in attending to a catheter, diarrhea from a nearby orifice makes the job infinitely harder.

At this point, Alan wore a semi-permanent Foley catheter to remove urine from his bladder, so he no longer needed to think about peeing. But defecating was a problem because he couldn't pull down his own pants. He needed help transferring from his wheelchair to the toilet, and he needed both hands to hold onto the grab bars on either side of the toilet. So I would pull down his pants for him, and when he had finished on the toilet, he would stand using the grab bars, and I'd wipe his bottom. The bidet toilet seat we installed during our remodel helped with some of the cleanup. But not nearly enough.

There is something about wiping your spouse's bottom that changes a relationship. I always tried to be matter-of-fact about it, because if our places were reversed, that's what I would want from Alan. No fuss, no complaining, just plain old assistance. But I felt sad to see Alan reduced to needing help with such a basic task.

During Alan's diarrhea weeks, I worked hard to prevent fecal contamination of his catheter, especially when I changed from the leg bag, which Alan wore during the day, to the larger night bag. After each bag change, I filled the bag I had just removed with a vinegar solution, let it soak for a while, and then rinsed it with plain water and hung it to dry.

Also during diarrhea weeks, soiled laundry multiplied like dandelions in a fertile field. I had always tried to conserve water, as we lived in a state with an average annual rainfall of only twenty inches. But when I balanced water conservation with keeping my husband clean, cleanliness always prevailed.

I fretted constantly that I must be doing something wrong, or why would Alan be getting so many UTIs? I washed my hands so many times a day that the ends of my fingers and thumbs cracked open. I made sure the nozzles on his catheter bags never touched bathroom surfaces. I used copious quantities of alcohol to clean the connecting plastic parts. But I must have been missing something important. I was sure it was my fault that he kept getting infected with nasty bacteria.

Each of us would breathe a big sigh of relief when Alan finished a course of antibiotics, knowing the diarrhea would gradually subside, and life would resume a more normal rhythm. And we would both cross our fingers, hoping we could keep him healthy for a good long time before another UTI struck.

The first clue I got that Alan was coming down with a UTI was typically that it became much harder to transfer him from his wheelchair to his bed, or the other way around. His legs got wobbly and couldn't support his weight. His feet stopped responding to the signals from his brain. Sometimes he developed a fever when he had a UTI, and sometimes he seemed confused. Sometimes his urine was cloudy or smelled different. But he always was harder to transfer first.

One night, I struggled to get Alan transferred from his wheelchair to his bed. He needed only to stand and pivot ninety degrees, which seems like it would be easy, but it was a lot to ask of someone with MSA, especially if an infection was sapping his strength.

I clipped his gait belt around his torso so I could hold him upright. With one of Alan's hands on the bed cane, a support device that attaches to the side of the bed, and the other grasping the floor-to-ceiling pole installed next to his bed, he was able to pull himself to a stooped but standing position.

"Take a half step to the side with your left foot," I coached him. He stared down at his foot and concentrated on getting it to move. It was almost as if the ball of his foot was nailed to the floor. He could lift his heel, and he could flex his knee, but moving the ball of his foot laterally was the challenge. It felt like an eternity before the foot finally nudged over an inch or two.

"Okay, turn your body. Stand up straight. Weight on your feet. Keep turning. You're doing great. Hang on tight to the pole. Move that foot just a little bit more. Keep turning."

I tugged on the gait belt to help him turn, and we finally managed to get him sitting safely on the edge of his bed—but it took a fair amount of grunting and groaning. I groaned inwardly, too, at the thought that this could be the beginning of another UTI. I grabbed the digital thermometer off the top of his dresser and ran it across Alan's forehead. The display turned red and flashed 100 degrees, another possible sign of an impending infection.

When Alan got up the next morning, Saturday, he had trouble transferring from bed to wheelchair, and his pee was cloudy at first, like proper British tea doctored with milk, but it cleared quickly. While he had some traditional signs of a UTI, Alan did not act particularly sick. I wasn't looking forward to spending the day in the waiting room at the urgent care clinic, surrounded by coughing, sneezing, sick people, and I didn't want to do it unless I was fairly sure it was required. So I took Alan's temperature every couple of hours. It hovered between 99 and 100 degrees, which was not low enough to be normal but not high enough to be a serious problem. I decided to watch and wait rather than taking him in for urgent care. On Sunday, nothing had changed.

On Monday morning, Alan's home healthcare nurse advised us to go ahead and have him tested for a UTI. I called his provider to see if I could deliver a pee sample I collected myself and have it tested. I had watched a nurse take a clean sample from Alan's catheter on a previous visit to the clinic, and it wasn't rocket science. Plus, I had a sterile sample cup stashed away. I felt confident taking the sample myself was the easiest way to get the job done. But I wasn't sure the medical team would agree.

After spending a half hour on hold waiting for the Urology Department to answer my call, I gave up and called the general advice/appointments line. My call was passed through various levels of triage, before being passed to the office of Alan's primary care physician. I told the whole story each time I reached a different person: Alan's neurological illness, his history of catheterization and UTIs, why I thought he might be coming down with another UTI, why I thought he didn't need an appointment with a doctor, only a urine culture. With each repetition, I had to work harder at being civil. *It's such a simple request. Why does it feel like so much work to get a straight answer?*

The last nurse I talked to insisted Alan needed to be seen by a doctor if he wanted a urinalysis, according to company protocols, but not a single primary care physician in the Boulder office had an opening that day. The nurse managed to squeeze Alan in with a physician's assistant by shortening the poor guy's lunch hour.

When we finally sat face-to-face with the physician's assistant, a man young enough to be our son, he asked Alan what was going on. Because it was so hard for Alan to talk, and because most people had difficulty understanding his slurred speech, he signaled to me to answer for him. Before I launched into the story, I bemoaned the fact that this would be the fifth time that day I had answered that question.

After I completed my recitation, the PA's first words were, "Next time you call with this type of request, you can say, 'My husband has a complicated medical history,' and tell them what you want. You don't have to explain the whole thing over and over."

I stared at him in disbelief. I am pretty sure my mouth fell open in wonderment. I was stunned by the idea that I could tell the medical establishment what I wanted, rather than wait for them to tell me what we needed. With the abundant resources at my fingertips via the Internet, it wasn't that I lacked knowledge, at least most of the time. It was because I had learned the hard way that medical personnel expected to be treated with deference. Here was a medical professional giving me permission to be clear and assertive.

Glory be.

And yes, it turned out Alan had another UTI. His sixth of 2019, and it was only April.

Sleep eluded me. I worried about Alan dying within weeks or months instead of living for another one to three years, which was his official prognosis at that point. My online research had uncovered a study detailing the cause of death for twenty-one people with MSA. A quarter of them succumbed to complications from UTIs. The fact that Alan already had had a UTI morph into sepsis, a serious systemic infection, made it seem plausible he would be one of those who dies from a UTI.

In addition to worrying about Alan, I stressed over how I was going get everything done in the limited time I had available the next day, a Sunday. We had made plans to meet Alan's daughters and their families at a local park in midafternoon to celebrate Alexis's birthday. I committed to making fruit pizza, which both of Alan's daughters, now in their forties, requested routinely for their birthdays. I was delighted to have a specialty they both enjoyed.

However, if you make fruit pizza too far in advance, the crust gets soggy, which ruins it. That meant I would have to make it after church, not before. But after the service our congregation was holding its annual meeting—which I had forgotten about when we made the plans with Alan's girls. Even if I prepped all the ingredients before we left for church, I was going to have a hard time assembling it when we returned from the meeting, while simultaneously taking care of Alan's needs and getting to the park at the appointed time. I knew better than to expect Alan to hurry. He was no longer capable of hurrying. I could run to the store and pick up a cake from the bakery, but Alexis was not a cake fan, and I had already promised her the fruit pizza. Over the last year, she had driven up from Denver at least two afternoons a month to spend time with Alan and to help out with chores like cleaning the garage. I appreciated her help and didn't want to disappoint her.

Tossing and turning, I worried about big things and small. When I hadn't fallen asleep in an hour, I turned on the light and picked up the book I was reading, *The Art of Dying Well* by Katy Butler. Butler's book is a practical guide to the topics you need to consider at each stage of your journey toward death. As I was reading, I stumbled across the very words I needed to hear. Butler advises readers to figure out what is important and do it. Let go of everything else. It sounded simple.

Relationships with family members are important, I decided. Keeping my word is important, so making the fruit pizza is important. A store-bought cake was not an adequate substitute.

It finally dawned on me that going to our church's annual meeting was not important. We could give our proxies to someone else to exercise and let go of it. I was embarrassed to admit it had not occurred to me earlier. Years ago, when I was president of the church board, getting people to attend the annual meeting was challenging. I had attended without fail every year to make life easier for the board president. I wasn't even sure who that happened to be that year.

I put down the book and turned off the light. Within minutes, I had drifted off.

CHAPTER 7

Alan spent 90 percent of his waking hours sitting in his power wheelchair. It would have been 100 percent, but in the evening, I helped him transfer to the couch where we sat together, snuggling or holding hands, as we watched TV. This snuggle time was as close as we came to intimacy in those days, unless you wanted to count the butt wiping.

Being in the wheelchair made it extremely difficult or downright impossible for Alan to participate in the activities he formerly enjoyed. Like cooking. Sitting in his power chair, he could no longer reach items in the cupboards or the pots and pans that hung from a rack attached to the ceiling. He couldn't safely reach the burners on the stove. His hands were not coordinated enough to use a sharp knife for chopping or slicing.

Occasionally, Alan joined me in the kitchen as I cooked. That's mostly what cooking together looked like then. But one day, I got inspired at Whole Foods and bought pork back ribs, which was one of the dishes *he* formerly cooked, not me.

After I carried in the groceries from the car and put the food away, I told Alan that cooking the ribs was his responsibility. He would have to decide on the recipe and tell me what to do, step by step. I would be his hands and feet, but he would need to call the shots. He flashed a big grin and started making plans.

First, Alan had me make a marinade for the ribs. He instructed me to put a glug of catsup and a slug of apple cider vinegar in a bowl, followed by a couple spoonsful of brown sugar, a shot of pepper, and a pinch of cayenne. Each addition to the recipe required a conversation. Exactly how much is a glug or a slug? How big a spoon should I use for dishing out the brown sugar? How many twists of the pepper grinder constitutes a shot? Back in the day, Alan could have made the sauce in half the time it took us doing it together, but communicating the requirements to an assistant takes more thought and endless explaining. But it was good, quality time spent together.

Next, Alan had to teach me how to fill the smoker fire box with pellets, how to light it, and how to prepare to cook on it.

Three hours later, we devoured the succulent, smoky, and spicy ribs, each of us congratulating the other on our mutual success. I was glad to learn to use the smoker, because when Alan was gone, I knew I might still want to smoke salmon for special occasions. And maybe ribs, now that I was an experienced ribs chef.

Paying attention to the small things that gave me pleasure, fleeting or otherwise, helped get me through each day. If I neglected to do so, I sank quickly in the mire of illness, the numbing sadness of losing my beloved in slow motion, the tedious repetition of rinsing catheter bags, doing endless loads of laundry, and cleaning up messes.

One day I made a list of things I noticed in a single morning:

The soft caress of my flannel pajamas against my shins before I even opened my eyes. The extravagance of light playing across the Flatirons as the sun peeked above the horizon and stretched its arms to embrace the day. The perfume of lilacs bursting into bloom outside my bedroom window. The rich aroma, the acidic goodness of that first swallow of coffee as it sloshed over my still-sleepy tongue and warmed my throat. The birds warbling joyously as I stumbled the length of the driveway to retrieve the day's newspaper. The hot water pelting my neck and shoulders, unsnarling my clenched muscles as I stepped into the shower. The soothing smell of lavender as I worked shampoo into my hair and massaged my scalp. The crisp outline of the Back Range, still swaddled in its winter wrap, fulgent against the blue, blue Colorado sky. The silky texture of dark chocolate as it melted into liquid pleasure on my tongue. The smile in Alan's blue, blue eyes as he watched me enter his room.

When I reached page twenty-four of Katie Arnold's *Running Home*, I had to put the book down and catch my breath. Lamenting her father's imminent death, Arnold asked herself, "And who will I be when he's gone?"

That is the very question that had been floating inchoate for months just under the skin of my consciousness. It was wrapped tightly around another question, like a bandage wrapped around a bleeding finger: *How can I possibly keep going after Alan's death? Surely, I will melt into a puddle of grief and never be able to take another step, utter another word, think another thought. How can I continue to exist when he is gone? And if I* can *pull it off, then . . . who will I be when he is gone?*

Unlike Arnold, who had lived with her father only for short stretches since her parents divorced when she was five, I had lived nonstop with Alan for the last twenty-four years. I had laughed and cried with him, slept with him, made love and fought (although rarely) with him. I had shared my pain and comforted him through his hurts.

I introduced him to the delights of raw oysters and sushi, and he taught me how to say, "I screwed up, I am sorry."

Most of the time we'd been married, I'd felt like I was my best self with Alan. One of the joys of being married to gregarious Alan was that, with very few exceptions, everybody loved him. And as his introverted wife, I had been included in that circle of love.

Would I be on the outside of that circle again when he was gone?

Who would I be when I was no longer a wife? Perhaps it was a failure on my part, but I couldn't imagine being a single woman, and especially a *dating* woman, again.

Before I met Alan, I remember the longing I felt to have a man with whom to share my life. Would I feel that longing again? I had been blessed with a great love. Maybe one is all we are allocated.

And who would I be when I was no longer a caregiver? I had been taking care of loved ones nonstop for almost a decade.

My mother's illness was advanced when she moved in with us in 2011. I bathed her frail body and washed her hair twice a week, and then we'd play "beauty parlor." She would sit in a chair under the heat lamp in our bathroom, and I would set her sparse hair in spiny, prickly rollers, like she had been doing for more years than I could remember. I helped her brush her teeth and get ready for bed each night, trying to squeeze in an extra dose of TLC.

My father's illness was more subtle initially, but he required care for a much longer time than my mother, six long years. And because our relationship had been so rocky, the care took more out of me. I was grateful for Alan's rapport with him, and for his willingness to lend a hand whenever needed.

But I had gone straight from taking care of my father to taking care of my husband.

So there I was, still cocooned in my identity of wife and caregiver, dreading the loss of those layers. I didn't know what would emerge on the other side. I suspected it would take courage to go on and even more courage to figure out who I would be next.

May 2019

I knew it was a bad sign when I had to shovel four inches of sloppy, heavy snow off the wheelchair ramp—on May 21, mind you—before I could get Alan to his doctor's appointment. And things went downhill from there.

Alan's morning appointment was with his urologist, a follow-up appointment five weeks after they finally placed his suprapubic catheter. The urologist had made a surgical incision a couple inches below Alan's belly button, through the skin and layers of fat, and inserted the catheter tubing through the incision into his bladder. For five weeks, Alan's pee had dripped out through the tubing into a collection bag that was strapped to his leg during the day or into the larger night bag that we hung off the bed frame. It was a relief to get rid of the Foley catheter, which was increasingly uncomfortable for Alan.

A suprapubic catheter is supposed to make a patient less prone to infection than if they use a Foley catheter, which is inserted into the bladder through the urethra. In Alan's case, it didn't exactly work that way: he had as many urinary tract infections after he had the suprapubic catheter installed as he had had before. And that was a lot. Since February, every time he was tested for a UTI, the urine culture revealed the pseudomonas bacteria, which is frequently a hospital-acquired bug. My theory was that he picked it up when he was hospitalized in

January for blood clots in his lungs. His doctors said it was likely he was colonized with pseudomonas at that point, meaning the nasty bugs had moved in permanently and nothing was going to make them change their minds. It also meant nothing I had been doing to keep Alan scrupulously clean had made one whit of difference.

When Alan arrived for his post-surgery follow-up appointment that snowy May day, he was being treated for his sixth UTI since January. Despite the infections, the suprapubic catheter had been working well. I had emptied two liters of urine from the night bag just hours earlier, the same as I had done every morning for the last five weeks. The doctor removed the old catheter tubing from Alan's bladder and replaced it with new—a routine task that needs doing every few weeks. He then flushed the tube with water to assure it was working properly. The urologist knew immediately that something had gone awry when Alan doubled over with pain. Replacing the tubing was not supposed to cause pain.

The urologist wheeled Alan into a procedure room, doused him with betadine and inserted a fiber-optic camera up his penis and into his bladder. From the inside of the bladder, there was no sign of the catheter and no sign of the incision the surgeon had made five weeks earlier. The urologist's best guess was that the original catheter had come loose and the hole in the bladder had quickly closed. The replacement tubing he had inserted never made it into Alan's bladder, so the water he had used to flush the catheter had gone instead into Alan's peritoneal space, the area around the outside of his bladder.

At that point, there were no good answers to what had gone wrong and no good solutions for fixing the problem. Alan and I were both crushed to learn they would not consider another surgery to reinstall the suprapubic catheter for at least five months. The only recourse was to reinsert a Foley catheter, the kind that had been causing Alan so much discomfort.

Hours later, when we finally made it home from the urology appointment, Alan got his wheelchair stuck in the snow that had fallen on the ramp while we were gone. He worked himself free, and he was glad to be home. Later, I noticed his power chair had left muddy tire tracks from one end of the house to the other.

Alan was quiet and listless as the afternoon wore on, which I attributed to his disappointment with the whole catheter fiasco. When I served a tantalizing pork tenderloin for dinner and Alan ate only two bites, it finally occurred to me that maybe I should take his temperature. Sure enough, he had a fever of 101 degrees. Alan was short of breath, and his heart rate hovered between 130 and 150. His normal heart rate was in the neighborhood of 70. I sent a quick message to the advice-line doctor who confirmed I should take him to the emergency room right away. In retrospect, I could have skipped this step. I knew he was sick and needed urgent attention. *Why did I feel like I needed someone else to tell me to take him to the ER?*

It was our fifth trip to the emergency room in 2019. Beverly had not yet returned from Uganda, so I was on my own again, wishing for moral support.

We learned, once again, that Alan had blood clots in his lungs. The ER doctor was also concerned with his unrelenting UTIs and with the possibility of infection in his peritoneal cavity—the space where the water likely went when the urologist tried to flush his catheter that morning. I was surprised when the doctor listed the peritoneal cavity issue as Alan's major problem, not the blood clots. Alan's blood tests showed he was once again on the precipice of sepsis.

The medical team pumped Alan full of IV antibiotics and started him on blood thinners and a saline drip. They admitted Alan to the hospital and moved him to a bed upstairs. By the time he was settled into his room for the night, it was well past midnight.

As I drove home in the wee hours of the morning, I remembered a similar after-midnight drive home from the hospital a few months earlier. As Beverly and I had rounded the turn into our neighborhood, a magnificent owl—with a wingspan almost as wide as my car—swooped down and flew in front of us as if he were leading us home. It had been years since I'd seen an owl nearby, and I took the breathtaking raptor as a good omen. But looking back now, I wonder.

Knowing that Alan was being monitored by professionals ratcheted down my anxiety a couple notches, but I was still too wound up to sleep when I finally made it to bed. I admit I was also relieved someone else would be wiping Alan's bottom and taking care of his catheter bags for at least a day or two. I welcomed a short break from those chores.

The next morning, after only three hours' sleep, I hurried back to the hospital by eight o'clock to make sure I didn't miss the doctor's rounds. I still had many unanswered questions. The hospitalist—the staff doctor assigned to Alan's case—didn't make it to Alan's room until after eleven, but I was glad I had arrived early to help Alan eat his breakfast. He was so weak he had trouble holding a fork or spoon, much less lifting a utensil to his mouth.

We groaned when the doctor told Alan he would have to be on blood thinners for the rest of his life. But we understood it was safer than repeated episodes of pulmonary emboli. After he poked around Alan's lower abdomen a bit, the doctor seemed less concerned about a peritoneal infection. He thought Alan would have more pain if he had a serious infection. But because Alan was so weak, the doctor ordered physical and occupational therapy consultations to evaluate his ability to transfer from bed to the toilet and back. We talked with him about how to tell when Alan needed to be treated for a UTI. Because he was now colonized with pseudomonas, a urine culture would always come back positive. I needed to be able to tell if Alan was sick from other signs and symptoms.

After the doctor left to continue his rounds, Alan's nurse remained behind to tell us that dying of a UTI is not a bad way to go.

"It is a peaceful death," she assured Alan.

She had noticed in Alan's chart that he had visited the palliative care team to discuss medical aid in dying. I found her words comforting in an abstract way, but not abstract enough to keep the tears from slipping down my cheeks. I was not ready to let him go. I knew the nurse was coming from a place of compassion and concern, but I felt annoyed at her for even suggesting Alan could choose to die at any time.

When the nurse left, I pulled the door shut and crawled into bed next to Alan, being careful not to jostle the IV tubing dripping antibiotics into his arm or crimp the tubing delivering oxygen to his nose. I nestled my nose in his neck, breathing in the soapy scent of his skin.

"How do you feel about the nurse's thoughts on dying of a UTI?" I asked, gripping his hand, hoping he would laugh off her comments and petrified he wouldn't.

Alan let out a big sigh. "I'm exhausted from all the trips to the emergency room. I'm tired of feeling so lousy all the time. I'm frustrated by not being able to talk clearly enough for people to understand me. I'm discouraged that I can't get my limbs to do what I want. And I hate it that I can't even wipe my own butt."

"Oh, Sweetie. You've been such a trouper for so long, putting up with so much crap without complaint."

"Well, I'm complaining now. It sucks. Big time."

"Of course it sucks. But that doesn't mean you're ready to die, does it?"

"I don't know." His voice was quiet. The gentle puffs of his oxygen equipment and the hum of his monitoring machines filled my brain with static, zapping my ability to think.

We lay there, side by side, for several minutes without talking, each of us feeling the new texture of the fabric of reality.

"How about this?" I finally ventured. "I'll check with you each time you come down with a UTI to make sure you want to be treated. I won't assume you want to take antibiotics. And I will support whichever decision you make. Is that what you want?"

He nodded, and the wrinkles in his forehead relaxed. Two minutes later, he fell asleep.

I gulped. I reminded myself that he was not saying he was ready to die. He was saying he didn't want me to assume he wanted to live. I needed to ask him at each inflection point. But I needed to be ready for either answer.

By Friday, three days after he was admitted, Alan was finally feeling better—I could tell because his sense of humor and his feistiness resurfaced. They finally sent him home on Saturday, still weak and needing lots of rest, but definitely on the mend.

The following morning after breakfast, we made a wheelchair tour of the yard and gardens, inspecting the tree limbs that had broken from the heavy snow load a few days earlier, checking to see how the lilacs and peonies had survived, lamenting the sorry state of the weedy flower beds and unplanted vegetable garden, and celebrating the glorious blooms—iris, roses, honeysuckle, soapwort, basket of gold, candytuft, anemones, alliums. So many amazing expressions of nature's abundant beauty. So much to be grateful for.

And so much to grieve.

Because Alan had a nurse who came to our home when his Foley catheter needed replacing, Medicare covered certified nursing assistants (CNAs) who showed up to give Alan showers three times a week. No catheter, no homecare nurse. No homecare nurse, no CNAs for showers. So I was grateful for his catheter for more than its ability to empty his bladder.

The two CNAs who came regularly couldn't have been more different from each other. Heather, who came on Monday and Wednesday mornings, was fiftyish, soft-spoken, borderline frumpy. Her sturdy ankles and clunky, mannish shoes peeked out below the bottoms of her high-water scrubs. Our Friday CNA, Missy, was young, effervescent, heavily inked, and the mother of a photogenic six-month-old son. Both were kind and caring individuals. However, sharing our normally quiet home with them early in the morning had taken getting used to. As I sat in the dining room, finishing my eggs and toast, the sounds of the CNA's voice flooded out from under the bathroom door like a creek overflowing its banks: Is the water warm enough for you? Do you want me to wash your hair first or your face first? Do you want to hold a washcloth over your eyes while I rinse your hair? Do you like to use cream rinse on your hair? Would you rather I use the bath brush or a washcloth on your back? Do you want me to dry you off on the shower bench or would you like to transfer to your wheelchair and dry off there? Do you prefer to use a comb or a brush on your hair? Do you want me to trim your beard today? Would you like to wear your sneakers or your sandals today?

I imagined the instructor for their CNA training telling students to let clients make as many decisions as possible, since they are probably feeling vulnerable and not able to control many aspects of their lives.

Missy, the bubbly Friday morning woman, asked all the questions so loudly I wondered if she was hard of hearing. More likely, half of her clients were, and the extraordinary volume was meant as a kindness. Her southern drawl, acquired by osmosis during her childhood in South Carolina, was charming at first, but it was not long before the drawl irritated me as much as the volume did. My crabbiness was not Missy's fault, I knew.

It didn't take me long to decide to take my morning walks while the CNAs were visiting.

A friend asked me why I didn't send Alan to a nursing home, since taking care of him at home was so much work. I knew the day would come when I would no longer be able to care for him at home, but for the time being, having Alan home with me was a gift for both of us. He would rather be home, in familiar, comfortable surroundings with some semblance of normalcy, than to be living among strangers. Home with his wife, who loves him.

I liked having Alan nearby, day and night, so we could share life's ordinary wonders and adventures in real time and talk about the little things when the spirit moved us. So we could appreciate the rainbows from the front porch together and watch the robins in the birdbath on the back deck railing together. So we could make a trip out to the raspberry patch at the end of our back driveway after supper to pluck sun-warmed berries and pop them directly into our mouths.

And I would rather have him home than have to go visit him somewhere else. When my dad was in assisted living, then memory care, I didn't mind short visits a couple of times a week, but more than that felt like a burden. Granted, my relationship with my dad was sometimes filled with friction, but it was more than that. It was being in a place that tried to pretend it was home but clearly fell short. The fake elegance and forced cheeriness grated on me. I felt assaulted by the Muzak and institutional odors: acrid, industrial-strength cleaning products with grace notes of the urine they were trying to get out of the carpet; cooking odors escaping the kitchen that evoked images of rubbery chicken and overcooked beef; the onslaught of perfume from elderly women who could no longer smell well enough to know they had overdone it.

But it was more than that. When I was home, I was in my element. I could start a pot of soup simmering on the stove and check it every half hour or so for as long as it took to extract all the goodness from the chicken bones and meld the flavors of the vegetables and aromatics. I could throw in a load of laundry and have it running in the background, while in the foreground I was refilling Alan's water container and talking to his medical team on the phone. I could run out the front door and weed the flower garden for a few minutes while he visited with a friend. I could slip into bed with him before the day started and fill my lungs with his sleepy scent, feel his limbs melting into mine.

When I was home, I was grounded and content. When I was at a nursing home—even one where kind medical professionals and their trained assistants took care of a man I loved—I was a visitor, an outsider. Not someone who could run to the kitchen and start a pot of soup.

The time would come when I would have no choice but to send Alan to a nursing home. At that point, I would do what needed to be done, and be grateful that nursing homes were available. But until then, he preferred to be home, and I was delighted to have him here with me, where he belonged.

When Alan first received his power wheelchair, we were close to being finished with the major remodel required to make our home truly wheelchair accessible. The remodel had taken almost two years, the first fifteen months working with an architect and fighting with the county to get our plans approved, and the last nine months getting it built. We ended up spending twice what we had originally budgeted, but the results are lovely. You don't walk into our home and think, "This house looks pretty good for a wheelchair-accessible home." You walk in and think, "What a beautiful home!"

At first, when Alan crashed his power chair into doorways and left long scratches down the newly painted drywall of our hallways, I assumed he would get better at driving the chair, at which point we could get all the damage repaired. However, his driving didn't improve. It got worse as his illness progressed. The woodwork around every doorway in our house sported ugly gouges. All of our kitchen and bathroom cabinet doors had such deep scratches I doubted they could be sanded down and refinished. I worried the doors would need to be replaced. All of our appliances were dented, and one stainless steel trashcan was so battered it was a wonder the lid still opened and closed. Most of our furniture was badly scraped, including several antiques.

At first, I was philosophical about all the damage. *It's only stuff,* I told myself. *I can get it fixed or replaced at some point in the future.* That worked for a while.

Sometimes, I lost my temper with Alan when he caught his

wheelchair controller on the drywall as he navigated a corner *and kept going*, a sure-fire recipe for a deep gouge. "Why don't you stop and back up and try to miss the wall on your next attempt?" I grumped at him. He never had an answer.

"Alan, just stop!" I yelled when he slammed into the same wall over and over again. The rational part of my brain knew it was his illness depriving him of his ability to drive like a sober person, but that knowledge didn't lessen my frustration.

I longed to have order restored, to have all the damage fixed, all the unfixable stuff replaced. But I knew it made no sense to fix or replace anything until *Alan was no longer here*. And I didn't want Alan to be gone, either because he had died or because he had moved to a nursing home. So when the urge to repair and replace hit me, I stifled it quickly, as if I were hiding a shameful secret.

Every week countless people told me, "You have to take care of yourself, Joanne, or you won't be able to take care of Alan." Some even reminded me of the necessity of putting on my own oxygen mask first, before attempting to assist others. I tried not to scoff or sneer at them, but I was sick of hearing it. I did not retort, *Oh! That never occurred to me,* with sarcasm dripping like hot candle wax from every word, but I thought it. I knew they meant well, so I stifled my annoyance and thanked them for their concern.

While I may not be the most impartial judge, I thought I did a good job of self-care. Tuesday afternoons, for example, I arranged a caregiver to keep watch over Alan so I had time to Take Care of Myself. It was my afternoon for appointments.

I had standing Tuesday afternoon appointments with two gifted therapists: my physical therapist, who helped me heal my body's aches and pains from straining to lift a man who outweighed me by almost 50 percent, and my long-term psychotherapist—the wise woman who saw and accepted me, who helped me deal with my childhood wounds, adult heartbreaks, and everything in between. I started seeing Kathy when my parents were preparing to move in with Alan and me. I knew I would need help to stay sane.

Between my two therapy appointments, I had just enough time to go for a quick walk. I pulled into the parking lot for a popular hiking and biking trail that is part of the Boulder County Open Space system. I donned my sneakers, grabbed my water bottle, and locked my car.

I veered right at the first fork in the trail to follow the dirt path next to South Boulder Creek. The oppressive July sun filtered down through the cottonwoods to create a kaleidoscope of flickering shadows on the path. Majestic views of the Flatirons and occasional glimpses of distant high peaks played hide-and-seek among the tree trunks. If I didn't dally, I knew I could reach a spot far enough from the road that the soothing burble of the creek would drown out the distant thrum of traffic. When I reached that magical spot, I wanted to linger in my momentary solitude and soak in the water's music, but if I slackened my pace even slightly, mosquitoes congregated to feast on my bare arms, my neck, my face. So I kept walking briskly, beyond the healing creek sounds and on to the paved trail where I turned back toward the parking lot. I listened to the bird calls and appreciated the radiance of the still-green teasels, backlit by the afternoon sun, and admired the feathery bursts of wild asparagus dotting the swampy areas beyond the fence.

A mere twenty-two minutes after I locked my car, I was back in the parking lot removing my sneakers and putting on my sandals. I had taken care of my body by walking an extra 2,500 steps, and I had temporarily quenched my thirsty soul with a tiny sip of nature.

Next, I spent fifty minutes sobbing in my therapist's office.

This was my Tuesday ritual.

Mid-July 2019

As it became increasingly difficult for me to transfer Alan from his bed to his wheelchair or from his wheelchair to the toilet without help, we started talking about the nursing home option. We visited Crestmoor Commons, a nearby senior living community that offered independent living, assisted living, skilled nursing care, and memory care. My father had spent about a year at Crestmoor Commons before he died, first on the assisted-living wing, and later in the memory-care unit, and we knew it was one of the best care facilities in our area. But neither of us was ready to take that giant step.

Instead, we bought a Sara Stedy sit-to-stand device to help with transfers. The Sara Stedy looked like a piece of exercise equipment you might find in a home gym—a simplified stair stepper, perhaps. To use it, I would roll the device into place, positioning the legs around Alan's wheelchair, and then I'd lock the wheels by clicking a lever with my foot. Alan would grab the horizontal handlebar and use his upper body strength to pull himself up to standing on the low platform. Then I would fold down a "wing" from either side behind his butt. Together, the two wings formed a seat that supported him while I rolled him wherever we were going. When we arrived, we reversed the process: I folded up the wings, and Alan used his arms to lower himself onto the toilet seat or the side of his bed.

The Sara Stedy eased the strain on my back muscles, made transfers safer for Alan, and made it possible for me to take care of Alan at home for a couple more months, which gave us enough time to adjust to the idea of him living elsewhere. But pulling himself up to standing using his arm and shoulder muscles became increasingly difficult for Alan. He pulled a muscle in his left rotator cuff, making the process painful. There were days when he couldn't stand up far enough for me to slip the wings behind his rear end. When that happened, we'd holler for Beverly to give us a hand, if she was home. Or we'd take a rest and try again and again until we were successful and quite often exhausted. A few times, Alan ended up on the floor, and we had to call neighbors for help.

It was clear things were not going to improve.

I wanted to make sure we were prepared when it came time to enroll Alan in hospice, so I started doing research into the various hospice organizations that served our area and provided in-home care. But choosing a hospice turned out to be more difficult than I expected. After getting recommendations from a variety of people whose opinions we valued, we interviewed representatives from four hospice organizations. For the most part, their offerings were similar because Medicare paid for their services, and Medicare had strict requirements the organizations had to follow.

The representatives from one of the hospices told us they would not support a patient who planned to take advantage of Colorado's medical-aid-in-dying law because their founder, a religious organization, expressly prohibited it. We promptly crossed that organization off our list. The representatives from the other three hospices were clear their teams could not be in our home while Alan took the prescribed lethal medication, but they said they would be able to support him up until he prepared to drink the cocktail and again after he had done so.

At that point, we didn't know if Alan would die suddenly before the need for medical aid in dying arose or if he would meet the criteria for using it when the time came. But Alan was clear: he didn't want that option to be taken off the table. It made sense for us to reject a hospice that wasn't aligned with Alan's views on such a fundamental issue.

We crossed another of the organizations off our list because of negative feedback from friends and rumors that its response times were slow.

Of the two hospice organizations remaining on our list, we had experience with one of them. Sort of. When my mother died, we used Family Hospice, and they did a great job. My favorite memory of their services was the harpist they sent over to play for my mother, who was a talented musician. The harpist filled my mother's room with gentle, soothing melodies and left a smile on her lips. Shortly after my mother's death, Family Hospice was bought by another company, and later that entity merged with yet another outfit. Soon after, most of the employees quit and formed a new organization named Trail Winds Hospice. Here we were, seven years later, evaluating Trail Winds as one of our finalists.

The other hospice organization on our list flubbed the first appointment. Their representative was supposed to arrive at our home at one o'clock. When no one had arrived by one twenty, I called the office to see if we had a misunderstanding about the schedule. The man who answered the phone apologized earnestly. He explained they were having technical difficulties with the app they used for scheduling appointments.

"I am going to make a couple phone calls and get right back

to you with a solution," he said. "Will that be okay for you?" Mentally, I was already crossing the group off my list, but I agreed to wait a few minutes for his call.

Five minutes later the man called back. "I can have a representative at your home in about an hour. Will that work for you?"

"I can't wait that long," I told him. "I have another appointment scheduled in an hour and a half, and that wouldn't give us enough time." I expected him to suggest we reschedule for a different day, but he asked for another few minutes to explore other options.

The man called back minutes later to tell me one of his representatives had just freed up and could be here in twenty minutes. The representative was a charming young woman who said all the right things, but that wasn't why we ultimately chose this organization. It was the responsiveness of the receptionist. He was committed to solving the problem and doing it quickly. He did a great job of turning lemons into lemonade. That's the kind of team we wanted working on Alan's behalf.

August 2019

Despite my best efforts to contain them, tears slipped down my cheeks as I stood in front of the card rack at the arts and crafts co-op. I blotted them with a used tissue I found wadded in the bottom of my purse. Surely I should know by now, I chided myself, to stock my purse with plenty of clean tissues when I left the house. I never knew when tears would erupt, and eruptions were happening more often.

I had driven across town to the co-op instead of perusing my neighborhood supermarket's card selection, because I wanted to find the perfect anniversary card for Alan, unique and sweet and loving, but not too flowery or overly mushy. But as I went through the motions of pulling each card out of the rack to inspect the artwork and read the sentiment, my brain was not really paying attention. It was struggling with the prospect that we were likely to be celebrating our last anniversary.

How can this marriage be almost over? How can my husband be dying? I was tempted to ask the other shoppers and the clerks behind the counter, but of course I didn't. I knew in my bones they couldn't answer these questions any more than I could. There was no good reason, no rational explanation.

If Alan lasted more than a year, he would probably be bed-bound, a potential condition that terrified him. He had made it abundantly clear he did not want to lie in bed, unable to move, or talk, or eat. Lasting until our next anniversary would be torture for him. I felt torn between not wanting him to suffer and not wanting him to leave me.

Relationship *firsts* are such fun to remember, to celebrate, to savor as a couple. Our first real date. The first time we kissed. The first time he cooked dinner for me. Our first Christmas, New Year's Eve, Valentine's Day together. Alan and I still chuckled about the first time we comingled our laundry—on a trip to Hawaii before we were married. It seemed momentous at the time, a declaration that yes, we were really a couple, because one doesn't comingle one's laundry with just anybody.

Lasts, however, are much harder to pin down, and in our case at least, they were wrapped up in throat-clogging wads of sadness—at least when we were aware they were lasts. I cannot name the last time we made love, because we assumed we would make love hundreds more times. We did not make a special note of it or write it on our calendars. It was long before we were aware

Alan had MSA, long before we knew the autonomic system controlling his erectile function and the urinary system would never again do its job adequately.

Yet I was acutely aware this was likely to be our *last* anniversary. Not surprisingly, nobody seemed to have made a card specifically for that occasion. I finally settled on one that said, "If I'd known I was going to spend the rest of my life with you, I would have started the rest of my life sooner." As I drove home, I realized it was not accurate to say I was going to spend the rest of my life with Alan. He was going to spend the rest of his life with *me*, but barring any sudden catastrophes, I would outlive him for who knows how long. But even that statement is a bit dubious, depending on your definition of "with me." We would still be married until the end of Alan's life. I would be with him in spirit, but it was unlikely he would be living with me in the house we had lovingly crafted into our home with umpteen remodels over the years. He would need to move to a nursing home soon, because we were careening downhill without brakes toward the point where I could no longer care for him at home. Some days his feet couldn't hold his weight long enough for me to clean his butt after a bowel movement, even when he used his arms to support himself on the grab bars on either side of the toilet. A local home healthcare agency sent aides to help me get him to bed every night, but it was becoming an increasingly difficult task even with two people and a variety of assistive devices.

Alan wanted to go out to dinner to celebrate our anniversary, a tradition we had enjoyed every year of our marriage. It sounded like a lovely idea, but I was concerned about logistics. At home, I could get him transferred from his power wheelchair into the car using our sit-to-stand device. But I couldn't take the sit-to-stand with us (it didn't fit in the car) so I didn't know how I would transfer him from the car into his manual wheelchair once we arrived in the restaurant parking lot. Or how I could get him back into the car when it was time to return home.

Friends kept telling me Uber had wheelchair-accessible vehicles available, and if true, it would be a perfect solution to the problem. Alan could roll his power chair directly into the Uber vehicle, and I wouldn't have to move him into or out of his wheelchair at all. I was skeptical we'd be able to arrange for a wheelchair-accessible vehicle, but I was hopeful. I was delighted when I checked the Uber website and found a mention of that option. A couple days before our anniversary, I returned to the web site and signed up for a wheelchair-accessible ride to the restaurant and a ride home two hours later. Even though it is only a ten-minute drive from our house to the restaurant, I set the ride reservation for forty-five minutes in advance of our dinner reservation to allow plenty of time for glitches.

On the evening of our anniversary, I checked to make sure our ride request was still showing on the website. I didn't see it, so I entered a new request on my phone an hour before our restaurant reservation. Fifteen minutes later, there was no sign of a driver picking up the request. I decided to give it a few more minutes, but also started brainstorming contingency plans.

"Alan, what would you think of getting takeout from the restaurant instead of eating out? I can go pick up the food, and we can have a lovely dinner here at home, with candles and a nice string quartet serenading us."

"Oh no! I really want to go out on a date with my sweetheart, do it up right. We might not have a lot of other chances to go on dates. Let's eat out."

How could I say no? I started thinking through who I could ask to meet us in the restaurant parking lot to help me transfer

Alan from the car to his wheelchair, but we had few friends who lived on that side of town, and none that I felt comfortable calling for a favor on such short notice. There was still no sign of an Uber driver picking up the ride request.

"I guess we'll wing it," I announced to Alan. I wasn't sure I could transfer Alan myself, but I decided to give it my best shot. I called the restaurant and told them we'd be a few minutes late for our reservation. Alan motored out to the driveway in his power chair, and I used the sit-to-stand to transfer him into the car seat, then stashed his power chair and the sit-to-stand in the garage. I heaved his manual wheelchair into the car trunk and headed for the restaurant, hoping beyond hope that my plan would work.

I pulled into the restaurant parking lot. All the handicapped parking spots in front of the restaurant were full, but there was one available halfway down the lot in front of a store that was closed for the day.

"This will do," I said to Alan, trying to stay positive. After parking, I hoisted Alan's manual wheelchair out of the trunk. It was a foldable transfer chair that weighed only twenty pounds, but it was unwieldy, and getting it into and out of our small trunk always felt like a wrestling match. Several gouges in the paint on the car's bumper bore silent witness to my struggles. I unfolded the wheelchair, put the cushion on the seat and rolled it to the passenger-side door that Alan had already opened. I positioned the chair at the proper angle and set the brakes. The easy part was done.

I reached across Alan to unbuckle his seat belt, then fastened the gait belt around his waist. "You ready to do this?" I asked.

"You bet. Let's roll." Alan sounded confident.

Alan pivoted in the car seat, and using his hands, lifted his feet out of the car onto the pavement. Using the car door handle as a brace, Alan pushed himself into a standing position while I steadied him with the gait belt. The next step, getting Alan turned around so his butt was in line with the chair, was the part that worried me most. He shuffled his feet in tiny sideways steps, turning almost imperceptibly with each shuffle, an awkward shadow of the shuffling he did in his younger years when his country-western-swing steps wowed the women at the Olympic Dance Hall and Saloon. Back when he was young and agile and at home in his body. Finally, he had turned far enough to release his grip on the door handle and grab the top of the door frame with his left hand. I held onto the gait belt with all my strength and helped him lower himself into the wheelchair seat.

"Whew! Good job!" We high-fived each other, and I pushed him across the parking lot. As we entered the restaurant, we were greeted with the citrusy smell of lemongrass mixed with subtle whiffs of garlic and by a hostess who asked if we were the Kellys. I was mystified by how she knew who we were, but I was too distracted to ask. She seated us immediately, and seconds later served us two frosty flutes of champagne.

"Wait. What?" I stammered. We hadn't ordered champagne yet.

"The champagne is a gift from Beverly," she replied. "Happy anniversary!" Now it made sense that she recognized us. When she arranged the bubbly, Beverly must have told her to be on the lookout for a man in a wheelchair.

When the hostess disappeared, Alan raised his glass. "Happy twenty-second anniversary to my trophy wife," he said with a smile.

"Happy anniversary to my arm candy," I answered as I clinked the rim of my glass on his. I couldn't remember exactly how we came up with those endearments for each other, but we'd been using them for two decades. Underneath our bantering, we both thought we had won the jackpot when we found each other. Alan told one of our neighbors years ago that he had married "way above his station." I'm not sure why he thought that, but I knew with every fiber of my being that *I* was the lucky one—although neither of us was feeling especially lucky as we watched his body and brain unravel.

Feeling pampered and sated after our dinner of seared scallops and fresh vegetables cooked to perfection, we shared a decadent dessert featuring dark chocolate, gooey caramel, and pecans. I don't remember what it was called, I only remember the rich gooiness, the crunch of the pecans, the rich chocolate caressing my tongue. As we had eaten, I had pushed my anxiety about getting Alan back into the car into the corner of my consciousness and pulled a curtain around it to wall it off so it wouldn't spoil my fabulous meal, my lovely evening with my sweetie. But as I pushed the dessert dish over to Alan one last time, the curtain snapped open and the anxiety reared its ferocious head. I started saying silent affirmations to calm myself: *We can do this. We got in here without problems. It will be just as smooth getting him back in the car as it was getting him out. We can do this.*

What I hadn't calculated in advance was that Alan would be exhausted, not only because it was late but also because he had just sat in his wheelchair for an hour and a half, which was hard on his body, while simultaneously focusing his attention, which required a lot of mental energy. And the champagne had done its magic on his cerebellum, the part of his brain devastated by his illness and the part of everyone's brain that is pickled by alcohol.

As I helped Alan into the car, he was only halfway through his shuffle-turn routine when his legs gave out, no longer able to support his weight. I wrenched him a bit farther around with the gait belt, but I was not able to get his butt onto the car seat. I stopped his fall to the ground with my knee, so all 175 pounds of him was perched precariously on my knee, which was wobbly with that much weight on it. I was not strong enough to move him into the seat and I didn't dare let go of the gait belt or attempt to move my knee. There wasn't a soul in the parking lot I could ask for help. The only solution I could think of was to let him slide to the ground so I could let go of the gait belt and get out my phone to call 911. It was not how I wanted our anniversary to end. As I prepared to admit defeat, a couple emerged from the restaurant and headed across the parking lot in our direction.

"Help! Please help!" I yelled. They sprinted the fifty yards and arrived out of breath. The woman of the couple sized up the situation instantly and helped me keep Alan from sliding lower. The man ran around to the driver's side of the car, yanked open the door and grabbed a handle on the back of Alan's gait belt, tugging him in the right direction. It took us several minutes of pushing and pulling to move what was essentially a 175-pound sack of tomatoes—which we did not want to bruise—onto the car seat. I thanked the couple profusely and, when they asked, gave them a one-minute summary of Alan's condition. I asked their names, but they evaporated as soon as the syllables hit my ear.

I sat in the driver's seat breathing deeply, saying a little prayer of gratitude that the kindness of strangers had allowed us to avert disaster. I would never try to transfer Alan without help again, I vowed. But I tried to push from my mind the larger implication of that decision: If I couldn't safely transfer him, he wouldn't be living at home much longer.

Not long after we pulled into the driveway, the aide arrived to help me get Alan into bed. When the aide left, I turned off the lights, locked the front door, and crawled into the hospital bed in Alan's room, in the small sliver of space on one side of his nearly immobile body. We held each other tightly.

It was early August, a couple of days before Alan's six-month check up with his neurologist. I waited until we'd finished dinner to bring up a subject that made me a little nervous.

"Before we see Dr. Kurtz, there's something I think we should talk about," I said. I passed him dessert—a bowl of sliced peaches, fresh from Colorado's Western Slope, the season's first, knowing it would give him joy.

"Oooh, yum!" Alan purred as he took a bite of peach. "What's up?"

"I'm thinking it might be time to ask Dr. Kurtz to refer you to hospice care."

Alan stopped shoveling peaches into his mouth and wiped a dribble of juice from his chin with his napkin. "Hmm. How come?"

"Because I know you want to donate your brain to the Mayo Clinic." Researchers at the Mayo Clinic in Jacksonville, Florida, were trying to unravel the mysteries of MSA, and they needed people with MSA to donate their brains to advance their work.

"Your brain needs to be harvested within twenty-four hours of death, or it can't be used for research. Not sure why, but that's what the website says. If you're in hospice when you die, the hospice doctor declares you dead immediately, and your body goes to the mortuary, which is where brain harvesting takes place. If you're *not* in hospice, I would have to call 911 when you die. The responders would take your body to the morgue, and it can take days for the coroner to release it to the mortuary. So if you want to make sure you can meet the twenty-four-hour deadline, you need to enroll in hospice as soon as you can."

"Are there any downsides to enrolling in hospice?" Alan asked.

"Well, once you are a hospice client, your hospice team is in charge of your medical care. You would no longer see your regular doctors."

"That's kind of a bummer."

"Yep. But if something urgent happens, you can always revoke your hospice enrollment. If you were to do that, you would automatically revert to your previous doctors again, with no waiting or paperwork. It's like your regular doctors are on standby. You can double-check that with Dr. Kurtz, but that's my understanding of how it works."

"Okay. I'm good with talking to Dr. Kurtz about hospice. Are there any more peaches?" The discussion had been easier on Alan than I had expected. I stepped into the kitchen and sliced another peach into Alan's bowl.

We shared our thinking with Dr. Kurtz at Alan's checkup, and he agreed it would be good to go ahead and enroll Alan in home hospice care. He was willing to attest to Alan's prognosis of six months or less, which is a requirement for hospice eligibility. And he confirmed my understanding of what would happen if Alan were to revoke his hospice enrollment.

Alan seemed unfazed by his prognosis. As with everything else, he just took it in stride.

Shortly after we signed the paperwork with the hospice organization we had chosen earlier, it occurred to me that Alan had met the first requirement for medical-aid-in-dying eligibility—a doctor declaring he had a life expectancy of six months or less. I had to sit with that thought for several days before I was ready to talk with Alan about it. I suspected he would be eager to apply for MAID, but was I emotionally ready to support him in that quest? I talked with my therapist about it, and I quieted my mind and asked the universe for guidance. Despite my reluctance, I knew what I needed to do.

We were sitting side by side on the front porch in the early evening, looking out over the railing at the yard and garden, at the neighbors walking their dogs down the street. The sun was setting noticeably earlier as we approached the equinox, but the evening breeze was still pleasant on our faces, and hummingbirds still buzzed the hyssop in my front flower beds.

"So, Alan, I've been thinking. . . ." I began, but hesitated to finish the thought. Did I really want to have this conversation on such a beautiful evening?

"Yes? Spit it out," Alan said.

"I've been thinking about you and medical aid in dying."

"Yes?" Alan moved his wheelchair closer to me.

"Dr. Kurtz has said you have six months or less to live. That's the first criteria for applying for MAID."

"Hmm, yes. Remind me what the other criteria are," Alan said, leaning toward me and taking my hand.

"You have to demonstrate the capacity to make good decisions on your own behalf and show that you can drink the cocktail by yourself. And jump through some hoops as far as paperwork and doctor visits are concerned."

"You're going to help me with all that, right?"

"Of course, Sweetie. But I think it might improve your chances of being approved if you went ahead and applied now instead of waiting until you've gone further downhill. What do you think?"

"I think you're probably right." Alan gave my hand a squeeze and added, "As usual." I knew he was trying to make me laugh, but all I could muster was a lukewarm smile. We sat silently in the accumulating twilight for a few minutes, holding hands, listening to the crickets serenading their potential mates.

"I'd be grateful if you'd go ahead and get the ball rolling for me," Alan said at last. "Okay?"

"I'll call the palliative care folks in the morning," I said.

"Good. Now let's go inside. I'm getting eaten alive out here."

When I called the palliative care team to tell them Alan was ready to proceed, the woman I talked to mentioned the possibility that the team would administer the SLUMS (St. Louis University Mental Status) test, and she scheduled Alan for an appointment five weeks out. As soon as I got off the phone, I found a copy of the SLUMS test online and downloaded it.

Even though it didn't seem to me as if the questions on the test had much to do with decisional capacity, I helped Alan practice several times a week. Alan struggled to name fifteen animals in one minute until we came up with strategies that helped. *Start with pets*—dogs, cats, goldfish, hamsters, guinea pigs. *When you run out of pets, move on to farm animals*—horses, cows, chickens, pigs. *As soon as you start to slow down with farm animals, switch to zoo animals*—lions and tigers and bears, oh my, giraffes, zebras, monkeys, snakes, hippopotami, elephants. *If you still have time left when you can't think of any more zoo animals, go for things that fly*—robins, parrots, owls, butterflies, bees. As Alan practiced, he got better and better at naming animals until we were both fairly confident he could name fifteen in one minute, at least on his good days.

One of the questions on the SLUMS test involved reading a short story, then answering four questions about it. I pounded the answers into Alan's brain: *The people's names are Jack and Jill. Just like the nursery rhyme. Jill is a stockbroker. She lives in Chicago, Illinois. She went back to work when her kids were teenagers.*

"I'm going to ace this part of the test," Alan said, relieved there was something that wasn't a struggle.

"Good thing, because these answers are worth two points each," I replied. "You're going to need those points to give you some wiggle room on the questions that are hard for you."

He seldom remembered more than three of the five items (*apple, pen, tie, house, car*) he was supposed to hold in his brain while he answered other questions. And no matter how hard he tried, he could not repeat a four-digit number backwards. He was fine with a three-digit number, but four digits stumped him every time. I must admit, I was not good at it either.

When it comes to taking care of your spouse, when do you call it quits and turn his care over to professionals? The Sara Stedy had bought us some extra time, but because of Alan's injured rotator cuff, it was no longer a good way to transfer him. Staying in bed 24/7 was not acceptable to Alan. We were running out of options.

I called Crestmoor and asked them to save a single room for Alan. Our plan was to move him there on October 2, a date two weeks away. But I found myself filled with doubts. Had I tried hard enough? Was I falling short on my promise to take care of Alan "'til death do us part?" Would people think I was a neglectful wife or a lousy person for ceding caregiving to someone else? I didn't *want* to care what other people thought, but deep down, I did. My therapist assured me there was a whole committee sitting up there in my brain, and each committee member got only one vote. The one who cares what others think was allowed to express her opinion, but obviously, she would be outvoted by the other committee members who had confidence we were doing the right thing for the right reasons.

Still, I wondered, if we didn't have long-term-care insurance to cover the cost of a nursing home, would I keep him home longer? We had bought our policies a decade earlier because both of my parents suffered from dementia, and we figured there was a good chance I would end up following in their footsteps. That could still be the case someday, but whether or not I end up using it, I was glad we had it for Alan.

Because, truth be told, I was exhausted.

CHAPTER 8

October 2019

On October 2, we moved Alan to the skilled nursing wing of Crestmoor Commons, one of the nicest nursing homes in our area.

Alan's room was on the first floor, and the windows looked out on a lovely shade-dappled patio with a koi pond. The staff was kind, and the food was usually fairly decent—they even had a gluten-free menu, so I could eat dinner with Alan without having to haul all my food from home. The decor in the hallways and common areas was elegant. Framed prints lined the wide hallways, and the custom upholstery in the seating areas picked up the colors from the prints, which were further reflected in the draperies. A talented interior decorator had had her way here.

Alan's room was small. To transfer Alan from his wheelchair to his bed or vice-versa, the bed had to be pushed to the side of the room to make room for the lifting device, the Hoyer. There was room for only a single visitor to sit, unless someone wanted to perch on the edge of Alan's bed. Eventually I brought in a folding chair from home, which gave us one more seating option. We stashed it in the corner, out of the way, when we didn't need it.

In the Caring Bridge update I wrote for Alan the day after he moved, I told friends and relatives we had a bunch of "hangnails" to deal with on the first day. I tried to keep the tone of the Caring Bridge blog upbeat and positive, but that day I had to bend the truth almost to the breaking point to do so. The true story is that I spent a good part of the first day with steam hissing out of my ears, as if my head were an overheated pressure cooker. Come to think about it, much of the first week was like that.

The problem started shortly after our arrival when a nurse assured me that hospice had given them Alan's list of medications and supplements, so I didn't need to worry about that piece of the settling-in process.

"It is all taken care of," she told me. "We ordered the drugs and supplements from our pharmacy, and we are good to go."

Maybe that's exactly what some family members want to hear, but for me, her smug "Don't you worry about a thing, little lady" attitude put me on high alert. Hospice had gotten the list of prescription medications and supplements from a spreadsheet I had created and had painstakingly updated with each adjustment to Alan's regimen for the last several years. I was worried about errors creeping in as the data was transferred from me to hospice and from hospice to the nursing home, and I was pretty sure all my verbal notes would need to be repeated. Did they know the vitamin C had to be chewable tablets because Alan couldn't handle large pills? Were they aware that because of Alan's genetic anomalies, the vitamin B had to include the methylated version of B12? Would they make sure the CoQ10 was the ubiquinol form of the supplement instead of the cheaper ubiquinone? Plus, I had brought Alan's remaining supplies of pills with me, and I certainly didn't want to see them go to waste.

The nurse reluctantly agreed to sit down with me to go over

the medications. As I suspected, several supplements were missing from her list, and a couple had incorrect dosages.

"Why is his melatonin listed at one milligram?" I asked.

"Because that's how our doctor wrote the order," she said.

"But it is supposed to be ten milligrams. That's what Alan's neurologist told him to take."

"Our doctor changed it to one milligram, and we have to go by what he writes in our orders."

This statement was my first hint of the lay of the land at Crestmoor Commons.

"Do you mean your doctor is changing Alan's dosages when he has never laid eyes on him and has never had a conversation with either me or him about it? That sounds like malpractice to me."

"I don't know why he changed it," the nurse whined.

"I don't care *why* he did it," I barked. "It is unacceptable. Get it corrected before Alan goes to bed tonight."

Under normal circumstances, I would be bending over backwards to defer to the person with more specialized education than I. I had grown up with a blunt, abrasive father who knew he was smarter than anybody else in the room, no matter what. And I had vowed decades earlier never to be like him. Instead, I spent most of my life attempting to emulate my mother's approach to life: placate, appease, defer. I was not always successful.

I didn't want to make enemies of Alan's nurses on his very first day there, but my inner "Father Bear" had emerged from hibernation. Or maybe the stress of the situation caused a break in the thin veneer of civility I normally wrap around myself like an invisible cloak. Whatever the underlying cause, I was too angry to be diplomatic.

The doctor in question had the contract to treat patients at

Crestmoor Commons, so we had no choice but to use him unless we wanted to pay out of pocket for all of Alan's medical care. I suspected Dr. D had little, if any, experience treating people with MSA. Almost everyone with MSA also has REM sleep behavior disorder, and published research reports recommend three to twelve milligrams of melatonin, along with clonazepam, for treating it. A lower dose of melatonin is apparently fine if you are taking it to help you sleep, but a small amount doesn't appear to do much to treat REM sleep behavior disorder.

When the nurses took Alan's vitals for the first time, they discovered his oxygen levels were low. Despite the fact that hospice had already delivered the oxygen concentrator, the nurses wouldn't let us use it. They had no orders for it. I quickly learned that "orders" rule the day in the world of nursing homes.

Within the first few days, I was shocked to watch a nursing assistant neglect to change her gloves after she cleaned up Alan's bottom and moved on to deal with his catheter. I was outraged to return to Alan's room in the late afternoon to find him frantically trying to reposition himself in his bed to reach his call button, which someone had left hanging from the drawer of his bedside table, well out of his reach. At home, we had bed canes on both sides of Alan's bed and a floor-to-ceiling pole with a trapeze that allowed him to pull himself into different positions in bed. He couldn't move in bed without some sort of assistive device. But at the nursing home, they had no orders for a bed cane or pole, which Medicare rules prohibit because they are considered a restraint. The only way to circumvent the prohibition was to get an assessment by a physical therapy practitioner who then deemed it a necessity. We worked for weeks trying to iron out who would pay for the PT assessment—his insurance company or hospice—and who would perform the PT assessment. Alan and I didn't really care. We just wanted the damn bed cane. I was tempted to bring ours from home and install it when no one was looking.

I was amazed that the nursing home team did not invite our hospice nurse to the first care conference they scheduled for a week after Alan arrived. I was aghast that I had to remind the nursing assistants several times that Alan's catheter bags were supposed to be changed out for new ones twice a week, by order of his urologist. I was irate when the helpers who put Alan to bed neglected to put on Alan's booties that prevented him from getting pressure ulcers on his heels.

Did I expect too much? Knowing that Crestmoor was one of the best nursing homes around—and one of the most expensive—I didn't think it was too much to expect the nursing assistants to practice good basic hygiene and good basic caregiving. I knew they were human and would make mistakes, as we all did. And I knew I would need to teach them to add an Alan-specific glaze to their base layer of training. But I had expected the base layer to be more robust.

One unsettling thought that hovered on the periphery of my consciousness was that all of my outrage and faultfinding could conceivably have been a result of my own reluctance to relinquish control. I had collaborated with Alan's doctors and caregivers for a long time, working with Alan to make the best decisions about his care. And now, all of a sudden, it felt like we were no longer in charge. Medicare had strict rules about what hospice could and could not do and what nursing homes could and could not do. And Crestmoor had its own rules. For example, I was not allowed to help Alan with transfers at Crestmoor, because if he were injured, even if his injury was my fault, the company's lawyers were afraid I might sue.

But I didn't feel like I could relax my vigilance yet. I spent most of my days and evenings with Alan, partly because I missed him, and our house felt so cold and empty without him in it. And partly because I felt like I needed to ensure the staff was taking proper care of him.

At the end of Alan's first week at Crestmoor, as I was getting ready to leave for the night, I turned off the reading lamp next to his bed and kissed him gently on the lips.

"Good night, Sweetie. I'll see you in the morning," I whispered as I stroked his forehead.

"Thank you, Sweetie," Alan whispered back.

"Thank you for what?"

"For fighting all the battles this week so I didn't have to. I know it wasn't easy for you."

Tenderness weakened my knees and threatened to flood my eyes. "Whatever it takes, Sweetie. You're worth it."

One of the biggest benefits of having Alan at Crestmoor is that they had an efficient and safe way to transfer him. First, Crestmoor nursing assistants wrapped him in a bright-blue, heavy-duty nylon sling, tucking it under his bottom and crossing the straps between his legs. Then they attached the straps to the Hoyer lift—a large, motorized machine with a rechargeable battery. With the push of a button, it hoisted Alan from his bed and swung him through the air, as if it were a carnival ride. The aides would roll the Hoyer into position so Alan hovered over his wheelchair and slowly lower him into place. Then they pulled the sling out from under him. Using the Hoyer was a major production each time.

"I know it looks like a carnival ride," Alan confided when the aides left, "but this Hoyer thing is not much fun."

"Well, dang!" I answered. "That's one of the rides they highlight in the Crestmoor brochure. Should we ask for a discount?"

"Very funny," Alan grumped.

"I'm sorry, Sweetie. Try me again. This time I'll be a better listener. Does it hurt when they transfer you with the Hoyer?"

"No, that's not it. I know it's easier on my body than using the Sara Stedy. It's just that it feels so, umm . . . *undignified*, I guess, to go swinging through the air in that contraption every time I need to use the toilet."

"Sort of rude, crude, and demeaning?"

"Yep, you got it. But not nearly as demeaning as having a whole cheerleading squad of people concerned about my bowel movements. I can't just poop in peace anymore."

"Hmm. I'm sorry, Sweetie. Is there anything the aides should do differently that would make the experience more pleasant? Or less unpleasant?"

"Nah. I just needed to bitch a little. I'll get used to it."

Alan was not alone in relying on the Hoyer lift for transfers. A Crestmoor staff member mentioned that seventeen of the twenty-three residents on his floor required the Hoyer, but most of them could use the smaller version of the machine. On Alan's floor they had only one large machine appropriate for tall people. Apparently, they considered Alan a tall person, even though he was only five ten. When people commented on how tall he was, which was often, Alan and I always exchanged one of those "looks" that married couples share, because we knew that statistically, he fell squarely in the "average" camp. But in any case, Alan frequently had to wait in line to use the tall-person Hoyer on his floor. Even when the machine was available, the other requirement was for two nursing assistants to be available simultaneously to execute the transfer. Of course, it seemed like all the residents wanted to be transferred at the same time.

All the waiting lent a different cadence to Alan's days. And mine.

Alan's appointment to be evaluated by the palliative care team to see if he met the criteria for medical aid in dying was at the end of the first week of October, his first week at Crestmoor. I had arranged a ride to the appointment for Alan in Crestmoor's wheelchair-accessible van, which made transportation much easier, and I rode with him. I brought along Alan's official written request to be allowed to die using Colorado's End-of-Life Options Act, which Alan had signed with a scribble. Beverly and I had witnessed his signature.

We had been practicing for the questions on the SLUMS test for weeks, and it turned out all of our practice was for naught: when we arrived for Alan's appointment, the doctor and social worker didn't administer the SLUMS test after all. Instead, the team interviewed him, which seemed to me to be a better barometer of his decisional capacity than naming animals or drawing clocks or answering questions about a hypothetical couple named Jack and Jill.

Alan was having a good day that day. Even though his speech was slurred, the team could understand him; he was charming and funny and sharp. I cheered him on silently. He demonstrated his ability to self-administer the drug by taking a deep drink from the water bottle he had brought along. Next, the team asked me to leave the room so they could ask Alan a few questions without my being present. They needed to be sure I wasn't pressuring him to end his life.

"On the contrary," Alan told me later he'd assured the team. "This is what I want, not what Joanne wants."

A week later, I arranged another trip to his provider's medical facility so Alan could meet with Dr. Kurtz, the second doctor who would assess his decisional capacity and ability to self-administer the drugs. The following week, I set up another meeting with the palliative care team, a phone visit this time, where Alan made his second official verbal request to be approved for medical aid in dying. With this second meeting, Alan finished the steps in the application process. Then, we sat back to wait for the answer.

With Alan living at the nursing home, I got to practice living alone before he was gone from the face of this earth.

Technically, I didn't live alone, because Beverly occupied our downstairs. Each floor had a separate entrance, but our downstairs living space was connected to the upstairs living space by a wide-open stairwell. I frequently sat on the top step, and Beverly stood at the bottom as we made plans or caught up on the day's activities. But Beverly had an active life, with lots of trips and hikes and meetings and occasional concerts and tea with friends. She was leaving in a week for a trek in Nepal with her twin sister and her sister's partner, and she planned to stop in Uganda on her way home to visit her friends at the clinic and to help a group of Ugandans build a piggery. She would be gone six weeks. But even when she was home, she was a friend and housemate, not an intimate partner. The aloneness I felt was mostly about missing Alan's presence in the house. It may be trite, but I feel it keenly: there was an Alan-shaped hole in our home. Beverly missed him too.

But the nice thing about this practice period was that I could leave the driveway and arrive in Alan's room nine minutes later without even breaking the speed limit.

As much as I missed Alan's presence at home, I *did* enjoy having more alone time. I felt guilty for finding it pleasurable. Over the last year or so of caring for Alan, I had craved time alone like an alcoholic craves her next drink. About as close as I got to alone time was the half hour I dedicated to my walk around the neighborhood each day. Most of the time, I kept my head down and hoped my neighbors wouldn't notice me so I wouldn't have to talk to anyone.

I spent about six hours each day with Alan at Crestmoor, but when I was not with him, I was not necessarily at home alone. Like most people, I spent a portion of my time running errands, shopping, going to appointments, and attending meetings of various sorts, none of which counted as alone time from my perspective. But when I *was* home alone, I soaked in the aloneness, the quiet, the peace, and recharged my batteries. I was not ready to declare a surfeit yet, but my intense craving for alone time had begun to wane.

Near the end of October, we got the results of Alan's evaluation for medical aid in dying: the palliative care team believed Alan had sufficient decisional capacity and the physical ability to self-administer the life-ending drugs. They approved his application. His prescription for the life-ending cocktail would be kept on file at the facility's pharmacy, and I could simply make a phone call to have it delivered to us.

"Thank God!" Alan exclaimed when he heard the news. "What a relief!" His eyes filled with tears, but his smile was wide. If he had had the ability to dance a jig, I think he would have jumped out of bed and done so.

"That's a big load off your shoulders, isn't it?" I replied. It was the best I could do.

"You bet it is! Even if I never use the prescription, I will rest easier knowing it's there."

On one level, I was glad for Alan. On another, I was stunned. As soon as I got to my car, the horrified part of me emerged from hiding: *Oh my God! What have I done?* By mapping the optimal timeline, providing emotional support, and helping him get to and from his appointments with the palliative care team, I had helped my beloved husband achieve his goal: He had the ability to legally end his life when he was ready. Always when we had talked about it, it seemed so abstract, so distant. Now it seemed too real, and I was panicking. There are few gifts more painful to give a loved one.

It had been less than a year since my friend Barbara had died using a medical-aid-in-dying prescription, and the memory was seared into my heart like a cattle brand: the pain of saying a permanent goodbye to someone you love, the intense relief that she no longer had to suffer. How could I go through this with the love of my life?

I couldn't undo what I had done, and even if I could have, I wouldn't. I didn't want him to suffer needlessly.

A few weeks after Alan's medical-aid-in-dying application was approved, I walked into his room at Crestmoor one morning to find him sitting in his wheelchair grimacing with pain.

"Oh, Sweetie! What's going on?"

"My butt. It hurts like hell."

I swung into action. I tilted his wheelchair seat back to take the pressure off his bottom and transfer his weight to his back. Then I pushed the button to call the aides to transfer him from his wheelchair to his bed. Getting him horizontal in bed always alleviated the worst of his butt pain.

While we waited for the aides to arrive, I asked him why he hadn't done those two things himself.

"My brain doesn't work when I'm in pain," Alan said. "I'm

tired of hurting. I'm ready to get my prescription filled so I can end it all."

"I'm sorry you're in pain, Sweetie." I said as I soothed his forehead. "But we can solve that problem pretty easily without filling your prescription. All you have to do is ask the nurse for some of the morphine in your comfort kit. That's what it's there for. I'm going to run down to the nurses' station right now and put in the request. You sit tight."

Alan closed his eyes and nodded.

Eva, Alan's nurse that day, dropped everything, grabbed a syringe of morphine from the drug safe, and had squirted it under Alan's tongue less than a minute after I'd made the request. And two minutes later, the creases in his forehead began to loosen their grip.

"Alan, next time, don't wait for it to get so bad before you ask for pain relief," Eva said. "We can talk to your doctor about scheduling regular morphine doses if we need to. But for now, you let me know when you're uncomfortable before it gets unbearable, okay?"

"It's a deal," Alan said, his words more slurred than normal, the edges smoothed off by the morphine.

The aides arrived minutes later and transferred Alan to bed, and minutes after that, he was asleep. I sat by his bed, holding his hand, watching him sleep, contemplating life and death, living and dying. Alan dying.

From then on, I made it my mission to make sure Alan's pain was controlled and his quality of life was as good as we could possibly make it so he would not want to die quite yet. I needed to prepare myself.

The painters came to touch up the gouges, nicks, and scrapes in the walls and woodwork of our home caused by Alan's power wheelchair. I called our plumber at the last minute and he scurried to replace the worst of the banged-up metal coverings for our baseboard hot-water heat registers in time to have the painters paint them as well.

And while I was at it (Alan calls these the most expensive words in the English language), I had the master bedroom painted a soothing pale green, softer than mint green, a whisper of crème de menthe mixed with a whole bowl of vanilla ice cream. When we finished our addition and remodel, I was stressed with trying to take care of Alan's increasing needs while trying to get us moved out of our temporary downstairs quarters and into our new main-level rooms, and I didn't have the mental bandwidth to choose a color for that room. I told our contractor to paint it off-white for the moment, and I would deal with choosing a color later. Now, a year later, I had to choose the color quickly when the painter called to say he had a sudden opening in his schedule due to bad weather and could I be ready the following afternoon? I ran to the paint store while Alan was preoccupied with a visit from a friend and narrowed it down to three choices. I bought a quart of each color and rushed home to paint large swatches of each on the bedroom wall. When I woke the next morning, the choice was easy: the palest green, the most calming color that carried just a hint of spring. I dabbed some paint on an index card to take to Crestmoor to show Alan. I knew he would approve. I had always had the final say on color choices, just like he had always had the final say on choices related to our cars. Still, I wanted him to see it before the painters started.

I replaced the metal kitchen garbage can, the kind with a foot pedal that raises the lid. The old one was dented beyond recognition by numerous collisions with Alan's chair. It looked like a piece of space debris battered by meteors.

Once the worst of the damage was repaired, I felt calmer, more settled at home.

Shortly after the repairs and painting were complete, my friend Annie and I went on a rare afternoon outing to see the Handweavers Guild Show, an annual showcase of the work of our area's finest fiber artists. Over the years, I had frequently picked out an item at the show for Alan to give me for Christmas: a hand-knit mohair sweater, a forest-green felted hat, a hand-painted silk scarf. This year, I fell in love with a wall hanging, a pleasing assemblage of wooden slats and strips of cloth and yarn that would look lovely in our newly painted bedroom. But as much as I liked it, I couldn't buy it. Why was I comfortable with painting the master bedroom, but not with buying a piece of art for it? I struggled to verbalize the blurry distinction between the two actions. Alan and I had discussed painting the bedroom a year earlier. We agreed it was something that needed doing. The purchase of a piece of art, we had not discussed. If Alan were fully functional, and we were each still full partners in our marriage, I would have taken a photo of the wall hanging and texted it to him. He would have texted back, "If you like it, buy it." Or "I'd be happy to buy it for you for Christmas." He was no longer capable of texting, his fingers too clumsy to hit the tiny keys. Even answering his phone was difficult for him.

If I made the decision to buy the wall hanging without Alan's input, it would feel too much like making the space my own. After Alan was gone, I would be able to give myself permission to do so. But it was too soon. I needed the space to still be ours.

November 2019

Alan's Foley catheter became increasingly problematic. The opening in the end of Alan's penis had torn from the constant friction from the catheter tube, and the tear had continued to widen over time. In addition, Alan had been increasingly uncomfortable sitting in his wheelchair. We had tried every kind of seat cushion we could find—different types of foam and donuts and cushions that had air pockets—and every different combination and permutation of stacking order of the cushions. I even made a custom donut out of some memory foam left over from a long-retired waterbed topper. Before that, we had upgraded the seat of his wheelchair so it could be leaned back to relieve the pressure on his bottom. Nothing helped. Alan spent less time in his wheelchair and more time in bed to alleviate the pain. A doctor suggested his catheter could be contributing to his discomfort.

Hospice reluctantly agreed to pay for a consultation with a urologist—not his regular urologist who was already familiar with Alan's long history of bladder problems and who was more knowledgeable about MSA than most medical professionals, but a urologist with whom our hospice had a financial agreement of some sort. But the soonest available appointment was more than a month out. We went ahead and made the appointment, but we were disappointed about the wait and the fact that we couldn't use Dr. Fisher, the urologist who had installed Alan's suprapubic catheter in April, the catheter that had mysteriously disappeared from his bladder. We were hoping Alan could try again to have a suprapubic catheter inserted, which would allow the tear in his penis to heal, and with luck, alleviate the pain in his bottom.

Dr. D, the doctor who served patients at Crestmoor, the physician whose judgment already troubled me, tried to convince us we should skip the suprapubic catheter and remove Alan's Foley catheter to let his pee drain into an adult diaper. I was aghast at that recommendation. I did not believe that Alan's MSA-damaged bladder would drain on its own, and I could not understand how sitting in wet diapers with an open wound could be a good thing. But Dr. D was convinced it would give the tear in his penis a chance to heal.

"The only way I would even consider agreeing to this plan would be if Alan's regular urologist, Dr. Fisher, approved it," I told Dr. D. I was pretty sure Dr. Fisher would nix the idea promptly.

"I'll call him and see what he says," said Dr. D.

Meanwhile, I reverted to my old habit of spending hours online doing research, this time on catheter-caused penis injuries and possible sources of Alan's butt pain that we hadn't considered. I came up empty on the penis injuries topic, but discovered an infection that could be causing Alan's butt pain: epididymitis, an infection of a tube at the back of the testicles that stores sperm. I knew full well it was unlikely, but I wanted him to be evaluated.

The next day, Dr. D called me to say that Dr. Fisher had given him a green light on his plan to remove Alan's Foley catheter and let his urine leak into a diaper. I was alarmed. *How could Dr. Fisher possibly go along with such a harebrained scheme? What was he thinking?* I asked Dr. D to hold off for a few days and left strict instructions with the Crestmoor nurses that Dr. D was not to touch Alan's catheter.

The hospice nurse visited Alan to check for epididymitis, and she quickly admitted she was out of her depth on the question. As I suspected, she said Alan would need to see a urologist for a definitive diagnosis. With the hospice nurse hovering at the end of Alan's bed, we discussed our options and decided quickly to revoke Alan's hospice enrollment so he could see the regular urologist, Dr. Fisher, not only to evaluate Alan for epididymitis, but to better understand his view on Dr. D's scheme and to discuss a new suprapubic catheter.

We were lucky to get a next-day appointment with Dr. Fisher and equally lucky to be able to arrange transportation to the medical facility in a wheelchair-accessible van on such short notice. The Crestmoor van could get him there at the appointed time, but it was not available to bring him back from his appointment. I called people I knew who had wheelchair-accessible vans until I found someone who could give us a ride back.

Dr. Fisher quickly determined that Alan did not have epididymitis. I was disappointed because it would have been a fairly easy-to-resolve infection that had the potential to make Alan much more comfortable rather quickly. But the exciting news from the visit was that Dr. Fisher was willing to schedule surgery for the following Wednesday, a day he normally had off, to insert Alan's new suprapubic catheter. We were overjoyed that he could make it happen so quickly.

When I asked Dr. Fisher what he had said to Dr. D about removing Alan's Foley catheter and letting his bladder drain into a diaper, he said "Oh, I told him he could try it if he wanted to, but it wouldn't work. Because of Alan's MSA-related bladder problems, it is not ever going to drain on its own. I told him to have another size-16 Coudet-tip catheter ready to go because he would need to insert it as soon as Alan's bladder was full."

When I realized how thoroughly Dr. D had mischaracterized his discussion with Dr. Fisher, I wanted to scream, to pummel the smugness off Dr. D's face with my fists.

From then on, when I saw Dr. D talking to family members in the conference room, I was tempted to rush in and warn the unsuspecting people of his capacity for deceit.

As I walked into Alan's room at Crestmoor one day in November, two nursing assistants were tending to him as he lay in bed. He had just finished telling the women how smart his wife was. I groaned inwardly.

I had spent most of my childhood trying to prove to my father how smart I was, because at our house, the only thing that mattered was how smart you were. The smarter you were, the more you were loved. The converse was also true. If you did something stupid, that dangling carrot of possible love was retracted swiftly and, I thought for sure, permanently. I spent most of my teen years trying to hide my intelligence from my peers. In the 1960s, it was not possible for a girl to be both smart and popular, and like many adolescents, I wanted desperately to be liked, to fit in, to belong.

As an adult, I discovered that smarts had to be coupled with a number of other attributes in order to be useful. What mattered was being accountable, flexible, friendly, honest, empathetic, creative, and kind. Which was a relief, because it seemed to me that the older I got, the worse my memory became and the dumber I felt.

So how did I respond when I found my husband bragging about my intelligence? First, I was embarrassed because I was sure bragging about how smart you are—or, for that matter, how smart your wife is—was never a good idea. All it does is make other people feel intimidated or resentful. Second, I was embarrassed because I was not at all sure it was true that I was smart any more. And third, even if it were true, it was not how I wanted people to think of me.

Before Alan moved to Crestmoor, I predicted it would take less than a week before all the staff was in love with him, and I was right. I had been watching Alan for years trying to figure out what it was that made everyone an instant fan, thinking maybe I could adopt some of his strategies. If you asked him, he would tell you he had no strategies, which I believed. It was not something he thought about; he was an authentic, kind, friendly, witty, and lovable man. He made people laugh and feel at ease. He was curious about other people and asked lots of questions about where they grew up, what they studied in school, how they got started in their careers. He wanted to know the stories behind each of their tattoos, what they cooked for dinner the previous evening, and what sports their kids or grandkids played.

His wit sat lightly on the tip of his tongue, just waiting to escape the confines of his mouth. As the nursing assistants wrapped him in his sling and hoisted him into the air with the Hoyer lift, one of the aides mentioned he was slipping sideways in his sling. "Say that five times fast," he quipped.

Another day, with a twinkle in his eye and a suppressed smile tugging at the corners of his mouth, he called a new aide a wimp because she wasn't as strong as her partner when the two of them pulled him up a few inches closer to the top of his bed. The young woman couldn't have stood taller than five feet, and she looked no more than sixteen, although we knew she was at least eighteen or she wouldn't have been hired. She smiled and introduced herself as Megan.

"Cool," Alan said. "I have a daughter named Megan."

"Really?" she asked. "How does she spell it?"

"W I M P," Alan replied without missing a beat.

I, on the other hand, can be sort of standoffish and stiff—never intentionally, of course, and likely a result of my innate introverted nature—and can't remember a joke for more than ten seconds even if my life depends on it, much less come up with an original witty remark in the moment. I wonder if my humor deficit is genetic or learned. I know some are born with a gift for languages or art or music. Others are dyslexic or tone deaf, and nothing they do is going to change that fact. I wasn't born with Alan's gift for being charming and funny, and I have come to the realization that while I can change how I react to people, no matter how much I analyze and emulate his techniques, I will never acquire his gifts.

But he gave me something even more valuable, the Pearl of Great Price: the knowledge that I am lovable, whether I am smart or not, for he loved me long and deeply. With Alan, I found my sense of belonging. I belonged with Alan.

Deciding to support Alan's wish to end his life using medical aid in dying was a gradual process, marked by frantic spikes of resistance. It was easier to accept when his death seemed distant, more abstract. It helped that Alan had been sharing his "we treat our pets better than we treat our elders" mantra for as long as I could remember, even before we were aware he had a terminal illness.

But as Alan's death came more into focus for me, I struggled. I desperately, passionately did not want him to die. It took me a while to internalize that he was going to die whether I wanted him to or not. In my saner moments, I realized my struggle was *not* about whether Alan used medical aid in dying or not. Given a terminal diagnosis, I believe we all should have the right to choose how and when our lives will end.

In late October, I reported to the Crestmoor nurses that the palliative care team had approved Alan's application for medical aid in dying, and one of the nurses made a note in Alan's medical file. The next time Dr. D reviewed Alan's file, he saw the note. As a resident of Colorado and a physician who works with a geriatric population, Dr. D had to be familiar with the MAID law, but he didn't act like it. When I met with him, he kept referring to Alan's ability to end his life as "euthanasia" and "assisted suicide." I explained to him that medical aid in dying was inherently different from euthanasia: With euthanasia, someone else—not the person who is ready to die—administers the drug that precipitates death. With medical aid in dying, the ill person is required by law to administer the life-ending drug himself.

And calling it "assisted suicide" clouded the issue, I maintained. When someone chooses suicide, they want to die.

"Alan wants to live to ninety-five, but he is terminally ill," I explained. Of course, Dr. D already knew Alan had a terminal illness, but I wanted to emphasize that Alan was not a healthy person who had suddenly decided he wanted to die. "Medical aid in dying merely gives him some control over how and when the end will occur, and by extension, how much suffering he has to endure."

These distinctions, which seemed clear and convincing to me, were lost on Dr. D. I wasn't sure if he hadn't heard me—I already knew he was not a good listener—or if he didn't understand the distinctions, or if he were intentionally trying to provoke me, or if he believed medical aid in dying was morally wrong and that being obtuse about it would change my mind. But he continued to use the offensive terminology. Finally, I had had enough.

"Do not call it 'assisted suicide' again!" I barked, letting my anger spill over.

"Umm, okay," he answered. His tone implied that he was baffled by the vehemence of my exclamation and a bit offended that I was treating him without the deference he thought he deserved. I had trouble focusing on whatever else he felt compelled to tell me from that point forward during our meeting. I pictured myself accidentally-on-purpose knocking his coffee over onto his laptop keyboard as I got up and left the conference room. I envisioned the look of surprise on his smug face as the brown liquid soaked the pages of his notebook, dripped off the edge of the table onto his trousers, and seeped between his laptop keys into the electronics beneath them, shorting the wiring in a shower of sparks. I don't know if you really get a shower of sparks when you spill coffee on a laptop, but I enjoyed the fantasy. I knew the momentary pleasure I would feel in carrying out that defiant act would be obliterated by the guilt I would feel later for stooping to such a childish deed.

Perhaps Dr. D was trying to uphold his oath to "do no harm," if somewhat obliquely. If he had said those words to me, we might have had a meaningful conversation about it. I would have asked him if he kept a suffering person alive, would he consider that doing harm or not. I am curious what his answer would have been.

The topic of medical aid in dying is still hotly debated among American Medical Association members, so he is certainly not alone, if indeed his objections were based on ethical concerns. A long list of national healthcare organizations have passed resolutions supporting a terminally ill patient's right to choose medical aid in dying, including the American Academy of Family Physicians, the American Medical Women's Association, the American Academy of Neurology, GLMA: Health Professionals Advancing LGBT Equality, the American College of Legal Medicine, the American Public Health Association, the American Academy of Hospice and Palliative Medicine, the American Medical Student

Association, many state medical organizations, and various nonmedical groups like the American Ethical Union, which promotes responsible and ethical living.

As of December 2021, eleven US jurisdictions—ten states and the District of Columbia—permitted residents to choose medical aid in dying. According to the Death with Dignity National Center, nine states and Washington, DC had passed death-with-dignity statutes. Those states are California (2015), Colorado (2016), District of Columbia (2016/2017), Hawaii (2018/2019), Maine (2019), New Mexico (2021), New Jersey (2019), Oregon (1994/1997), Vermont (2013), and Washington (2008). Each year, more states consider medical-aid-in-dying legislation.

Montana has not passed a medical-aid-in-dying statute, but in 2009, Montana's Supreme Court ruled that state law did not prohibit a physician from prescribing medication to hasten a terminally ill patient's death. As a result, the residents of Montana have access to medical-aid-in-dying prescriptions.

At present, seventy-two million people, or about one in five Americans, live in jurisdictions that permit medical aid in dying. I believe it is only a matter of time before medical aid in dying is legalized in most states and welcomed by a majority of physicians.

After we ate lunch together, whether Alan sat in his wheelchair in the Crestmoor dining room or had a tray delivered to his room and ate propped up in his bed, I typically tidied up his room a bit and helped him get ready for his nap. I closed his venetian blinds, which effectively blocked the sunlight to create a gentle twilight. I filled the reservoir of his CPAP machine with distilled water and helped him position the nose pads and straps of the CPAP mask. I lined up his essentials on his adjustable-height bed table so he could reach them when he awoke: water mug with straw positioned correctly for a lefty, glasses, phone, TV remote, tissues, and the controller that raises or lowers the bed and adjusts the position of the head and foot. I lowered his bed as low as it would go, so if he were to fall out, he would be less likely to hurt himself. I made sure he had his call light pinned to his shirt, covered his eyes with his eye mask, turned off the reading lamp, and kissed his forehead before I shut the door to his room and headed out.

But one afternoon, I had to leave a little earlier than usual to run an errand and make it to my therapy appointment on time, so I left the nap-preparation duties to his aides. I was about halfway through my therapy session when my phone rang. Normally, I didn't answer my phone during a therapy appointment, but I would check the caller ID. If it was Alan or the Crestmoor nursing staff calling, I would pick up the call.

"My glasses broke," Alan said when I answered. "The little screw that holds the lens in place has fallen out, and I can't find it. Will you bring your repair kit and come fix it for me?"

"Sweetie, I'm in the middle of my session with Kathy now. Press your call button and ask the aides if they have a repair kit, and I will call you back just as soon as I am finished here. Okay?"

After I had dried my tears and tucked my grief away, written my check, and scheduled my next appointment with Kathy, I returned to my car and called Alan back. Because of his lack of coordination, it was hard for Alan to answer his phone. My call went to voicemail the first two times I called, but on the third attempt he managed to answer. I asked if the aides had fixed his glasses. "I couldn't call the aides because I can't reach my call button. It's on the floor next to my bed." A spark of anger flashed through me, undoing a good chunk of the equanimity I had reached in my therapy session.

During the first week Alan was at Crestmoor, several times the aides had neglected to place the call button where Alan could reach it. I had asked his case manager to find a way to solve the problem, and she suggested having the aides clip the button to his shirt. Most of the time, the aides remembered, but when they didn't, it was a big problem. Maybe some of the nursing home residents had more flexibility and coordination than Alan did, so reaching a misplaced call button was not a big deal for them. But Alan couldn't turn in bed or scoot his body even an inch or two to extend his reach. I had reminded the aides repeatedly to double-check that his call light was securely fastened to his shirt before they left his room. Every time.

"Okay, Sweetie," I said. "I'll call the nurses' station and see what I can do." I had not planned to return to Crestmoor that afternoon, as Alan's daughter, Alexis, was arriving at four o'clock to visit and have dinner with him.

I dialed the nurses' station, but nobody answered. I left a message on voicemail and drove home from my therapy appointment. When no one had returned my call twenty minutes later, I tried again, and once again my call went to voicemail. Another twenty minutes later when I still hadn't gotten a return call, I called the receptionist at the Crestmoor front desk and asked her if she could get a message to the nurses on Alan's wing. "All I can do is call over there and leave a message, just like you've already done," the receptionist whined. Now I was indignant. I was writing checks each month for almost $12,000 (even though much of it was reimbursed by Alan's long-term care insurance, Crestmoor was still getting paid that much), and this was the best they could do? Surely the receptionist could have lassoed someone to make the thirty-second walk over to the skilled nursing unit when my husband had been ignored by staff for hours. I was sorely tempted to give the woman a lecture on customer service, but I decided solving Alan's problem was a higher priority.

I called Alan once more to see if anyone had stopped by with a repair kit while I was busy making calls.

"Nope. Haven't seen anyone in three hours now."

I grabbed the glasses repair kit from the shelf in my office closet and stomped out to the car. Fifteen minutes after I pulled out of the driveway, I had driven to Crestmoor and fixed Alan's glasses, only minutes before his daughter was scheduled to arrive.

I debated: Do I ignore this, knowing the staff was doing its best? The half of me that learned how to be an adult from my mother wanted to let it go with a gentle reminder. Or do I march into the executive director's office and give him a piece of my mind? Which is what the half of me that learned how to be an adult from my father was chomping to do. It didn't take me long to decide I needed to bring it to someone's attention, because it was not safe for disabled residents to be completely ignored for three hours. But I reminded myself I didn't have to be nasty about it.

With Alan happily watching TV with his newly repaired glasses perched on the bridge of his nose, I went looking for the social worker who is Alan's case manager. Her office was empty and locked. She'd apparently left for the day, but her boss, Jeff, whose office was right next door, was sitting at his desk. I poked my head in and asked if he had a minute. When he invited me into his cozy office, I sat down in a straight-backed chair next to the door and burst into tears. I told him no one had been in to check on Alan in three hours and related the story of his broken glasses and the out-of-reach call button.

"Is Alan okay?" Jeff asked. I was relieved his first concern was Alan's wellbeing. I nodded as I searched my pockets for a Kleenex and came up empty-handed. Jeff handed me a box of tissues as he apologized for Crestmoor's staff falling down on the job. If he'd been a jerk, I probably would have stopped there and returned home with a knot of anger still festering inside. But his kindness—the concern for Alan, the tissues, the apology—loosened something that had been dammed in my chest behind a flimsy scrim of coping.

"My real fear is that Alan will get too frustrated," I confessed, my words a slurry, awash in a flood of tears. "I am so scared." I was gasping for air. "He has been approved for medical aid in dying, so he can choose to die at any time. I'm not ready for him to die. I don't want him to get frustrated or be in pain or to be sad or mad. I want him to choose to live."

Until I stuttered the thought into words, I didn't realize how desperate I was, how fear was driving my frantic attempts to make Alan's life as cheerful and pleasant as possible.

Jeff stood there looking flustered, like he had no clue what to say. He disappeared for thirty seconds and came back with Eva, my favorite nurse on Alan's unit. As she pulled up a chair next to mine, she made soothing little cooing sounds as if she were a mother comforting her crying toddler. It didn't matter that Eva was young enough to be my daughter. She took my hand in hers and comforted me until my sobs subsided and I could breathe again.

The following day, the assistant director of nursing stopped me in the hall and apologized for her team's shortcomings. She also reported procedural changes she had implemented to assure her aides would check on all residents immediately before and after shift changes to prevent the gap we had experienced the previous day. When I told Alan about the exchange, he said she had stopped by his room earlier and had the same conversation with him.

Crestmoor staff had responded appropriately to the situation, but they couldn't solve the problem I wanted them to fix.

December 2019

When I returned to Alan's room in the late afternoon, he was almost always sitting up in bed watching TV, the reflected light from the big screen dancing across his face, flirting with his rumpled sheets. Sometimes, the aides had been in to open the blinds and refill his water mug, and sometimes I did those jobs myself.

Two weeks after the glasses repair incident, when I returned to Alan's room after his nap time, it was still dark and quiet. I assumed Alan was still sleeping, so I tiptoed in, easing the door shut behind me.

As I snuck across the carpet, his voice startled me. "Hi, Sweetie," he said with tenderness rippling off the edges of his words.

"Why are you sitting here in the dark? Is something wrong?" It wasn't only the darkness that seemed odd, but the fact that he didn't have the TV on. He always watched TV when I wasn't there with him.

"I've been thinking," he answered. "It's time. I'm out of juice."

I immediately knew what he was telling me, and I knew it would be futile to try to talk him out of it. He was in pain so much of the time and was relying more and more on morphine to make it through each day, each night.

I knelt on the floor beside his bed with my head on his chest, his shirt soft against my cheek. As I wept, Alan stroked my hair gently. When my tears finally slowed enough that we could talk, we agreed not to share the news with anyone until we had a plan for what his death would look like, when and where he would do it, and who would be there. Then we'd need to figure out in what order to tell family members and friends and make a list of the people he'd want to see one last time in person.

We did not talk about his decision again for several days, as the reality sifted down, slow motion, through the dense matter of our brains, though our arteries and veins, down, down into the nucleus of the cells that make our hearts beat.

I have no memory of those days, except this: It is less than two weeks until Christmas, and I am irritated, even agitated, by all the festivities and joviality going on in my peripheral vision: the incessant carols, the insipid cards piled in drifts on my dining room table, all of them wishing me merriment and joy and happiness, each wish a wound.

I want to eviscerate the plastic reindeer—the one with the blinking red nose that decorates the lawn of a house I am obligated to pass on my drive home from Crestmoor. I fantasize about doing the job with a chain saw. And the fifteen-foot-tall, inflated snowman glowing in a yard around the corner from our house elicits dreams of slipping out of the house at midnight with a blowtorch. I imagine the boom, the release, the tiny pieces of plastic floating silently back to earth like lazy snowflakes. I have no capacity for frivolity, for joy, nor can I fathom anyone else's.

All of my nerve endings jangle, raw and exposed like the pulp of a cracked tooth.

Like an addict, I want, I want, I want. I am drowning in want and petrified by the intensity of it. I want Alan to be healthy again. If I can't have that, I want to rub lotion on the soles of his feet, between his toes, up his shins, his thighs, imbedding the feel of his skin on my fingertips. I want to memorize the texture of his beard on my cheek. I want to burrow my nose in his neck to sniff his scent, to imprint it permanently on my olfactory receptors. I wonder if there is a product I could order from Amazon to capture his smell, like an olfactory photograph or digital scent recording—perhaps a tiny vial, a lacrimatory for the pheromones of my lover. Of course, I could keep a T-shirt he has worn under my pillow, but I know the scent would fade eventually, and one morning I would awake and find it blank, expired, void. And my heart would break again into shivers of glass, a thousand needled shards.

The intensity of my *don't wants* terrifies me too: I don't want Alan to suffer. I don't want him to leave me. I don't want him to die on my watch, to stop breathing, to grow cold and stiff and waxy-skinned. I don't want to grow old without him.

I have known for a long time this day would come, this day of peeking around the corner and seeing the end, the reality of the beast staggering upright on its hind legs, roaring. Now that it is here, I am not prepared for it. It makes my knees buckle and knocks the breath out of me as if I have fallen from a high nest and thudded onto my back, stunned and helpless.

And yet, I keep putting one foot in front of the other. I breathe in, I breathe out. Alan is counting on me to help him pull this off, and I cannot let him down.

When I was finally able to face talking with Alan about his dying day, I attempted to crawl into bed with him so we could be as close as possible as we began to formulate a plan. To pull this off, I needed to be touching him with more than just my hands. I realized immediately that lying side by side in Alan's narrow bed was not going to work. With Alan in the middle of his single bed, there was simply not enough room for me to squeeze in next to him. I walked around to the far side of the bed and tugged with all my strength on the slip sheet underneath him. I was able to move him over about three inches. Next, I pulled a folding chair over to "my" side of the bed and lowered the bed so it was at the same height as the chair seat. With the folding chair as my backstop, I had just enough room to lie on my side and snuggle up in the crook of Alan's arm.

"Can you wait until after the first of the year to die?" I asked. "If you die now, it will ruin Christmas for your daughters and granddaughters for decades to come."

"And you too, maybe?" I couldn't see his face from my curled-up position, but I could hear the smile in his voice.

"Maybe." I smiled too.

"Okay, as long as we can schedule it as soon as possible after New Year's."

Months earlier, Alan had invited his eldest granddaughter, fifteen-year-old Kaitlyn, to be present for his death. He wanted to invite his other three granddaughters to be there, too, but I urged him to wait and talk with his daughters first, to give them a say in the matter. That conversation hadn't seemed urgent until now.

With his granddaughters as potential participants, we decided to plan Alan's death for a weekend so the kids wouldn't have to miss school. And we needed to choose a weekend where the girls would be with their mothers, as both of Alan's daughters had shared-custody agreements with their ex-husbands. The earliest possible date that met the criteria was January 11.

"That sounds like a good day to die," Alan said. "And in case I haven't already made it clear, I want to die at home. In my own room."

"I don't know if I can make that happen, Sweetie, but I'll see what I can do." I couldn't quite imagine how I would manage to take care of him at home, even for a single day, because I had no way to get him from his bed to the toilet. We didn't have a Hoyer lift at home.

But I also couldn't envision him dying in that tiny room at Crestmoor, with flocks of strangers—nurses and aides, yes, but also visitors coming to see other residents, rehab providers, activities staff, the carpenters working on the nurses' station remodel, the building maintenance crew, and more—scurrying around like ants in the hallway on the other side of his door. For that matter, it felt like an impossibility that I would be able to drive home afterward, or even put on my coat and make it to the parking lot.

We would have more privacy if Alan died at home and more flexibility for creating a sacred atmosphere. But the most important reason for arranging for him to die at home was this: It was what Alan wanted. At this point, he had so little control over his life, his body, his environment, that it seemed important to do everything I could to make his wishes for his death come true.

When you are planning a major life event like the birth of a child or a wedding, you have at least a vague sense of how others have done it before you, what the gamut of options is, what you need to consider. There are books, consultants, articles, blogs, and well-meaning relatives who are glad to offer advice. But that wasn't the case for planning Alan's death via medical-aid-in-dying prescription. The palliative care team had prepared us well in the mechanics of the actual dying—the interval Alan had to wait after his last meal, the timing for taking the medication that prevents vomiting, how to prepare the poisonous drink—but that seemed like a very small part of the whole process of Alan leaving this world, perhaps analogous to signing the marriage license when you are planning a wedding. It is critical, for sure, but it is a drop in the bucket in the grand scheme of things. We didn't have a blueprint for the big picture.

We did have a couple of experiences with people we knew who had ended their lives using medical aid in dying, one from a distance—the woman from our support group who threw the big party the night before she died—and one closer and more recent, our friend Barbara. But Barbara's situation was different, as she had no children or grandchildren who were available to participate, and she was a practicing Buddhist, not a Christian. There wasn't much from her death that fit Alan's situation.

We had to figure out from scratch what Alan's death would look like.

The first thing I needed to do was to find a new hospice organization to help us. We had taken Alan out of hospice during the first week in November because it was the only way for him to be able to see his regular urologist, Dr. Fisher, who performed Alan's second suprapubic catheter surgery. Everything had gone well—but it did not alleviate Alan's pain as we had hoped. Alan was scheduled for a follow-up appointment with the urology team a few days before Christmas.

As soon as I got Alan back to his room at Crestmoor after the follow-up appointment, we were ready to have hospice involved in his care again. We had had a string of problems with the first hospice we had used—including a revolving door of nurses, not all of whom were competent at the simple task of changing Alan's catheters, a task that needed to be completed every three weeks. So we decided to use a different hospice organization. I called Trail Winds Hospice, the organization we had come close to choosing initially. One of the advantages of Trail Winds was that they had a doctor on staff who would come to Crestmoor to see Alan, alleviating us of the need to use Dr. D, the "house" doctor whose shaky ethics and loathsome bedside manner I continued to dislike.

After I gave Trail Winds a brief picture of Alan's situation, I asked my most important question: "Can you help me get my husband transported home from Crestmoor on Saturday, January 11, and can you support him in dying at home that day using his medical-aid-in-dying prescription?" The woman who answered the phone said she would have to make a couple of calls and would get back to me shortly. When she called back, she warned us that hospice staff couldn't be in our home when Alan took the life-ending drugs—which was the caveat of all the hospices we had talked to—but other than that, they could provide an ambulance to bring him home, and they could support him at home that day. So I asked them to enroll Alan right away.

Next, we needed to make sure the date would work for Alan's daughters and granddaughters. I didn't think they had any plans to be out of town since the Christmas and New Year's holidays would be over, but both Megan and Alexis traveled for business sometimes, and I did not want to assume their availability. I was dreading having the conversation with them because I knew it would be difficult for them to hear their dad was calling it quits. They, too, knew it was coming, but that didn't mean it would be easy.

Initially, we considered waiting until after Christmas to share the news with Alexis and Megan so their holiday wouldn't be ruined. But ultimately, we decided it would be kinder to give them as much time as possible to prepare themselves.

After brainstorming possibilities for how to tell them, Alan and I decided on a three-way FaceTime call, so both girls would hear the news simultaneously. I texted them to set up a time for the call, and asked them not to have their kids join them. Both girls figured out immediately what the topic would be.

Using my creative balancing technique with the folding chair, I joined Alan in bed for the call so we could both see and be seen as we talked into the camera on Alan's iPhone. Alan shared his decision with the girls, and we all cried together. Both girls confirmed they'd be available on January 11 and would plan to come to our house for the day. We talked about which of Alan's granddaughters might want to come. Alexis wanted to talk with the hospice social worker before she decided if her daughters, aged twelve and ten, were mature enough to handle being there for their beloved grandfather's death.

I told both of Alan's girls to let me know when they wanted to come visit their dad during the remaining weeks. They had first dibs on visiting times. We asked them not to share Alan's plan with anyone until we told Chris, Alan's brother, who was on a cruise in Asia with limited phone and Internet availability. We did not want Chris to learn about his brother's imminent death from someone's well-meaning Facebook post.

Next, I called our minister, Scott, and told him what we were planning. He confirmed he would be available to come pray with us and support us on January 11.

Finally, before finalizing the date, I called the diener, the autopsy specialist who would harvest Alan's brain, to make sure he was available. I knew of only one diener in the Greater Denver area, and Alan's brain needed to be harvested within twenty-four hours of his death, so there was not a lot of room for error. The diener gave me a thumbs up on the date.

The bones of Alan's dying plan were in place.

CHAPTER 9

December 2019

As close friends came to visit Alan at Crestmoor, he would share his plan for ending his life with them. I listened to him tell the news over and over to different people, and while I think it became easier for Alan to tell, it never became easier for me to hear.

"You already know I applied for medical aid in dying a couple months ago," he said to Andy and Linda, the first friends he told about his plan. Andy sat on one side of Alan's bed in the upholstered chair, while Linda occupied the folding chair on the other side, squeezed in the narrow space. She massaged Alan's hand as she listened. I sat in Alan's wheelchair near the foot of his bed, where I had a good view of the others.

"Well, I jumped through all the hoops, and they approved my application in late October." He waited a few beats to let that idea sink in before continuing. Crestmoor kept the rooms warm to make sure the residents were comfortable, but the heat and the crowded room made me feel like there wasn't enough air in the room. I fought the urge to bolt out the door.

"I've decided I am ready to use my medical-aid-in-dying prescription to end my life."

Keep in mind that I am reporting this conversation as if Alan's speech sounded normal, but it didn't. Most days, his illness made his words so garbled, so slurred, that people had to pay close attention to understand him. Bartenders would probably be good at deciphering Alan's speech. Stone-cold sober, Alan talked like someone whose car keys should be confiscated without delay. As his cerebellum continued to degenerate, his speech went from mildly loopy to out-of-control, falling-down drunk.

When Alan made his announcement, Andy and Linda jerked their heads around to look at me, their eyes brimming with tears. They knew this day was coming. I couldn't think of a good way to respond compassionately to them. I was too steeped in my own pain and sadness to take on theirs. I merely nodded, confirming the reality of Alan's news.

I felt torn with each repetition, desperately wanting Alan's suffering to end, but even more desperately wanting him to live. I knew I was being selfish in not wanting him to die, that the most loving choice was for me to support wholeheartedly his quest to die. I longed for a third option: an instant cure for his illness that would not only stop the degeneration but would restore all the functionality he had already lost. My rational adult self knew that wasn't going to happen. But that didn't stop me from resorting to magical thinking. I simply wished for a happily-ever-after ending, where Alan lived pain-free and disability-free well into his nineties. Sometimes I seesawed between the rational and magical. Sometimes the seesaw jerked back and forth so fast it left me dizzy. I had to keep reminding the aching, nonrational part of myself that Alan was going to die soon from his illness anyway, that in supporting his wish to die sooner rather than later, I was supporting his desire to endure less prolonged suffering. If it were me with the debilitating illness, I would choose less suffering over more suffering. And I would want my spouse to support me in that choice.

We asked everyone we told not to share the news broadly, because even though we had left multiple messages on Alan's brother Chris's phone, we still hadn't heard back from him. But word seeped out among our local friends, and soon requests for visiting times came pouring in. To make sure Alan got a chance to say goodbye to all the people *he* wanted to see, I asked him to help me make a list of the must-see folks. We mapped out two to four visiting slots per day, planned around mealtimes, Alan's need to rest, scheduled shower times, and other activities already on the books, like visits from his hospice team and his daughters and granddaughters, which took precedence over almost everything else. And we saved some precious time for just the two of us.

When we had filled up almost all the visiting slots and there were still dozens of people Alan wanted to see and who wanted to see Alan, we decided to hold a gathering in one of Crestmoor's large meeting rooms—the one right next to Alan's room—for all the rest of the people. We did not invite our closest friends whom we had scheduled for private visits with Alan, only the people we couldn't squeeze in individually—friends from church, neighbors, some of Alan's old work colleagues, and home maintenance clients who adored him. I sent emails and text messages and made phone calls to these friends to invite them to a gathering on January 8, three days before Alan planned to die. I mostly blurted out the facts when I called: "Alan doesn't have much time left, and if you would like to say goodbye, you are welcome to join us at a gathering at Crestmoor." I debated whether I should cushion the news, to make it as gentle as possible or leave an opening for the recipients to express and process their emotions, but ultimately, I decided I couldn't take care of that many people. I'd call, drop the bomb, and run. I also didn't mention in my calls or texts that Alan would be ending his life using medical aid in dying, because I worried that would open the door to a bigger conversation than I wanted to have on the phone or via text.

I asked each person to bring a memory to share with Alan. Crestmoor's kitchen staff agreed to provide appetizers, wine, and sparkling water, and I hoped the rest would take care of itself. We invited people to come for a single hour, because I knew Alan would have a hard time sitting in his wheelchair for any longer than that, and—even though he loved a good party—he would be completely exhausted by all the activity.

Finally, a few days before the gathering, Chris called to say he and his wife had returned from their trip and had gotten our messages. When I left the messages for them, I had not shared the news that Alan had a firm timetable for dying. I had asked them to call me at their earliest convenience. So I broke the news to Chris, the eldest of the three Kelly brothers, who at the age of seventy-four would end up being the only one still living. Their youngest brother, Paul, had died four years earlier when he was fifty-nine, after he developed lymphoma. Alan, who was already ailing but still driving at that point, had flown to Phoenix when Paul was dying and helped Paul and his son through the final days.

At that late date, Chris, who lived in Hawaii, could not arrange to get to Colorado to see Alan once more, but he promised to come for the celebration of life, which we had planned for February 8. We scheduled a phone meeting so the brothers could talk one last time.

Finally, with Chris fully up to speed, we didn't have to try to keep word from leaking.

Alan's new hospice team was a delight. I wished we had chosen Trail Winds initially. In addition to the other kind and empathetic staff we worked with, we were impressed with the Trail Winds staff doctor who made house calls at Crestmoor.

The Trail Winds doctor introduced himself as Jim. He was young, dark haired, and wiry. He looked as if he might be a runner or a rock climber, and he exuded an air of humility. "What can I do to lighten your worries and make you more comfortable?" he asked each of us on his first visit. I was touched to be included in his circle of care and heartened by his attitude.

Jim had already consulted with the palliative care team, so he was up to speed on medical aid in dying and all the details of preparing the prescription drug. He referred to it as "aid in dying," not "euthanasia" or "assisted suicide." He made it sound like a humane option for limiting suffering instead of an ethically deplorable act. He wanted to review what Alan's final day would look like.

"How would you like me to refer to the day Alan will die?" he asked me.

"We just call it 'January eleventh.'"

"If it's okay with you, I'll call it that too."

"That would be fine." I was impressed he had asked. It was a simple thing, but it demonstrated his commitment to doing what felt right to *us*.

Jim recommended Alan attempt a trial run of drinking four ounces of water within two minutes to make sure he could do it. He scheduled a time to meet with Beverly and me together to go over the instructions for preparing and administering the medications one last time. He wanted everything to go smoothly for us. All of us.

January 3, 2020

On the first Friday night in January, eight days before Alan would die, I brought Alan raw oysters for an appetizer because I knew it would bring him joy. When we met, Alan had never tried raw oysters, but once I introduced him to the delicacy, he was smitten. He spent the next twenty-five years working hard to make up for the lack of oysters in his life for his first forty-six years.

Alan was listing hard to the right that day. I kept pushing him upright, and the next thing I knew, he would be leaning over again. It's hard to feed yourself when you are propped up in a hospital bed at a forty-five-degree angle front to back, and you are leaning to the right at about thirty degrees off vertical. Plus, Alan's coordination was off more than usual. He managed the oysters well, but when his dinner was delivered, he struggled. Piling rice on his fork was hard enough, but then lifting that fork into the air and bridging the gap from plate to mouth was almost impossible. He could barely even drink by himself. When he lifted his glass, the straw hit the bottom of his chin every time. He had to use two hands and focus all his attention on the task to get the straw all the way into his mouth. I hoped the nurses didn't notice his struggles. I was afraid they would make a note in his record, and somehow it would get back to the palliative care team who might decide he no longer met the criteria for medical aid in dying—that if he couldn't get the straw in his mouth, he couldn't self-administer the prescription drug that would end his life. I noticed myself thinking this and wondered when I had turned the corner to root for Alan to be able to end his life when he chose. To have the good death he craved.

Rather than watch Alan struggle to eat, I fed him. We made it through the curry and rice, the overcooked broccoli. The aides did not include a dessert on his tray, so I wandered down to the dining room and surveyed the choices. I selected a slice of blueberry pie and asked the kitchen attendant to warm it up and add a dollop of vanilla ice cream on top. I knew what Alan liked.

Alan smiled when he saw what I'd brought him. His mouth eagerly anticipated each bite as I scooped in fork loads of pie and ice cream. He closed his eyes and made small noises, gentle coos of pleasure, little mews of appreciation. When we got to the final bite, the ice cream was all gone and there were no berries left, only a bite of dry crust, which looked completely unappetizing to me. I started to clear away his plate.

"Hey, what are you doing?" Alan demanded.

"You don't really want that bit of plain crust, do you?"

"You bet I do! And when I'm done, I'll have one of the chocolates from the top drawer of my dresser."

One evening in the final week as Alan and I lay snuggled in his cozy bed, I asked him if he had any regrets. He thought a minute before answering, "Two."

"One, I regret not being a better parent." I suspected that one was coming because we had talked about our parenting experiences many times before. Perhaps it is human nature to remember all the times you lost your temper or meted out an overly harsh punishment, the times you let something trivial get in the way of something truly important. Perhaps it is also human nature to aspire to perfection in the critically important role of parenting—which sets us up for failure before we even start.

I knew Alan's daughters thought he was a wonderful dad.

Alan's good friend Dave Smith, like Alan, had been a single parent with custody of his two kids back in the 1970s when it was highly unusual for dads to end up with custody. Dave and his boys moved in with Alan and his daughters when Alexis and Megan were eight and six years old. Dave's boys were four and two at the time. The two divorced dads and four kids shared a house for several years.

Dave talked about what a parenting role model Alan was during those years. "When the boys were acting up, and I would get frustrated, Alan would always say, 'Don't you hate it when they act their age?' He reminded me repeatedly that you had to expect kids to act like kids. And when Friday night would roll around, I'd try to talk Alan into going out with me to the Olympic Dance Hall and Saloon for a couple of drinks, maybe pick up some women, do some country western swing dancing. Alan would say, 'Nope, I've got plans.' The plans were usually to cuddle up with the girls and watch a movie or play some games. He was much more settled into fatherhood than I was, much more mature."

With glowing testimonials from his daughters and from his former housemate, all of whom had front-row seats to Alan's parenting style, I had a pretty good idea Alan was being overly hard on himself. But I didn't try to convince Alan he was unrealistic in regretting his inability to live up to his own standards. I simply listened and accepted what he had to say about his experience from his perspective. I asked him if he needed to talk to his girls about that regret, to get some closure around it.

"I'll think about it," he said.

"Okay, what's your second regret?"

"This one is harder to explain." He was quiet for a minute before he attempted to articulate his thoughts. "I kind of let life happen to me." He hesitated again. "I wish I had lived more intentionally."

Slightly baffled, I lifted my head from the crook in his shoulder and swiveled my neck as far as it would go so I could look him in the eye. "Can you give me an example?" I asked.

"Well, with all my jobs, I never had a vision of where I wanted to go, what I wanted to be doing. I took the first thing that came along that would pay the rent, put food on the table, and let me pay the electric bill."

Again, I didn't try to convince him his regret was off base, but the memory that flooded me was the time when Alan lost his job in the plastics industry, and it took him almost two years to decide he wanted to be a handyman and then another year gathering the tools and skills he needed to launch his business. It sure seemed to me he had acted with great forethought, great intentionality, to choose his final career path. But I didn't bring it up. Once again, I didn't see it as my place to talk him out of his regrets.

Instead, I said, "I think a lot of people live their lives that way, Sweetie."

"Maybe so. But I wish I had done it differently."

I filed that thought away to contemplate later with respect to my own life: Was I living my life with sufficient intentionality? What were the things I still wanted to accomplish in the time I had remaining? At that point, it was difficult for me to see how I was going to survive the next month. Examining my past behavior and planning my future was not an immediate priority.

"Are you unhappy with how your life turned out?" I asked.

"No, no. Not at all." He sounded surprised by my question. "I've had a good life with lots of love and lots of laughter. I feel incredibly blessed."

"And I have been blessed to be a part of your life for all these years," I replied. "Thank you for loving me so well."

"Same to you. That's been the best part." We held each other tightly until the nursing assistants showed up to help Alan put on his pajamas and brush his teeth.

Alan's final days at Crestmoor fizzed by in a blur, each day sublimating, going directly from solid to gas without a visible transition, without leaving a visible trace.

I gave notice to his case manager that Alan planned to vacate his room on January 11, and she spread word, first among facility administrators, then nursing staff, and finally the news trickled down to the nursing assistants. Apparently, Alan was the first person at this Crestmoor location to choose to end his life using medical aid in dying. Of course, the staff were inured to the reality of people dying, but usually it happened more organically, more haphazardly. Alan was a novelty in deciding the timing of his passing. Knowing the date of his death in advance proved to be awkward for me and for Alan's daughters too.

"How do I ask my boss for the day off on January tenth?" Megan asked me. "It feels really weird to tell him my father is going to die the next day, and I want to spend some extra time with him."

Other than suggesting she could call it a personal day, I had no advice for her. I had already faced a couple of similar situations without coming up with a good solution.

Staff members stopped me in the hall to give me hugs. The nurses seemed to respond more quickly to Alan's requests for morphine, and they offered more freely to give him the higher doses in the range prescribed by his hospice doctor. They were intent on making him as comfortable as possible—not that they hadn't been focused on keeping him comfortable before we announced Alan's decision, but it seemed they felt a greater sense of urgency about it. Maybe they worried less about him becoming addicted, with the end so close at hand.

The nursing assistants started a rivalry to see who could build Alan the biggest, most elaborate ice cream sundae. It started innocently enough, when Lisa brought him a sundae with scoops of both chocolate and vanilla ice cream, a drizzle of chocolate sauce, and a few walnuts scattered over the top.

"Thanks for bringing me a sundae," Alan said. "You know, yesterday, Megan made my sundae with a banana on the bottom, and that was mighty nice." Alan's eyes sparkled with mischief.

"Oh, she did, did she?" Lisa asked with a raised eyebrow.

The next day, when it was Megan's turn to bring dessert, Alan told her that Lisa had made his sundae with three scoops of ice cream.

"Is that so?" Megan asked.

The following day, Lisa showed up with bananas under the ice cream *and* whipped cream piled on top of the whole creation.

Not to be outdone, Megan ran around the corner to the grocery store the next day on her break and bought a jar of maraschino cherries out of her own pocket to give herself a leg up in the competition. Alan kept egging them on.

I had a picture in my head of people on the cusp of dying, mere shadows of their former selves, desiccated, emaciated, all skin and bones with haunted, deeply shadowed eyes. My mother and my friend Barbara both looked that way in their final weeks. But not so with Alan. He put on close to forty pounds in the last year of his life and weighed more than he ever had before. He freely shared his philosophy with anyone who asked: *Life is short. Eat two desserts.* And, of course, he wasn't getting any exercise to burn those extra calories. His wheelchair was powered by a rechargeable battery that required him only to push a small lever in order to move, and when he wasn't in his wheelchair, he was in bed. As his belly grew, I teased him about eating for two, but how could I find fault when he had so few pleasures left to enjoy?

One evening before I headed home, one of the younger nurses who worked the night shift stopped by to say goodbye to Alan. This was her last shift before she left for a week's vacation, and she realized Alan would be gone when she returned. The thought was more than she could bear. She stood next to Alan's bed, holding his hand in hers, choking back sobs. I don't know if she cried saying final goodbyes to all the residents under her care or if it was Alan's relative youth—at seventy-one, he was a decade or two younger than most of the residents of the facility—or his kind and fun-loving nature that touched her so deeply. I got up from my chair on the far side of Alan's bed and wrapped my arms around her in a grandmotherly hug. *It must be emotionally draining,* I thought as I held her, *to have almost all your clients die on your watch.* She was still so young; perhaps she hadn't yet developed a thick skin, a barrier to protect herself from falling in love with her patients.

January 11, 2020

I hadn't slept much for several weeks. Despite the pills my doctor prescribed to take the edge off my anxiety, my brain kept performing do-loops until the wee hours of the morning. I'd finally fall asleep an hour or two before my alarm went off. Then I'd drag myself out of bed, grab a cup of decaf coffee—I never indulged in caffeinated coffee because I didn't like how jittery and manic it made me feel—and try to revive my brain as I stood in the shower and let hot water pelt the back of my neck.

On the day Alan had decided to die, Saturday, January 11, I set my alarm for earlier than usual. Despite my lack of sleep, I felt focused and alert when I woke up. I could not let my emotions seep to the surface because we had a firm schedule to meet, a busy day ahead. Alan needed to finish breakfast, the last meal he would ever eat, by nine o'clock, when the medical transport team was scheduled to arrive at Crestmoor with an ambulance to bring him home. Calculating the schedule from there, I needed to be up by six o'clock to shower, cook and eat breakfast, and clean up the kitchen, in order to be at Crestmoor by seven thirty, which would allow me to get Alan to the dining room by eight o'clock, assuming no big glitches. This was always a shaky assumption considering Alan's limitations.

I had invited Alan's friend Chris—his former roommate during the time Alan and I were first dating, the guy who owned the weight bench that was the only piece of furniture in the living room the first time Alan cooked for me—to share Alan's last breakfast with him. When Alan was healthy, Chris and Alan had met for breakfast fairly regularly, usually ending up at a Mexican restaurant that served enormous breakfast burritos, oozing with melted cheese and topped with copious quantities of green chili, each of which easily exceeded the caloric requirements for a normal adult for an entire day, if not longer. Once Alan gave up driving, Chris would swing by the house and pick him up for their breakfast jaunts. When getting Alan in and out of Chris's monster pickup truck became next to impossible, Chris bought a used, low-to-the-ground Honda Civic solely for transporting Alan to and from breakfasts. But, eventually, getting Alan in and out of *any* vehicle became a struggle for all parties involved, so Chris would bring take-out burritos to our house, and the two of them would chow down in the dining room while I made myself scarce—usually by escaping to the garden or heading out for a walk—so I wouldn't inhibit their "guy talk." And for the last three months of Alan's life, while he lived at Crestmoor, Chris would bring burritos and eat breakfast with Alan in the Crestmoor dining room, usually at a table for two off to the side.

Alan liked the idea of burritos with Chris as his final meal. I planned to finish packing up Alan's belongings while the two of them ate. I wanted everything to be ready for our friends Liz and Dave, who would arrive a little later to transport the boxes and suitcases to our house. I didn't want to pay for an extra day of Crestmoor room rental if I could avoid it, and I knew better than to think I'd be able to go back later the same day—after Alan died—to pick up his belongings myself. I recognized it as a great opportunity to allow someone else to help, and Liz and Dave were happy to lend a hand. Alan had gotten to know them when their daughter participated in the Sunday School class he'd taught twenty years earlier. They both loved to hike, garden, and read, so we had a lot in common.

Figuring emotional support would be helpful, Chris enlisted Alan's daughter Alexis to join them for breakfast. Chris texted me when he reached the Crestmoor parking lot so we could meet him in the dining room. I helped Alan steer his power wheelchair down the wide hallway. Alan could no longer steer a straight course, and it was safer for the other residents and staff if I steered for him. Some days he got testy when I insisted on taking over the controls, but today he was beyond worrying about the details.

Alexis was already pouring champagne for mimosas when we arrived at the table, and tears were already slipping down her cheeks. I was glad to be leaving Alan in Chris's and Alexis's hands, because I knew it would be hard to keep from crying myself with the two of them blubbering away, and I worried that once I started, I might never stop. I needed to be strong for Alan's sake, and I still had a lot of logistics to manage. After Alan was situated at the table with his bib fastened securely around his neck, I scurried back down the hall to finish packing his room.

As nine o'clock approached, I had to work harder to keep the panic from rising in my gut. I walked down the hall to the dining room once more and accompanied Alan back to his room, his last jaunt in his wheelchair.

Before we even made it to his doorway, Alan started moaning. "My butt hurts like hell. Get the aides to help me back to bed. Now. Please."

"Sweetie, the ambulance is going to be here any minute to pick you up and bring you home. Are you sure you want to be transferred back to bed?"

"I don't care if it's only for a few minutes. I hurt too much to stay in this chair for one more second."

"Do you want me to ask the nurse to get you some morphine?"

"No, I don't want to feel all dopey. Just get me horizontal as fast as you can."

I tilted his wheelchair seat back to take the weight off his bottom and turned on his call light to summon the aides for the transfer. Then I stood in the hall outside Alan's door to round up the aides as quickly as I could. Transferring Alan required two aides, but if I could find even one, I could help her until the second aide arrived. Technically, it was against the rules for me to assist, but usually they let me help them get the sling situated underneath him and get the Hoyer lift moved into position. Once they hooked the sling's loops over the hooks on the Hoyer, they wanted me out of the way. After pacing the hall for a few minutes, I waved down an aide, and the second was not far behind. We were lucky the Hoyer lift was available. The aides set to work and had him situated comfortably in his bed a few minutes later.

However, as soon as Alan was lying down and the aides had departed, he smiled sheepishly and announced he needed to use the toilet. "All that greasy, spicy Mexican food got my innards all fired up. It was mighty tasty, but now I'm in a hurry to go, go, go." I turned the call light back on and once again flagged down the two aides to transfer him from his bed to the toilet. Again, the aides wrapped him in the sling and lifted him into the air using the Hoyer. They rolled the Hoyer into the bathroom and lowered him onto the toilet. The aides hovered in the hall outside his room until Alan was ready to be cleaned up and transferred back to bed.

Alan let out a big sigh of relief to finally be horizontal in his bed after all those transfers in quick succession, at which point two ambulance attendants arrived with a gurney—a stretcher on wheels—to take Alan home. Once again, the Crestmoor aides wrapped the Hoyer sling around Alan and used the lift to hoist him into the air and deposit him onto the gurney. At this point, every square inch of Alan's tiny room was full. In addition to the gurney and the pile of suitcases and boxes I had packed, his floor was crowded with two Crestmoor aides, the Hoyer, two ambulance attendants, Chris, who hadn't left yet, and me, although Chris and I were really standing in the hallway because of the lack of space inside the door.

"Wait a minute," I said to the ambulance attendants. "How are you going to get Alan from the gurney into bed at home?

We don't have a Hoyer lift. Are the two of you strong enough to lift him?"

"Hmm. Good question," the attendant said. "Will there be other strong people at your house when we get there?"

"Beverly and I will be there, but neither one of us is known for our strength," I said. I wanted to add that we were known for our beauty and brains, but decided it wasn't a good time for jokes.

"I can help," said Chris, who was definitely on the burly side. "I'll drive over and meet you at your house."

"If we use a mega-lifter, we should be able to lift him at your house with three strong people," said the attendant.

"What's a mega-lifter?" I asked.

"It's a stiffer sling, sort of like a giant pancake spatula, that has handles on the sides so we can get a good grip. We just need to lift Alan with the Hoyer one more time to slide the mega-lifter underneath him before we leave here." One of the attendants ran out to the ambulance to retrieve the mega-lifter while the Crestmoor aides once again wrapped Alan in the Hoyer sling.

So on his last day alive, Alan set an all-time personal record for the largest number of Hoyer transfers, six in total, before nine thirty in the morning.

Chris and I made it to our house before the ambulance pulled into the driveway. I stood in the doorway and watched the attendants roll Alan's gurney up the sturdy ramp Alan had built only a few years earlier. While I was overjoyed to have him home, the reason for his return filled me with such paralyzing grief I could not stop and think about it. I watched Chris and the ambulance attendants grab the handles of the special sling and heave Alan into his bed.

Once Chris and the ambulance attendants left, a big smile

sprouted over Alan's face. He burbled with delight about how good it felt to be in his own home, in his own bedroom again. To be able to look out the window at the wintery landscape of home, at the feeble January sun doing its best to brighten the day. To see all the photos of his grandchildren we hadn't taken to Crestmoor, the ones on the top of his dresser. To drink in the pleasure of having his favorite books lined up side by side on his bookshelf. To reacquaint himself with the comforting scent of home. He had been gone for a little more than three months, but it seemed far longer to both of us.

Beverly stuck her head in the door of Alan's room to welcome him home. "Thanks for bringing home those hunky ambulance attendants," she said, without pointing out that they were young enough to be her grandchildren.

"I'm always looking out for you," Alan responded with an ornery smile.

Liz and Dave arrived with the rest of Alan's possessions from the nursing home. They stashed most of his gear in the garage, but I asked them to bring the clothes on hangers inside, into the walk-in closet, and hang them up. Liz and I were standing in the closet laughing over the fact that in the three months Alan had been living at the nursing home, I had completely taken over his half of the closet. Suddenly, we heard Alan yelling from his room across the hall, using his best attempt at a Brooklyn accent: "Hey! Keep the noise down in there! We got people trying to die in here!"

Alan was hours away from drinking the poisonous cocktail, and he was still doubling us over with laughter.

As soon as Liz and Dave pulled out of the driveway, the Crestmoor wheelchair-accessible bus stopped by to deliver Alan's power wheelchair, which I had arranged the previous week, and Alan's hospice team arrived to give him a sponge bath. While Josh, the tall, tattooed aide who was in his early twenties, washed him and combed his hair, Cara, the hospice nurse, walked through the plan one last time with Beverly and me and reviewed the contents of the hospice comfort kit—a collection of drugs we could use to keep Alan calm and pain-free. Cara was juggling her time between Alan and another client who was also dying that day, although the other client had not planned the date in advance like Alan had. We decided Beverly would stay in touch with Cara using text messages and phone calls to update her and get questions answered. That way, I could stay by Alan's side and keep my focus on him, and Cara could be at her other patient's bedside while still staying in close contact with us.

Our friends Andy and Linda arrived before Cara and Josh left. Andy, the best man at our wedding twenty-two-and-a-half years earlier, had been another one of Alan's frequent breakfast partners over the years. Linda, his wife, another retired nurse, loved to take care of people. She had showered both of us with kindness as Alan's health degenerated. I had offered them the opportunity to be at our house while Alan died, not to take care of *him*, but to take care of the rest of us who were gathered to support him. They said they felt honored to be asked and readily agreed to make lunches for us and to make sure we stayed hydrated as we sat with Alan while he made the transition from life to death. They were on call to run errands or offer hugs or do whatever was needed to help us get through the day.

As soon as breakfast was finished, Alexis had zipped home to Arvada to pick up her elder daughter, Olivia, who was twelve and a half. She and Olivia made it to our house just as Megan arrived from Littleton with her elder daughter, Kaitlyn, fifteen.

Linda took their coats and hung them in the hall closet, and they scooted down the hall to give their dad and grandfather hugs.

Minutes later, Scott, our minister, arrived. The full send-off team was now assembled. We hadn't had that many people in our house for a long time, but each person loved Alan and had an essential role to play, and I was grateful for their presence.

Other than asking Scott to lead us in a prayer, I had not planned any sort of ceremony, as Alan had asked me to keep things simple. The only structure we had was dictated by the pharmacist's instructions: Alan had to wait five hours after finishing his last meal to take the life-ending cocktail, and he had to take two medications an hour before the final one, one to prevent nausea and one to prevent anxiety. He had finished breakfast at nine o'clock, so he would take the two preliminary medications no sooner than one o'clock, and then consume the final cocktail an hour later.

The house filled up with the tantalizing aroma of homemade chicken soup, a comforting backdrop for the activities about to unfold. Linda had made a gluten-free chicken-and-rice batch for me, texting me in advance about each ingredient to make sure it was safe. She also had made a large pot of chicken noodle for everyone else to share. She must have spent two days shopping and prepping all the food she brought. She kept the soups hot all day so we could sneak into the kitchen and fill a bowl whenever we were hungry.

We all trooped into Alan's bedroom and held hands around his bed. Scott led us in a prayer, and then we went around the circle taking turns expressing thanks for Alan and blessing him on his journey.

"Thank you for being the best daddy a girl could ever wish

for," Alexis said as she dropped the hands she was holding to wipe her wet cheeks with a tissue.

"Thank you for always offering me sound advice, whether I wanted it or not," Megan said, making all of us, including Alan, smile. Offering advice was one of Alan's gifts or character flaws, depending on your point of view.

"I could always count on you for honest feedback to my sermons," Scott said. "Sometimes it wasn't what I wanted to hear, but it was always sincere and respectful. I am grateful to you for that."

"Thank you for bringing me coffee in bed every day for more than twenty years," I offered. That was as close as I could come to thanking him for what I was most grateful for—for loving me so completely—without succumbing to the sobs that hovered just under the surface. I was afraid to start sobbing so early in the day, fearing once the spigot was turned on, I'd never get it turned back off. I wasn't ready to let go yet.

I wanted private time to say goodbye to Alan, so after the thanks-giving circle, I suggested each family member take twenty minutes alone with him. Alexis went first, then Megan. Beverly disappeared downstairs and serenaded us with a Bach suite on her cello, the rich melodies floating up the stairs, swirling around us, mingling with the soup's perfume. The rest of the assembled troops retreated to the living room. Olivia and Kaitlyn, glad for the break from the emotional intensity, buried their faces in their phones, while the adults made polite conversation and snacked on the cookies Linda had made.

Finally, it was my turn to be alone with Alan. I closed his bedroom door and climbed in next to him in that narrow sliver of bed, nestling my head in the crook of his shoulder as I'd always done. I'd held it together for longer than I thought possible that day, and I couldn't keep my grief tamped down for another second.

"How am I going to survive without you here to love me?" I wept. He held me tightly.

"I promise I'll be loving you from afar," he whispered.

"I guess that will have to do." I realized this would be the last time I would nuzzle his warm neck.

"I'm going to carry you with me in my heart for as long as I live," I promised.

When my sobs subsided, I sat up and gently stroked his forehead, something I knew he found comforting. I tried to memorize his eyelids with my lips and sear the light in his eyes into the backs of my retinas. I couldn't think about how the day would end. I forced myself to stay in the present.

When my private time with Alan was over, he asked me to bring in his granddaughters. He was pleased the two older girls had decided to bear witness to his departure. Both girls were still glued to their phones in the living room, and when I told them it was their turn, that their grandpa wanted a few words with them, they looked at me with terror on their faces. Kaitlyn shook her head.

"You can go in together if you want," I said, hoping to find a way to talk them into it. Kaitlyn looked at me as if I had two heads, a look she normally reserved for her mother. Olivia's eyes filled with tears.

"Please. It would mean a lot to your grandpa if you came in to talk with him for a couple minutes," I said. Kaitlyn looked at Megan, her mom, with a mixture of desperation and defiance on her face. As much as I wanted her to talk with Alan for *his* sake, I understood her reluctance. I had had my first close contact with death in my twenties, when my first husband's grandfather died. And I had felt the same urge to hide from it as Kaitlyn did.

"I told her she didn't have to participate in anything she didn't want to," Megan explained to me. I turned my attention to Olivia. I knew Alan would be devastated if neither granddaughter came in to say goodbye.

"Please, Olivia," I begged. "I will go with you." Tears streamed nonstop down her face, but she didn't resist when I took her hand and pulled her behind me as far as the dining room, where we stopped to grab a fresh supply of tissues. She stood there next to the table and sobbed, looking at her shoes, crying like a child but perched on the verge of womanhood, overcome with embarrassment and heartbreak, lips quivering.

"It's okay to cry," I told her. "It is a really sad day, that's for sure." She nodded, and I reached for her hand once more as we walked the last few steps down the hall and into Alan's room.

"I couldn't talk Kaitlyn into coming in," I told Alan as Olivia and I stood next to his bed. I held his hand with my right hand and Olivia's with my left. Her tears continued without a break, and she continued to study her shoes.

"Do you have some words of wisdom for Olivia?" I asked.

Alan nodded but paused a minute as he gathered his thoughts. Then he spoke slowly, but with more clarity than I'd heard from him in a long time.

"Olivia, when you have important decisions to make, I want you to reach down inside and find the best Olivia that lives deep inside you. Ask her for advice. Ask her to help you make good choices. Then listen to what she says. Do you think you can do that?"

Olivia nodded. She lifted her eyes from the floor for just an instant to look her grandpa in the eye, acknowledging his gift. I was glad to be there with her, to witness my husband at his most inspired. I marveled at his wisdom and wondered where those words had come from. Olivia and I stopped in the dining room again on our way out to exchange our wet and wadded tissues for a fresh supply. I gave her a long hug. We stood side by side and let our tears fall without restraint, without words.

As the time approached for Alan to take the two preliminary medications, we gathered as a group in his room once more, although Kaitlyn and Olivia stayed behind in the living room. Beverly tells me she brought Alan's pills into his bedroom and we bowed our heads together to bless them. I don't remember this, but I'm not surprised that details have spilled from my memory. She says she asked for guidance in preparing the medications and affirmed that the drugs would produce the desired effect, that they would "take him where he wanted to go."

As soon as Alan had swallowed the Ativan to prevent anxiety and the antiemetic to prevent his throwing up the final cocktail, we took up the positions we would maintain for the next four hours: I stood on the far side of Alan's bed, in the narrow strip between his bed and the wall. At some point, Beverly—or maybe it was Linda—came up behind me and slipped a stool under my bottom so I could sit instead of stand. Megan perched on a stool somewhere behind me at the end of Alan's bed, her hand slipped under the blanket so she had a firm grip on her father's ankle. Alexis parked herself in Alan's recliner, off in the corner, and next to her in a folding chair sat Scott. The long side of Alan's bed that faced the open door of his room didn't have a permanent occupant. Beverly, Andy, and Linda each came in at various times and occupied that space temporarily. I hoped that maybe Kaitlyn or Olivia would venture in for a visit, or that Alexis would come out of her corner to offer her dad a hug. Someone started the Willie Nelson play list we had set up on an iPad in my office, which was next to Alan's room.

Once I was in my position next to his bed, Alan grabbed my hand, squeezing hard, and he didn't let go. My fingers promptly fell asleep. I don't think Alan was afraid. I suspect the firm grip was intended to reassure me that all was well. It would be in keeping with Alan's character to be worrying about me, not himself, as he prepared to die.

I am sure we talked, but I have no memory of what Alan or I or anyone else said. I felt like I was in an alternate universe where time was fluid and the normal laws of physics were suspended.

At two thirty, Beverly poked her head into Alan's room. "Are you ready for me to mix up the cocktail?" I could hear a note of nervousness in her voice. I knew she loved Alan like a brother, and despite her cheerful demeanor, this day—and her role in facilitating Alan's death—was hard for her.

"I am," he said, with the gravity of someone making a solemn vow. Beverly disappeared back into the kitchen, and Alan increased the strength of his grip on my hand, something I would have claimed was impossible if I hadn't felt it myself.

Several days in advance, Beverly told me she had laid out the medicine and mixing equipment on the kitchen counter and visualized the steps she needed to take: Measure the apple juice, pour it into the amber glass bottle with the prescription powder, shake and swirl it until the powder dissolved, pour the liquid into the mug, check for lumps, mix more with a spoon if lumps are present, insert the wide-bore straw into the mug, and serve. Like a world-class athlete, she visualized the whole process from start to finish until it felt like second nature to her. It was a simple process, but it was one she didn't want to mess up. I was glad we didn't have to open up hundreds of capsules, as Michael had when Barbara used her medical-aid-in-dying prescription a year earlier.

On the day of Alan's death, when Beverly actually performed the steps she had visualized, everything went smoothly until she poured the mixture from the amber bottle into the mug. Lumps were everywhere, like a batch of turkey gravy gone horribly awry, and getting rid of them was harder than she expected. Knowing Alan had to drink the cocktail within minutes, she felt pressured to conquer the lumps quickly. She stirred like a hyperactive bartender as her anxiety level climbed.

Beverly didn't tell me in advance that she had added a step of her own to the process: insert a toothpick into the liquid and touch the toothpick to her tongue.

When the lumps were tamed, Beverly brought the mug of poison into Alan's room and held it out to him, a reluctant offering. Alan released his grip on my hand and accepted the mug, holding it reverently with both hands. He hesitated only long enough to look me in the eyes, then lifted the mug in the direction of his mouth. Beverly stepped back, and we all held our breath as we watched Alan take that first gulp through the fat straw.

Beverly was the only person in the room who was not surprised when Alan spat out the straw. She already knew the cocktail tasted disgusting. *Bitter* and *metallic* were the words she used to describe it when she told me the next day about tasting the concoction. She also confessed how much she regretted skipping the optional step of adding stevia to the mixture. I had pointed to the bottle of stevia on the top shelf of the cupboard earlier, but by the time she realized how desperately it was needed, it was too late to go looking for the step stool. The clock was ticking.

After Alan spit out the straw and I reminded him he had only two minutes to drink the rest, he held the straw to his mouth once more and drank until the mug was empty, closing his eyes and grimacing, but consuming every last drop. From that point forward, my eyes did not leave his face. Beverly brought him a glass of plain apple juice, a "chaser" to wash away the vile taste. She offered to bring him a shot of tequila, but he shook his head. All he wanted was a little morphine to take the immediate edge off his pain. Using a syringe, Beverly squirted the liquid under his tongue, and it wasn't long before the creases in his forehead softened and his jaw muscles relaxed.

My best guess is that it took Alan about twenty minutes before he started to fall asleep. He was already starting to nod off when his eyes fluttered open, and he looked directly at me.

"I love you," I whispered, my eyes riveted to his.

"I love you," Alan mouthed back. Andy, who was standing in the doorway at that moment, witnessed Alan's final words, our last exchange, and wept. He had witnessed our vows on our wedding day, and now he was witnessing our final affirmations of our devotion. We had loved each other unceasingly—sometimes fiercely, sometimes tenderly—until death hovered at the door.

Alan did not open his eyes again. Leaning forward on my stool, I continued to stroke his forehead gently, lovingly, for a long time. Despite the fact that Alan appeared to be sleeping—perhaps he had slipped into a coma by then—he did not loosen his grip on my hand.

We didn't know how long it would take Alan to die. The timeline prepared by the palliative care team said it could take anywhere from eight minutes to thirty hours after he drank the cocktail.

The late-afternoon light from the window behind his bed splashed painterly highlights on his forehead, his nose. I wanted to take one last photo of him while he was still alive, but somehow it seemed sacrilegious, and I couldn't let go of his hand to grab my phone for a photo. I could not let go of his hand for any reason.

For a while, Alan made his infamous dying-horse noises as he breathed. I wasn't concerned because I knew that's what Alan's breathing sounded like when he slept without his CPAP machine. But the nurses in the room, Beverly and Linda, having never heard the sounds before, were concerned he was choking. Beverly slipped into the kitchen and texted Cara, who suggested giving Alan atropine, one of the drugs in the hospice comfort care kit meant to dry up excess saliva secretions. After the atropine, the room was peaceful, if you could ignore Willie's guitar twanging in the background.

Alan held on to my hand until I pried my fingers from his more than three hours after he'd swallowed the cocktail, after his breathing had slowed and then stopped altogether, after his heart had stopped beating, after his skin cloaked itself in the waxy sheen of death. The late afternoon winter sun slipped behind the Flatirons, and the handful of candles flickering on Alan's dresser took over the job of lighting his room.

Alan had died at a time he chose, in his own room. He died just the way he wanted to die: tenderly, without pain, surrounded by people who cherished him.

Beverly and Linda had filled plastic bags with ice earlier in the day, and after Alan died, they packed the bags around his head to keep his brain cool until the diener, the brain harvester, could do his work.

The next thing I knew, everyone had gone home except Beverly, who hung around upstairs for the rest of the evening. Everyone probably said goodbye to me, but I don't remember much after Alan stopped breathing. I must have left his side to walk people to the door, because I remember returning to Alan's room and laying my head on his still-warm chest. As I did so, the last of the air in his lungs escaped. In my daze, I thought he had just exhaled. I jerked up, expecting him to sit up and say, "Just kidding!" with a mischievous grin lighting his face. Adrenaline coursed through my veins, and it quickly cleared my head. I felt foolish and was glad no one else was present to witness my folly. I returned my head to his chest and listened to the silence. The forever stillness.

I have friends who speak of being able to feel the presence of a newly departed spirit hovering around the body or even hovering around their loved ones for days or weeks after their deaths. I had not sensed that presence when my parents or my friend Barbara had died, but I figured if I could sense it with anyone, it would be Alan, my soulmate. I closed my eyes and quieted my mind. I opened my senses to feeling Alan nearby, or at least a numinous presence. But all I sensed was a void, an emptiness that felt vast and unfillable.

The hospice nurse and chaplain arrived, followed a bit later by the undertaker. Because I felt so dazed, so disconnected, I was glad I had followed the step-by-step instructions from the Brain Support Network. Months in advance, I had prepared the detailed paperwork to authorize the donation of Alan's brain and provide instructions for the diener. The undertaker, a big, burly man who must have played football in his younger years, took the envelopes of papers from me when he wheeled Alan's body out the door. Somehow, he had managed to move Alan's body from his bed onto the wheeled gurney by himself. I stood in the doorway and watched him roll the gurney holding Alan's sheet-draped body down the front ramp. The full moon hovered over the treetops to the northeast, illuminating the lump of Alan's body on the gurney with a ghostly glow. I had a clear sense, already, that it was only Alan's body that was leaving home for the last time. Alan's soul had departed hours earlier for another realm.

CHAPTER 10

January 12, 2020

When I awoke on Sunday morning, I felt lighter. I'm sure the good night's sleep helped, but it was more than that. I felt like a burden had been lifted: the burden of Alan's suffering. He had stayed alive longer than he wanted to at my request, so I had felt responsible for his pain.

I poured myself a mug of coffee, grabbed the Sunday newspapers from the driveway, and crawled back in bed. In the old days, Alan and I shared coffee and newspapers on Sunday mornings, the first half of our weekly Sunday-mornings-in-bed ritual. The second half of the ritual required no props or beverages, only our naked bodies. It seemed like a lifetime ago. Even though the idea of reading the newspaper in bed sounded like a luxurious treat, I was unable to read more than a sentence or two of any article before my attention dissipated. My attention did not wander; I wasn't thinking about other things. My brain was not functioning. I remembered how stunned Michael seemed immediately after Barbara died and felt a surge of kinship. *So this is what it feels like after you lose your soulmate, after you help your lover die.*

I didn't answer my phone all day Sunday. There was nobody I wanted to talk to. I skipped the online church service I normally watched with Alan on Sunday mornings. I let Beverly drag me out for a hike, but the gusty wind disquieted me. I felt lightheaded and ungrounded, so we cut it short. I gave myself permission to be unproductive, to only sit and not do, not think. My body ached from sitting on a wooden stool beside Alan's bed, leaning forward so I could stroke his forehead, his cheek, his hair, sitting, leaning in the same position, my eyes locked on his, for four hours the previous day. My heart ached from saying a permanent goodbye to the man I loved.

January 15, 2020

Ushering Alan's body out of this world felt like an important act of stewardship. I wanted to bear witness, to be present until his body turned to smoke and ash. It might never have occurred to me to ask to watch, but in December I had read Kate Braestrup's memoir *Here If You Need Me*, and in it she witnesses the cremation of her husband's body after he is killed in a car accident. She brings family members and friends with her to the crematorium, and they sit on a comfortable couch in a private viewing room, telling stories about her husband and laughing and crying together as his body is incinerated. At least that's how I remembered the story. When I went back to read the story again, months after Alan's death, I discovered there was no mention of a couch or a private viewing room, and the stories and laughing and crying were associated with washing and dressing her husband's body for the wake, not the cremation. I must have envisioned the scene at the crematorium the way I wanted it to look.

But the private viewing room with the comfortable couch was the picture I had in my head when I told Mike, the undertaker, I wanted to be present for the cremation of Alan's body. He agreed to make those arrangements.

Mike instructed me to meet him at nine o'clock at a crematorium in Lafayette, a city a couple of miles to the east of us. The facility he normally used for cremations was not set up for witnessing, he told me. Apparently, it was a big industrial facility with no amenities for visitors. So on the Wednesday morning after Alan died, I headed to Lafayette in search of the address Mike had given me. I drove by the place twice before I spotted Mike's hearse parked out front and figured out I had arrived. I'm not sure what I expected it to look like, but this definitely wasn't it. The crematorium was located across the street from a middle school in the center of a small strip mall of mostly empty stores, although a couple of units appeared to be occupied by nonprofit organizations with not much to display in the windows other than a few hand-lettered signs.

I opened the front door and walked into a large, sparsely furnished room with nondescript industrial carpeting. On my left was a conference table surrounded by comfortable-looking padded chairs, and to my right was the facility manager's desk and credenza. In front of me was an eight-foot-high wall that went up only halfway to the sixteen-foot ceiling above, which was cluttered with pipes, vents, and industrial-looking fluorescent light fixtures. Mounted in the shorter wall was a small, shoulder-height window and a single door leading to the much-larger back room. A display of urns decorated the wall behind the conference table, adding the only splash of color and civilization to the dull room.

As I walked in, Mike greeted me warmly and introduced me to Michelle, the crematorium manager, who busied herself at her desk while Mike and I took care of some final paperwork at the conference table. When we were finished, Mike led me to the small window in the wall that blocked off the back room. Michelle walked through the door and opened the curtain blocking the window so I could see the furnace, which they referred to as the *retort*.

Alan's body lay wrapped in several layers of semiopaque plastic inside a body-sized, lidless cardboard box next to the furnace. I knew it was Alan because I could see the fire-engine red of his shirt through the film of cloudy plastic.

I debated asking Michelle to unwrap the plastic so I could have one last look at him, but decided against it. I didn't know what shape his face would be in after the diener removed his brain, and I decided I would rather not take the chance that it would be disfigured. I preferred to remember him intact.

Mike stood with me at the window as I watched Michelle roll the box containing Alan's body up a small ramp equipped with metal rollers and into the open door of the furnace. She lowered the metal door and began pushing buttons and entering numbers on the control panel above and to the right of the retort door.

"May I push the button to start the furnace?" I asked Mike. He opened the door to the back and relayed my question to Michelle.

Michelle poked her head around the corner. "Sorry, but you're not allowed in the back room. It's corporate policy." Disappointed but not surprised, I returned to watching her through the window. She moved efficiently, automatically, as if she had performed this job hundreds of times, which she probably had. When she had finished setting up the controls, she turned to the window and asked me if I was ready. I nodded, and she pressed the button to start the flames inside the closed retort. Immediately, the digital temperature readout on the control panel started to climb and the time-remaining counter began to rotate through the seconds. One set of numbers climbing and one set falling. That's all there was to watch.

Michelle emerged from the back room, pulling the door behind her with an air of finality. "Do you want to come back around three o'clock to pick up Alan's remains?" she asked.

"No, I'll stick around and watch and take them with me when I go." Michelle's eyes widened in surprise. It was obvious this was not the response she was expecting.

"There's really nothing to see from here on out."

"That's okay. I want to be here until the process is complete." I wasn't sure why I needed to be there, but I did. Although I knew Alan was dead, I wanted to walk his body—a body I had loved and caressed and held, a body I knew almost as well as my own—I wanted to walk it to the end of the road. All the way home.

"If that's what you want, you are welcome to stay. I have some things I need to take care of, but just ask if you need anything."

Mike shook my hand one last time and left me standing in front of the window. I considered pulling over one of the chairs from the conference table, but the window was too high off the floor. If I sat, I would be too low to see through the glass. So I stood. And thought of Alan. I tried to picture him arriving in the afterlife, being met and welcomed by the shimmering souls of his mother, father, and brother. I had read Eben Alexander's *Proof of Heaven* years earlier, and his detailed account of his near-death experience had stuck with me. Although it was hard to imagine Alan's soul without his body, I pictured a glowing orb of Alan-ness floating blissfully through a "giant cosmic womb," enfolded in love.

Periodically, Michelle's phone would ring and shake me out of my reverie. Her desk was only ten feet from where I stood, so I heard every word of her half of conversations. People calling with questions about their contracts. Suppliers calling with questions about orders. Mortuaries calling to schedule cremations.

When Michelle had trouble getting her computer to communicate with her printer, I was tempted to offer advice. But this was not my problem to solve. I wanted to focus on Alan as I watched the flames consume his flesh, as I breathed the wood smoke and communed with a cast of circling hawks, but since that was not a possibility, I settled for staring at the digital readouts on the retort. I let my mind drift to memories of Alan organizing daily crack-of-dawn plunges into the lake at my parents' summer cottage. He would wake my daughter Sarah's kids, Francesca and Ethan, goading and prodding them until they had their suits on. I'd sit on the sunporch, wrapped in my robe, sipping my coffee, as I watched the three of them shivering on the dock, mist rising from the still water around them as they worked up their courage, birds twittering in the thicket of blueberry bushes hugging the shore. Alan always dove in first, followed closely by the kids. They would splash and laugh, swim to the float and back, and emerge wide awake and ready for breakfast.

Later, when the IT consultant arrived to solve Michelle's printer problem, I found it difficult to ignore him, because he was so physically close to where I stood at the little window. I pulled my attention back to Alan again, remembering him crafting a cradle for Kaitlyn before she was born. That cradle would be passed back and forth between his daughters as each new grandchild joined the family. I recalled him measuring and remeasuring, his face lit by an inner light. I could see him sawing planks, assembling parts, his excitement palpable. He sanded endlessly, transmitting love into the wood with each stroke of the sandpaper. He stained and oiled it until the surface glowed. He showed it off to friends, so proud you might think he'd invented cradles.

At ten o'clock, Michelle announced she needed to open the furnace door momentarily to make sure Alan's body was positioned optimally under the burners.

"Okay, good," I said. "It will give me a chance to see inside the furnace."

"Umm, sorry, but no. I need to pull the curtain. Corporate policy."

"How could it hurt for me to see?"

"We've had people flip out, so we don't allow anyone to watch me open the door anymore." She pulled the white cotton curtain across my little window, but she left the tiniest crack between the two panels. I'm sure it was unintentional, but I was grateful for the shimmering sliver of a view. All I could see was Michelle's back and the red-hot firebrick that lined the furnace, not unlike the interior of the kiln I had used for firing pottery when I was in my twenties. When the cremation process was finished, the temperature of the retort, approximately two thousand degrees, would be about the same as my kiln had been at the end of a bisque firing.

Through my tiny peephole, I watched Michelle's back as she moved quickly, using a shovel to shift things around inside the retort. Then she slid the furnace door closed, put away her tools and heat-resistant gloves, and reopened my curtain. I did not confess that I had a sliver of a view, nor did I flip out. With my view of the control panel restored, I stood and watched the numbers change on the two digital displays and returned my thoughts to Alan, this time replaying memories of the rich tastes, the lazy afternoons lingering over plates of cheese and olives and bottomless glasses of wine as we toured Tuscany in celebration of our tenth wedding anniversary. Of watching Alan's face light up as he crushed grapes at the Poggio Argentiera winery near Montalcino. Of winding, cobbled streets in ancient hilltop towns, of making love on a bed with squeaky springs in a rustic farmhouse near Lucca, wooden shutters thrown wide to the Tuscan sky, a gentle breeze laced with rosemary, our bodies melding.

Around eleven o'clock, foot traffic on the sidewalk in front of the crematory started to pick up. Michelle got up from her desk and pulled the drapes across the plate-glass windows to prevent gawking from middle schoolers on their lunch hour. Michelle announced she'd have to pull the curtain on my little window until the lunch period was over, otherwise the kids might gather at the door and stare in.

"Oh, come on," I objected. "All they would see is the furnace with the little digital numbers on the control panel. How can that hurt?"

"We don't like them staring in the glass door. I'm sorry but I need to close the curtain." She disappeared into the back room and yanked the curtains closed over my window, leaving no sliver of a view this time.

I sighed and took the opportunity to sit at the conference table and rest my feet. I pulled out my thermos of decaf coffee and made myself comfortable. As I sat, I decided to offer Michelle some feedback. I'd spent years in marketing focusing on optimizing customers' experiences, which frequently involved focus groups to discover what customers were thinking and feeling. I was going to offer her a focus group of one.

"Michelle, would you be interested in some ideas for making this place more user friendly?"

"Umm. Sure. What are you thinking?"

I shared two ideas: bar stools so customers could sit at the window, and a drape to give customers a bit of separation from the office area and a sense of privacy.

Michelle listened politely. "Okay. I'll pass your suggestions on to the owners," she said without sounding like she meant a word of it.

Finally, forty-five minutes later, the early lunch period was over, and Michelle reopened the curtain on my little window. I resumed my watch, but it didn't last long. I barely had time to delve into a memory of Alan cooking lobsters for our dinner club, glee on his face as he emerged from the kitchen with a platter piled high with their red bodies and tangled claws, when the bell for the late lunch period sounded, and a second wave of youngsters descended. Again, Michelle pulled the curtain across my window.

And at one o'clock, she kicked me out. "I have an errand I need to run," Michelle explained. "The retort has reached temperature, so I am turning it off and letting it cool. When I get back, I will sweep the ashes into a container for you. You can come back at three to get them."

She didn't mention putting Alan's bones into the grinder first, which I knew was a requirement because Kate Braestrup's book had described the oversize blender used for that purpose—which she had actually seen at the crematorium in Maine where her husband's body was cremated—and I had, of course, Googled the cremation process before I set foot in the place. But I didn't put up a fuss. I was tired of pushing to be involved in a process where my presence was tolerated but hardly welcomed. I packed up my thermos and my tote bag and headed home.

When I returned at three o'clock, Michelle handed me a plastic shoe box shrouded in a forest-green velvet bag. I was surprised at how heavy the box was and how warm it felt in my arms. I hurried home and crawled into bed, hugging the box to my chest like a hot-water bottle, feeling Alan's warmth embracing me for the last time.

February 8, 2020

How long had I known Alan was dying? Perhaps three years in my rational brain, but longer in my bones. With that much advance notice, you might think I'd have formulated at least a rough sense of what his memorial service, his celebration of life, should look like. But I hadn't. Even with the experience of helping to plan Barbara's service, only a year earlier, I didn't start to cobble together ideas for Alan's service. I had not been ready to make the leap from thinking of Alan alive to thinking of Alan here no longer. Now that he was gone, I could start to plan.

Shortly before Alan's death, I had asked him what his wishes were for a memorial service.

"I don't have any particular wishes," he said. "Memorial services are for the people left behind, so you can do whatever feels best to you."

"No special requests for music?" I was almost reluctant to ask, fearing he might name a Willie Nelson classic.

"Nope. Whatever you want is fine with me." I breathed a sigh of relief.

The day he told Pat Foss, the woman who cleaned his fish tank religiously, about his plans to end his life, he mentioned to her he'd always liked the poem about the ship on the horizon that is sometimes read at memorial services. Pat knew exactly what he was talking about and sent me a copy of the poem, "Gone from

My Sight," by Rev. Luther Beecher. I would never have found it without her help. I was glad to have a place to start.

Beverly agreed to be in charge of music, and I suggested she recruit Marie, a talented vocalist and friend from church, to help. We discussed some possible songs to include, and then I stopped worrying about that part of the service. Beverly and Marie loved Alan, and I trusted them to create beautiful music with which to celebrate him.

I started working immediately on the slide show of Alan's life and hoped the rest would fall into place. I had created a slide show for both of my parents and for Barbara. I loved shuffling through old baby photos, snaggletooth school pictures, snapshots of proms, graduations and weddings, of vacations and offspring, creating a visual history of a lifetime. But for Alan's slide set, what I loved most was reliving all the memories of our lives together. I spent days parked on the couch, wrapped in a fleece blanket, poring through the pages of our photo albums, and more days going through all the photo folders on both of our computers and phones. I laughed and cried and longed to have him at my side to share the memories.

I invited Alan's daughters to speak at the service. Alexis declined but Megan agreed to a short tribute to her dad. If I had guessed in advance, I would have laid odds it would be the other way around. Megan was the introvert and Alexis the extrovert, never reluctant to stand before an audience. Andy, our best man, and Dave Smith, Alan's former housemate, each agreed to say a few words.

But who was going to give the main eulogy? I wanted to do it myself, but I wasn't sure I could pull it off. I waited for the perfect volunteer to step forward, but it never happened. A week before the service, I wrote a eulogy. My daughter Sarah agreed to be my backup; if I couldn't get through it, she would read it for me. Finally, we had a plan. I met with our minister, and we finalized the service.

Sarah and her wife, Babe, arrived from New York, along with Sarah's kids, Franny and Ethan, and Franny's husband, Connor. Fortunately, Beverly didn't mind us using the extra rooms downstairs. We had a houseful, but everyone had a comfortable place to sleep. As he had promised, Alan's brother, Chris, flew in from Maui, and he stayed at Alexis's house. It snowed the day before the service and Chris didn't own boots or a heavy winter jacket, but he survived the Colorado weather with a minimum of grumbling.

On the day of the service, the Colorado sun made a comeback, and its rays reflected off the previous day's accumulation, doing its best to add a cheerful note to the celebration. Beverly played her cello as we showed the slides of Alan's life, and then Pat started us off by reading the poem Alan had chosen. When it was my turn, I stood tall behind the lectern and shared with our assembled friends and family members how blessed I felt to have been married to Alan. I talked about his brave decision to end his life using medical aid in dying, and I shared the story about Alan saying, "We got people trying to die in here!" I shared a video of him laughing uncontrollably over something silly Beverly said to him just two days before he died, his *joie de vivre* still erupting as he prepared to die. At least half my talk was devoted to thanking all our family and friends and neighbors for their acts of kindness to Alan and me over the last several years.

The best part of the service was when Scott opened the mic for our guests to share stories about Alan. Alan's college roommate, also named Allen (only spelled wrong), who had flown in from Arizona for the service, told stories of playing bridge and hearts with Alan when they should have been studying, and about Alan being there for him through all the challenging times in his adult life. Barbee, a mother of one of the boys Alan had taught in Sunday School, talked about the important life lessons her son learned from Alan, both during Sunday School and later, when Barbee hired Alan to help her son, then a teenager, fix a hole he had punched in a wall. Alan worked with the young man every day after school for an entire week to teach him about drywall repair and listen to him talk about his relationships, his frustrations, and his fears. Vivian, a woman Alan had dated when his girls were young and who had flown in from Seattle for the service, told us that Alan was the only man she ever dated who asked her if she needed to use the bathroom before they left the house. So many people had touching or funny stories to tell.

I held it together for the service and for the reception afterward. I kept my tears at bay until I changed from my dress clothes into my sweatpants and curled up on the couch, safe at home at the end of the day. Sarah and her family waited on me for the rest of the evening, bringing me bowls of soup and cups of tea and keeping me supplied with tissues.

Once again, the full moon blessed me with its benediction as I headed off to bed. I'd sent Alan's body down the ramp with the undertaker on the previous full moon. On this one, I'd celebrated his life with a flock of others who held him dear.

It didn't occur to me until later how lucky we were that Alan's determination didn't waver, that he stuck to his original schedule for dying. If he'd waited another month, which I was rooting for him to do, we wouldn't have been able to have an in-person celebration of life because of COVID-19 restrictions on gatherings. If he'd waited another two months, I wouldn't have been allowed to visit him at Crestmoor during his final days. So, in retrospect, his timing was perfect.

March 2020

In early March, much sooner than I expected, I received Alan's brain neuropathology report from the Mayo Clinic in Jacksonville, Florida, which is one of several Mayo Clinic locations in the US, the one where the neuropathology laboratory is located. The language in the report was highly technical and filled with the names of various structures of the brain. For example, "The pontine base has moderate to marked neuronal loss and gliosis with atrophy and demyelination of pontocerebellar fibers and many synuclein immunoreactive glial inclusions." They did provide a summary in more-understandable English, which did not stop me from looking up all the unfamiliar terms online. But the bottom line was simple: Alan's clinical diagnosis of multiple system atrophy was correct. In addition to the overwhelming evidence of MSA, Alan's brain showed a few early signs of Alzheimer's pathology.

The confirmation of Alan's MSA seemed almost anticlimactic. A friend from our support group, a man named Gary, died two months before Alan. Six years earlier, he had been diagnosed at the Mayo Clinic in Rochester, Minnesota, with progressive supranuclear palsy (PSP), another nasty disease in the atypical Parkinsonian family. When his wife got his brain pathology report, she was surprised to learn that Gary did not have PSP after all. Instead, he had an illness that had never before been described in the literature: corticobasal degeneration with pallido-nigro-luysial degeneration (CBD-PNLA). Each of the atypical Parkinsonian illnesses involves degeneration in different areas of the brain and different proteins that are misfolding. CBD involves the cerebral cortex and the basal ganglia, and the misbehaving protein is tau. CBD in itself is exceedingly rare, with an incidence of less than one new case per year per 100,000 people, but it is the associated PNLA degeneration (atrophy and neuronal loss in the globus pallidus, substantia nigra, and subthalamic nucleus, which are all components of the basal ganglia) that set Gary apart from other cases of CBD. Gary was apparently only the third patient known to have this novel pathological finding. His neuropathology report sent ripples of excitement through the research community and through the members of our support group.

By comparison, Alan's report was tame. It was pretty much what I expected. His degeneration was mainly in the cerebellum and brainstem, and the primary errant protein was alpha synuclein. The Mayo Clinic Neuropathology Laboratory will save Alan's brain tissue and use it for research into MSA to learn what causes the illness in hopes that someday they will be better able to diagnose, treat, and prevent it.

Why was Alan stricken with this rare and nasty illness? If someone told me my odds of winning a lottery jackpot were approximately 1 in 200,000, I would not bother to buy a lottery ticket because of the long odds. And if someone quoted those same odds to me as my likelihood of being stricken with a progressive, fatal neurological condition, I would feel confident I wouldn't be the person who would fall ill. Yet Alan was that person. I think of a vulture plucking him randomly and unexpectedly from the nest of our marriage and bashing him against the rocks of disability. Why did the vulture pick him and not me? Why did the vulture pick him and not some other unsuspecting victim?

There is some evidence that environmental toxins may play a role in the development of MSA, and if that's the case, it is certainly possible that Alan's years in the plastics industry, his years of breathing fumes from industrial solvents, played a part in his being stricken with the illness. One of the members of our support group believes his MSA was caused by exposure to Agent Orange when he served in Vietnam. Apparently, the Veterans Administration has decided his illness is service related, because they are paying him benefits and even bought him a wheelchair-accessible van.

I *am* glad we donated Alan's brain, because I think it is important for some good to come from his suffering. And I have faith the researchers will keep plugging away until they find answers.

Over the next few weeks, Alan visited me frequently in my dreams. I dream that Alan and I are at a hotel, a big, fancy one with lots of rooms and lots of meeting halls and restaurants. Alan is healthy and handsome and horny. He grabs my arm and steers me out of the elevator and down the carpeted hall, his hand hot on my skin. When we arrive at our room, we start to rip off our clothes and jump into bed, but we discover the room is swarming with secret service agents who are making sure the room is not bugged because the Obamas are staying next door.

Alan and I head down the hall, looking for a vacant room, but every room we enter is occupied with members of the Obama entourage. In the last room on the hall, we find Michelle herself. She is more beautiful in person than I remember, but then again, I have never seen her in person before. We don't have to explain our problem to her. She already knows. She is kind and compassionate, telling us her experience is that sometimes, no matter how hard you try, you just can't find a private place for love to happen. She says she is familiar with the problem, but she doesn't offer to help us come up with a way to solve it, even though I think she should, since it's partly her fault we're in this predicament.

I wake up missing Alan, wanting Alan with every cell in my body.

Another night, I dream I am settling into bed in a dark room. I have locked the door and pulled the security chain across the door frame and hooked the knob into the slot where it belongs. As I am drifting off to sleep in my dream, I hear someone turning the door handle and see the door crack open, letting in a thin line of light from the hallway.

"Who's there?" I call, knowing the chain will keep the door from opening more than an inch. But to my surprise, the door continues to open, long past where the chain should have caught it. The backlit outline of a man is standing in the doorway. The man's bulk and stature are similar to Alan's when he was healthy, but the door has swung closed behind him and I can't see him well.

"Is that you, Sweetie?" I ask. There is no response. The man pulls his sweater off over his head. The man moves like Alan used to, but more importantly, his presence feels like Alan.

"Alan, if that is you, please say something." The man silently unbuckles his belt and starts to pull down his pants.

"Alan, if that is you, just say my name. That's all, just my name." There is no answer. The man finishes undressing and starts to crawl into bed with me. It feels like Alan, but I am scared because he won't say my name. *Maybe he doesn't know my name.*

"Alan, why won't you say my name?" I scream. And my

scream wakes me up. In my wakened state, I am heartbroken by my own stupidity. If I had only controlled my panic, I could have held my husband in my arms, even if only in my dreams.

Months later, when I cleaned out Alan's closet, I found a box of VHS tapes, most of them unlabeled, although some of them had gum residue on their spines as if they had been labeled at some point but the labels had vanished. I wondered if the video of our wedding might be on one of those unlabeled tapes, but I no longer owned a VCR to play them.

My heart ached so badly for him, I wondered if I would survive. Suddenly, nothing was more important than finding our wedding video. I had to know exactly what we promised each other that day, and I wanted to watch him kiss me.

I emailed my friend Byron. He had been Abraham Lincoln at Daryl's Halloween party all those years ago. He had always been an electronics geek, and if anybody still had a VCR player, it would be him. He responded, yes, I was welcome to come to his house and use his equipment to view the contents of my VHS tapes, and if I found what I was looking for, he would be glad to convert the file into a digital format for me.

Most of the tapes turned out to be homemade copies of shows from the history channel, and the quality was poor. But about halfway through the box, I found the wedding video. I was ecstatic. Byron converted it to MP4 format and uploaded it to his Google Drive the next day.

How young we looked! Our faces were unwrinkled and our bodies fit and firm. Alan looked nervous, and I looked as if I was radiating joy and love to all, like a good fairy sprinkling invisible fairy dust on all our friends and relatives. My four-year-old granddaughter, Francesca, stole the show as the flower girl. She kept dropping roses from her basket as she walked down the aisle in her pale pink dress. She stopped to pick up each rose she dropped, handing it to someone sitting in the nearest aisle. It took her a while to get to the front of the sanctuary.

Alan and I followed Franny. I was not interested in having my father, or anyone else for that matter, "give me away," because you can't give something away unless it belongs to you. As a single woman, I didn't relate to ownership. So Alan and I walked together down the aisle.

I watched us making our vows several times until I captured each word. Here are the promises Alan and I made to each other on our wedding day:

> *I accept you as you are, baggage and all. I promise to treat you with respect and compassion and to do my best to keep our relationship current and honest. I promise to make my own spiritual and personal growth a priority and to support you in yours. I promise to be your loving and faithful partner as we face life's lessons and challenges together. May I always be conscious of how blessed I am to have you in my life.*

Early in the morning, when I go out to retrieve the newspaper from the driveway, the world is still except for the birdsong, and the sun is starting its climb in the blushing sky. I stand in my slippers, wearing an old flannel shirt of Alan's for a robe, eyes closed, and I wait.

I wait for a chickadee to call, "Hi, Sweetie."

And when he finally sings to me, I call, "Hi, Sweetie" back to him.

RESOURCES

Compassion & Choices

Compassion & Choices offers free resources to help people get the end-of-life care they want. The *End-of-Life Decisions Guide and Toolkit* guides users through considering their priorities, discussing them with medical providers and loved ones, and making a plan. For people interested in medical aid in dying, the *Find Care Tool* helps them locate a facility, medical team, or hospice that supports this option. And for practicing physicians seeking to better serve their patients, *Doc2Doc* provides confidential phone consultation with a medical professional experienced in end-of-life care.

compassionandchoices.org

Death with Dignity National Center

The Death with Dignity National Center promotes death-with-dignity laws in the United States, both to provide an option for dying individuals and to stimulate nationwide improvements in end-of-life care. The organization offers information, education, and support about death with dignity as an end-of-life option to patients, family members, legislators, advocates, healthcare and end-of-life care professionals, media, and the public.

www.deathwithdignity.org

The Conversation Project

The Conversation Project offers free tools, guidance, and resources to help people begin talking with loved ones about their wishes for care through the end of life, so those wishes can be understood and respected. The website includes an excellent blog, *Talking Matters*, which includes a list of recommended books on death and end-of-life care.

theconversationproject.org

Medical Aid in Dying Blog

Join us for a moderated discussion about current news and issues related to medical aid in dying. Share your story, your advice for others, and your opinions about what's happening in the world of death with dignity.

joannetubbskelly.com/blog

STATE-SPECIFIC ORGANIZATIONS PROVIDING SUPPORT AROUND END-OF-LIFE CHOICES

End of Life Choices California
https://endoflifechoicesca.org

End of Life Choices Oregon
https://eolcoregon.org

End of Life Washington
https://endoflifewa.org

Patient Choices Vermont
www.patientchoices.org

Maine Death with Dignity
www.mainedeathwithdignity.org

RESOURCES FOR PEOPLE WITH MSA, PSP AND CBD

Multiple System Atrophy Coalition

Provides education and support for people affected by multiple system atrophy and funds patient-centric research into the illness.

www.multiplesystematrophy.org

CurePSP

Provides information and support for people with PSP, MSA, and other neurodegenerative illnesses.

www.psp.org

Brain Support Network

Helps people with MSA, PSP, LBD, and CBD donate their brains for research.

www.brainsupportnetwork.org

ACKNOWLEDGMENTS

So many people stepped forward to help as Alan's health deteriorated. I am deeply grateful to the kind and competent physicians on his team, especially Dr. Avrom Kurtz, Dr. Mark Fisher, and Dr. Laura Hughes. These dedicated physicians led the way, but they were backed up by dozens of other healthcare professionals—physical, occupational, and speech therapists; nurses and nurse's aides; physician assistants; and more—who eased Alan's journey. While I can't name everyone individually, I would be remiss if I didn't call out Susan Lankford and Minda Papson, who always left us smiling; Alison Hoffmaster, who gave us hope; and the many helpers at Dignity Care who gave us a hand, day after day.

Special thanks to the Trail Winds Hospice team who supported us in Alan's last weeks: Dr. Jim Romano; Cara Leisher, RN; Josh Thompson, CNA; and John Smith-Lontz, MDiv. You wrapped us in a loving embrace that I still feel today.

To our tribe, the members of our MSA/PSA/CBD support group: Thank you for walking this path with us, for sharing your trials and frustrations, your tips and tricks, your joys and triumphs. Thank you for laughing at Alan's jokes and for telling more than a few of your own. You made our journey more bearable. Special thanks to Helenn Franzgrote for facilitating the group.

I will never be able to adequately thank our community of friends and neighbors, who overwhelmed us with their generosity and kindness: Beverly Lyne, Andy and Linda Lattanzi, Chris Disch, Pat Foss, Dave Morden, Liz and Dave Abbott, Chriss Meecham, Paul and Cass D'Agostino, Christine Cappello, Sue and Ron Blekicki, Tommy Thompson, Brian Mueller, Susan Gallagher, Dave Smith and Kathy Lower, Bob and Jerene Anderson, Michael Chapman, and Dave, Danny, and Dylan Cuyler. Thank you to Annie Russell, Julie Legg, Anne Weiher, and Kathy Narum for helping me stay centered through the years leading up to Alan's death, and to Rev. Scott Schell and Rev. Sue McQueen for their spiritual support.

Unending showers of gratitude to my writing group members, Sylvia Keepers, Becky Tarr, Nana Mizushima, and Kerstin Lieff, who poked and prodded me into writing more compelling scenes, and who wormed their ways into my heart in the process. Gratitude also to Rachel Weaver from Lighthouse Writers Workshop; Carolyn Forché who handled my tears with sensitivity as she helped me hone my manuscript as part of Pam Houston's Manuscript Bootcamp; and to Brooke Maddaford who helped me tighten the story as I neared the finish line.

Thank you to Brooke Warner, publisher at She Writes Press, for her vision in creating an alternate publishing platform and for helping women tell their stories. Thanks also to project manager Samantha Strom, copy editor Jennifer Caven, proofreader Chris Dumas, and to designer Gerilyn Attebery for making a stunning cover from the beautiful photo by my friend Claudia Courtney.

Gratitude to Alan's daughters Alexis Hamilton and Megan Brugger for their love and support of their dad during his illness. He loved you with every fiber of his being. And to my daughter, Sarah Dufoe, thank you for listening so patiently.

ABOUT THE AUTHOR

Photo credit: Gretchen Troop

As a kid, Joanne Tubbs Kelly moved around a lot, but she always felt at home when she had her nose stuck in a book. As an adult, she provided marketing communications services to high-tech companies. Now that she's retired, she lives in Boulder in the home she and her husband, now deceased, remodeled from top to bottom. She delights in puttering in her garden and walking and hiking where she can wallow in the beauty of Boulder's Flatirons and Colorado's high peaks. Whenever she's not in her garden or out walking, you can usually find her up to her old tricks: hiding out somewhere with her nose stuck in a book.

SELECTED TITLES FROM SHE WRITES PRESS

She Writes Press is an independent publishing company founded to serve women writers everywhere. Visit us at www.shewritespress.com.

Memories in Dragonflies: Simple Lessons for Mindful Dying by Lannette Cornell Bloom. $16.95, 978-1-63152-469-1. A daughter uncovers the hidden gifts of the dying process as she cares for her terminally ill mother in her final year—a journey that results in a spiritual awakening and an appreciation of the simple joys of life, even in death.

Bless the Birds: Living with Love in a Time of Dying by Susan J. Tweit. $16.95, 978-1-64742-036-9. Writer Susan Tweit and her economist-turned-sculptor husband Richard Cabe had just settled into their version of a "good life" when Richard saw thousands of birds one day—harbingers of the brain cancer that would kill him two years later. This intimate memoir chronicles their journey into the end of his life, framed by their final trip together: a 4,000-mile, long-delayed honeymoon road trip.

Bound: A Daughter, a Domme, and an End-of-Life Story by Elizabeth Anne Wood. $16.95, 978-1-63152-630-5. When Elizabeth Anne Wood's aging mother—a charming, needy, and passive-aggressive woman who has only recently discovered the domme within her—falls terminally ill, it is up to Wood to shepherd her through the bureaucracy and unintentional inhumanity of the healthcare system, as well as the complicated process of facing death when she has just begun to truly enjoy life.

Warrior Mother: A Memoir of Fierce Love, Unbearable Loss, and Rituals that Heal by Sheila K. Collins, PhD. $16.95, 978-1-93831-446-9. The story of the lengths one mother goes to when two of her three adult children are diagnosed with potentially terminal diseases.

Green Nails and Other Acts of Rebellion: Life After Loss by Elaine Soloway. $16.95, 978-1-63152-919-1. An honest, often humorous account of the joys and pains of caregiving for a loved one with a debilitating illness.

The Space Between: A Memoir of Mother-Daughter Love at the End of Life by Virginia A. Simpson. $16.95, 978-1-63152-049-5. When a life-threatening illness makes it necessary for Virginia Simpson's mother, Ruth, to come live with her, Simpson struggles to heal their relationship before Ruth dies.